THE GOD OF THIS HOUSE

INVENTING CHRISTIANITY

Series Editors
L. Stephanie Cobb
David L. Eastman

In the second and third centuries, insiders and outsiders alike were grappling with what it meant to be Christian. In this period, there were shifting and competing centers of clerical and textual authority and disagreements over group boundaries, interpretive strategies, and ritual practices. Inventing Christianity examines the numerous ways in which early Christianity was "invented"—that is, given definition and boundaries—by different people in different times to different ends. The series contributes to the study of second- and third-century Christianity by exploring how the very notion of Christianity developed and redeveloped in multiple forms and through cultural interactions.

OTHER BOOKS IN THE SERIES:

Michael Flexsenhar III, *Christians in Caesar's Household: The Emperor's Slaves in the Makings of Christianity*

Jared Secord, *Christian Intellectuals and the Roman Empire: From Justin Martyr to Origen*

Blake Leyerle, *Christians at Home: John Chrysostom and Domestic Rituals in Fourth-Century Antioch*

ADVISORY BOARD
Nicola Denzey Lewis
Kim Haines-Eitzen
Robin M. Jensen
David Konstan
Jeffrey Siker
Jeanne-Nicole Mellon Saint-Laurent

THE GOD OF THIS HOUSE

Christian Domestic Cult Before Constantine

CAROLINE JOHNSON HODGE

The Pennsylvania State University Press
University Park, Pennsylvania

Library of Congress Cataloging-in-Publication Data

Names: Johnson Hodge, Caroline E., author
Title: The God of this house : Christian domestic cult before Constantine / Caroline Johnson Hodge.
Description: University Park, Pennsylvania : The Pennsylvania State University Press, [2025] | Series: Inventing Christianity ; 4 | Includes bibliographical references and index.
Summary: "Examines how early Christians, from the first to early fourth centuries, developed household rituals similar to traditional Roman domestic cult practices. Through supplications, offerings, and gestures, they engaged with divine forces, creating what can be described as a Christian household cult that shaped health, family, and livelihood"—Provided by publisher.
Identifiers: LCCN 2025010330 | ISBN 9780271099873 hardback
Subjects: LCSH: Christian life—History—Early church, ca. 30–600 | Christian life—Rome | Jesus Christ—Cult—Rome | Households—Religious aspects—Christianity | Households—Rome | Rome—Religious life and customs
Classification: LCC BR195.C5 H57 2025 | DDC 270.1—dc23/eng/20250415
LC record available at https://lccn.loc.gov/2025010330

Copyright © 2025 Caroline Johnson Hodge
All rights reserved
Printed in the United States of America
Published by The Pennsylvania
State University Press,
University Park, PA 16802–1003

The Pennsylvania State University Press is a member of the Association of University Presses.
It is the policy of The Pennsylvania State University Press to use acid-free paper. Publications on uncoated stock satisfy the minimum requirements of American National Standard for Information Sciences—Permanence of Paper for Printed Library Material, ANSI Z39.48–1992.

Dedicated to my parents, Frank Johnson (in memoriam) and Caroline Frances DuBose Johnson.

I am grateful to both for giving me a lifetime of support and love, as well as a delight in learning.

CONTENTS

List of Illustrations *viii*

Acknowledgments *ix*

List of Abbreviations *xi*

Introduction: "My God and the God of This House" *1*

1 Honoring the Gods in Households: Daily-Life Religious Practice in the Ancient Mediterranean *14*

2 Doorways, Bedrooms, and Kitchens: A Sampler of Everyday Christian Practices *27*

3 Amulets, Spells, and Gems: Seeking Protection and Healing in the Name of Christ *48*

4 Foreign Gods and Unsupervised Worship: Wives, Slaves, and Power *71*

5 "Peter and Paul, Keep Us in Mind": The Cult of the Dead Among Pre-Constantinian Christ Followers *95*

Conclusion *122*

Notes *129*

Bibliography *160*

Index *183*

ILLUSTRATIONS

1. Clay figurine, female, orans position *19*
2. Aedicula shrine in atrium of House of the Red Walls, Pompeii *22*
3. Aedicula shrine with figurines in atrium of House of the Red Walls *23*
4. Bloodstone gem, obverse *60*
5. Bloodstone gem, reverse *61*
6. Constanza gem *62*
7. Line drawing of Alexamenos graffito *63*
8. Januarius inscription *105*
9. Photo of *mensa* slab on top of Tomb G, Kapljuč *106*
10. Aerial view of Tomb G in basilica and earlier cemetery *107*
11. Reconstruction of Tomb G on floor of fourth-century basilica (below pulpit) *107*
12. Reconstruction of Tomb G in three phases *108*
13. Reconstruction of *triclia* at *ad catacumbas*, under San Sebastiano *110*
14. Fragments of graffiti from *triclia* under San Sebastiano *111*
15. Reconstruction of the Basilica Apostolorum *113*

ACKNOWLEDGMENTS

I am particularly grateful to colleagues who have been conversation partners over the years: Barbara Borg, Michael Flexsenhar, David Frankfurter, Paula Fredriksen, Verena Fugger, Felicity Harley-McGowan, Andrew Jacobs, Ross Kraemer, Nicola Denzey Lewis, Markus Oehler, Joe Sanzo, Stan Stowers, and Dan Ullucci. My thanks also to various scholarly communities where I have presented portions of this work, including Boston Patristics, the Redescribing Christian Origins section of the SBL, the Archaeology of Religion in the Roman World section of the SBL, the Sacra Privata conference, COMCAR 2018, the Women's Studies in Religion Program at Harvard Divinity School, and David Frankfurter's graduate students at Boston University in March 2019. My thanks to those who read portions of this project: Denise Buell, David Frankfurter, Mahri Leonard-Fleckman, Tat-siong Benny Liew, Ross Kraemer, Ellen Perry, Joe Sanzo, Kat Shaner, and Dan Ullucci. Academic work is always enriched by collaboration and conversation, and this project is better for the insights and comments of all of these colleagues.

Two fellowships gave me time to research and write: the Women's Studies in Religion Program at Harvard Divinity School and a Faculty Fellowship at College of the Holy Cross. I am also grateful to Holy Cross for regularly scheduled sabbaticals. An O'Leary Fellowship and a Whiting Fellowship supported research-related travel. Monica Berry was a great travel companion—thank you for crawling around in the catacombs with me!

Three student research assistants gave invaluable help: Victoria Tutino, Michelle Hu, and Marya Macuk. Sabine Guerrero offered timely assistance with some German translations. Erin Beall was a formidable editor and footnote formatter. The library staffs of Clapp Library at Wellesley College and at Dinand Library at College of the Holy Cross were always generous. I offer special thanks to Jennifer Whelan for helping me track down obscure sources.

I am grateful for the generosity of those who helped with the images for this book: Jackie and Bob Dunn at Pompeii in Pictures, the Kelsey Museum, the British Museum, the Pontifical Commission for Sacred Archaeology, and Everpresent. Special appreciation goes to Marty Martinage, who produced line drawings of several difficult-to-access materials.

My thanks also to those at Penn State University Press, including the series editors Stephanie Cobb and David Eastman, who expressed interest in this work some years ago. Tristan Bates, Josie DiKerby, Maddie Caso, and Laura Reed-Morrisson have been ever helpful and patient.

Portions of my work here have appeared in articles published over the years. Portions of chapter 1 were originally published as "Household Worship" in Behind the Scenes of the New Testament: Cultural, Social, and Historical Contexts, edited by Bruce W. Longenecker, Elizabeth E. Shively, and T. J. Lang, copyright © 2024. Used by permission of Baker Academic, a division of Baker Publishing Group. Chapter 4 builds on parts of the following articles:

> "Daily Devotions: Stowers's Modes of Religion Meet Tertullian's *ad Uxorem*," in *"The One Who Sows Bountifully": Essays in Honor of Stanley K. Stowers*, edited by Caroline Johnson Hodge, Saul M. Olyan, Daniel Ullucci, and Emma Wasserman (Providence, RI: Brown Judaic Studies, 2013), 43–54.
> "'Holy Wives' in Roman Households: 1 Peter 3:1–6," *Journal of Interdisciplinary Feminist Thought* 4, no. 1 (2010), https://escholar.salve.edu/jift/.
> "Married to an Unbeliever: Households, Hierarchies and Holiness in 1 Corinthians 7:12–16," *Harvard Theological Review* 103, no. 1 (2010): 1–25.
> "Mixed Marriage in Early Christianity: Trajectories from Corinth," in *Corinth in Contrast: Studies in Inequality*, edited by Steve Friesen, Dan Showalter, and Sarah James (Boston: Brill, 2014), 227–44.
> "'Wife, Pray to the Lar': Wives, Slaves, and Worship in Roman Households," in *The Struggle over Class: Socioeconomic Analysis of Ancient Christian Texts*, edited by G. Anthony Keddie, Michael Flexsenhar III, and Steven J. Friesen, Writings from the Greco-Roman World Supplement 19 (Atlanta, GA: Society of Biblical Literature Press, 2021), 73–94.

My deepest thanks goes to my family: Annie, Peter, Tom, and of course, Hazel. Their companionship and love have sustained me throughout. I am particularly grateful to TPH for regular conversations about every aspect of the project and, most importantly, for a wonderful three decades of shared life.

I dedicate this work to my parents, Frank (*in memoriam*) and Fran Johnson. Their own lifelong love of learning, curiosity about history and religion, enthusiasm for travel, and steadfast support of me have given me the resources and inspiration to do this work.

ABBREVIATIONS

Journals, Series, Collections

ANF	*The Ante-Nicene Fathers*. Edited by Alexander Roberts and James Donaldson. Revised by A. Cleveland Coxe. 10 vols. Buffalo, NY: Christian Literature Publishing, 1885–97
CIL	*Corpus Inscriptionum Latinarum*. Berlin, 1862–
CSEL	Corpus Scriptorum Ecclesiasticorum Latinorum
ICUR	*Inscriptiones christianae urbis Romae*. Edited by Giovanni B. de Rossi. Rome: Officina Libraria Pontificia, 1857–88
ILCV	*Inscriptiones Latinae Christianae Veteres*. Edited by Ernest Diehl. 3 vols. Berlin: Weidmann, 1925–31
LCL	Loeb Classical Library
NPNF	Nicene and Post-Nicene Fathers
P.Ant.	*Antinoopolis Papyri*. Edited by C. H. Roberts, J. W. B. Barns, and H. Zilliacus. London: Egypt Exploration Society, 1950–67
PG	Patrologia Graeca. Edited by J.-P. Migne. 162 vols. Paris, 1857–66
PGM	*Papyri Graecae Magicae*. Edited by Karl Preisendanz. Stuttgart: B. G. Teubner, 1973–74. English translation: Betz, Hans Dieter. *The Greek Magical Papyri in Translation*. Chicago: University of Chicago Press, 1986
PL	Patrologia Latina. Edited by J.-P. Migne. 217 vols. Paris, 1844–64
P.Oxy.	*Oxyrhynchus Papyri*. Edited by Bernard Grenfell, Arthur Hunt, et al. London: Egypt Exploration Fund, 1898–

Origen

Cels.	*Contra Celsum*
Or.	*De oratione*

Tertullian

An.	*De anima*
Apol.	*Apologeticus*
Bapt.	*De baptismo*
Cor.	*De corona militis*
Exh. cast.	*De exhortatione castitatis*

Idol.	*De idololatria*
Marc.	*Adversus Marcionem*
Mon.	*De monogamia*
Nat.	*Ad nationes*
Or.	*De oratione*
Res.	*De resurrectione carnis*
Scorp.	*Scorpiace*
Spect.	*De spectaculis*
Test.	*De testimonio animae*
Ux.	*Ad uxorem*

All biblical translations are from the NRSV; I note any amendments. Greek from Nestle-Aland *Novum Testamentum Graece*.

INTRODUCTION

"My God and the God of This House"

The scene is set at the front step of a house in the city of Iconium (in modern-day Turkey) in the first century CE. We see an elite young woman named Thecla, who left her fiancé and her household duties to follow Paul, returning years later to the household where she first heard Paul preach. She falls to her knees and begins to pray: "My God and the God of this house, where the light shone upon me."[1] Here, as though marking the front doorway with her kneeling body, Thecla proclaims that her god—the god of Christ and of Paul—belongs to this house. With these words, recounted in the Acts of Thecla (second century CE), Thecla speaks a familiar language in the daily life of the ancient Mediterranean world: she addresses the divine being who watches over the household, just as others did in their own spaces. Through supplications, offerings, and gestures, people interacted with the myriad powerful beings that influenced their health, families, and livelihoods. In the Acts of Thecla and in other texts like it, Christianity emerges in the spaces of the household: bedrooms, dining rooms, hallways, and courtyards.

In this book, which takes its name from Thecla's prayer, I argue that those who followed Christ invented a household cult in the second, third, and early fourth centuries that shared many of the characteristics of traditional domestic devotional practices of the ancient Mediterranean world. Like the scene in the Acts of Thecla, these daily devotions included prayers, offerings, or gestures that both preserved and adapted traditional practices. I use the term "household" or "domestic" broadly, covering practices that actually took place not only where people resided but also in other unsupervised spaces, such as street-corner shrines, tombs, and shops. David Frankfurter defines domestic religion in terms of a "cluster of concerns and orientations" rather than as a practice involving a specific space.[2] These concerns might include interacting with ancestors, securing protection, seeking aid in procreation, marking holidays, and performing the mundane tasks of daily life (such as food preparation and other work) that require divine assistance.[3] Practices related to these concerns, performed by members of households, took place in a variety of domestic and "extra-domestic" spaces and involved many of the basic activities of daily life.[4] In this study, therefore, I understand the domestic cult in an expansive way and use adjectives like "domestic" and "household" along with broader ones, such as "everyday" and "daily-life," to describe the religious practices I document.

Despite this broad scope, I am not claiming that the Christian domestic cult was organized, universal, or even necessarily intentional. Rather, I argue that followers of Christ, like everyone else in the ancient world, interacted with the divine in ways that made sense in specific times and places. To do so, they incorporated the vocabulary and gestures of households in the Roman empire, which were conveniently flexible and various. Unlike communal rituals, these daily devotions were typically not interpreted or supervised but belonged to the kind of intuitive and innovative worship that took place in doorways, at hearths, in shops, or at tombs.

Not Doctrine, Not Church: A New Angle

Historically, scholars have typically focused on the ideas of Christianity; beliefs, texts, doctrine, and interpretation have occupied our attention for centuries. Indeed, these intellectual practices have defined what Christianity is. As I explain below, I understand these intellectual pursuits as one type of religious practice among many in the ancient world. Far more common, in fact, are interactions with the divine that did not rely on interpretation or right thinking but instead were intuitive, shared practices of exchange with the gods. Rituals of eating, offering, and expressing thanks are the most common. These kinds of practices, which have been understudied and undervalued, are the focus of this book.

When scholars have examined Christian practices, they have focused on communal ones. There is general agreement that the first corporate worship took place primarily in domestic settings; thus we imagine baptisms and meals taking place in ancient households, as believers gathered to discuss scripture or hear the latest missive from a traveling teacher.[5] The household, therefore, is viewed as the birthplace of the *ekklesia*, often translated as "church" or sometimes "house church."[6] Traditional scholarly reconstructions posit that these early gatherings of believers eventually evolved into the institution of the church in the fourth century. The ancient household is indeed relevant for thinking about early liturgical traditions, structures of authority, art, and architecture.[7] In this study, however, I focus not on the rituals in communal settings but on the daily lives of believers outside of the *ekklesia* gatherings, especially those who were living (and therefore worshiping) among non-Christians. How did Christians honor their god at home, in shops, in neighborhoods, or in fields—or in other unofficial contexts?

In recent decades, there has been fruitful work done on "unofficial" Christian practices in the fourth century and later.[8] Even after Constantine and the building of public, imperially funded churches, Christians continued to worship in their homes and at burial sites. Sometimes this caused tension with what was emerging as the official church, as bishops and others were suspicious of unsupervised worship in households and aimed to control it. My project complements these later studies by documenting Christian household rituals in the second, third, and early fourth centuries and suggesting that these practices were critical to the growth of Christianity as a whole.

My contention is that alongside the development of communal worship, and alongside the debates over belief and doctrine among educated believers, a Christian domestic cult also evolved in the early centuries as followers of Christ integrated their worship into their daily lives. Sometimes these believers were heads of households and could direct the religious behavior of other household members, but sometimes they were subordinate members, like wives or slaves, in non-believing households. I seek to capture something of the lives of these people. Furthermore, these strains of Christianity did not develop in isolation; instead, they mutually influenced and shaped each other in interesting ways, especially in the third century, when the church leaders (or some leaders in certain places) began to wield political power. A larger contribution of this study, therefore, is to enrich our understanding of the development of Christianity, shifting our focus to practices and people not usually examined and then seeking to understand the larger whole in a new way.

Evidence for a Christian Household Cult

Perhaps the biggest challenge I face is the availability of evidence, both for this period (second, third, and early fourth centuries) and for people like women and slaves. For a variety of reasons, we do not have abundant, explicitly Christian evidence of daily-life religion in the first few centuries of the Common Era. One reason is that early Christian authors, for the most part, are not concerned with these practices; therefore, the best evidence we have for early Christianity mostly does not address daily-life religion. When these practices are addressed, it is often to criticize or censure them, which is still useful to us as long as we recognize and account for these rhetorical aims. This sort of evidence is discussed in the chapters that follow. Another reason is that quotidian practices tend not to produce durable evidence that would leave a trace for us centuries later; libations, prayers, and gestures often do not leave a mark. The archaeological evidence that does survive is not typically marked as belonging to any particular cult. Drinking vessels and jars, for example, are both objects of everyday use and ritual objects for making offerings. Thus the evidence is both everywhere and nowhere! A third reason relates to modern scholars, who, echoing ancient Christian writers, have not traditionally valued this facet of Christian history, so evidence has been ignored or sometimes destroyed.[9]

Long story short, the data collection to build my case has not been easy. But this is all the more reason this book is important; it documents a side of early Christian life that is simply hard to access. Underlying my search is the basic assumption that, despite the scant evidence left to us, early Christians still buried their dead, prayed for healing, and celebrated life passages even during the first few centuries, well before these rituals were connected to the institution of the church.[10] I also recognize that many of these Christians grew up as non-Christians, so they participated in traditional family celebrations at least before if not also after their interest in Christ began. Thus an important body of evidence is the household religious practices of non-Christians, the traditional household cult. As I show, these familiar, traditional practices form the basic fabric out of which Christ followers wove their own cult practices. This process defines a fascinating period—during the second, third, and early fourth centuries—marked by transition, innovation, and adaptation.

And this is indeed borne out by the most important body of evidence collected here: sources that are marked as Christian. In the first and second centuries, most of this evidence is textual: letters, stories, and essays that refer to Christians worshiping in households or other unofficial venues. Starting in the third century (although some would argue earlier), we have a material record of Christian daily-life religion, both at burial sites and in the form of amulets and gems. Other evidence includes spells with Christian symbols and names as well as church manuals that mention practices outside of communal worship. And even though published Christians tend not to concern themselves with daily practices, there are a few exceptions, especially when these writers worry about what Christians—especially Christian wives married to unbelievers—are up to. Moral literature and the canons of church councils in the fourth century, often using a discourse of censure, offer bits and pieces that, when considered within the larger context of household religion in the Roman empire, we can use to imagine a Christian household cult.

Thus the materials I take up in this study come from a wide variety of sources and regions within the Mediterranean world.[11] This is in part because of the limitations described above and in part to point out patterns across different parts of the Roman empire. These patterns support my larger claim that Christ followers developed a household cult that fit into a broad understanding, even if locally inflected, of how to interact with powerful beings in daily life (more on this below). My interest has not been to promote a universal picture of a Christian household cult but to demonstrate the innovation, adaptation, and appropriation that repeatedly shows up in a variety of contexts where those loyal to Christ lived their lives.

Theorizing Everyday Religion

Any attempt to talk about daily-life religion must contend with the fraught history of scholarship on what has often been called "popular religion," a category that is usually defined in relation to "official religion" or "authentic religion."[12] Scholars experiment with a variety of terms for this category of religious practice—popular, lived, local, folk—and in some cases these represent attempts to avoid (or at least to acknowledge) the implicit judgment that it is a lesser form of religiosity. This dichotomy (official/popular, in its various iterations) proves to be a hard one to shake, and it reveals the extent to which we have absorbed normative claims about what "true" Christianity is, or even what religion is.[13]

Yet there is also something important and persistent about this category of religion. In many cultures and historical moments we find a vibrant, ongoing, and diverse collection of practices, often related to basic human needs and life passages, that not only stands in contrast to but also interacts with what is considered the "official" religious tradition of that time and place. Even as these daily-life practices represent innovation and local adaptation, they also tend to contain consistent features, such as common conceptions of divine beings and similar modes of interaction with these beings.

In recent years, scholars have attempted to redescribe these practices so as to avoid judgments about authenticity and instead to contextualize them, along with all religious practices, in terms of human social behavior. This has been an important contribution by Stanley Stowers, who challenges historians to reconceptualize religion as a "social kind."[14] This approach combines the insights from cognitive science (about how human brains work), social ontology (about how human sociality works), and the environment or context (in this case, the agricultural economy of the ancient Mediterranean world) to propose a model of religion that makes sense of the widespread evidence for practices of exchange between humans and divine beings. Accounting for both diverse inflections and persistent features, this model reorganizes the way we understand religion in the ancient world. Instead of focusing on beliefs, singular traditions, or institutions, Stowers suggests we think in terms of multiple religious modes (or subkinds) that are organized around different practices. One mode is connected to the daily-life practices discussed above, and the other is related to intellectual practices such as reading, writing, and interpretation. Each of these, in turn, has an offshoot mode created by the institutionalization of each set of practices.

These modes, which derive from human behaviors and social interactions, allow us to look at religion in the ancient Mediterranean world from a fresh perspective and thus lay the groundwork for my claim that Christians developed a household cult. By removing "Christian" or "Roman" as defining categories of religion, this theoretical perspective allows us to see how certain types of practices cross those boundaries.[15] A brief description of the modes or subkinds here will serve as a reference point for subsequent chapters, where I apply them to specific examples.

The first and most basic mode, which Stowers calls "the religion of everyday social exchange,"[16] is the primary focus of this study. This mode includes practices that were ubiquitous in the ancient world, as they involved the basic activities of eating, drinking, working, and socializing. Instead of a set of ideas or beliefs, as we might intuitively understand religion today, this mode comprises a variety of practices that evolve out of reciprocal relationships with the divine. That is, in the ancient Mediterranean world, people imagined that any number of divine beings might interfere with life in positive or negative ways. Theodore de Bruyn describes this perception: "The world of the ancients was populated by a host of subordinate spiritual beings. They served as assistants to higher deities; as protectors of particular places, people, and things; as messengers; and as agents in human affairs, working on behalf of higher deities or human petitioners for good or for ill."[17] It was important, therefore, to maintain relationships with these beings through religious acts such as prayers and offerings. Stowers has explained this as a system of exchange; for example, the gods give things to humans (crops, wealth, offspring, health, etc.), and humans express thanks through offerings and festive meals.

This system of exchange is not so different from human social interaction. Stowers asks:

> Who in the ancient Mediterranean did not know how to give gifts, prepare food for others, share in celebratory meals, clean up a place for others, talk to others, request from others, ask for help, get someone powerful to help you, appease the hostile, make promises, honor and praise, sing for someone, seek information about another's disposition, whether kindly or hostile, and seek expert or insider advice? Simply add the idea that the other person involved was a god, ancestor, hero, angel, dead martyr, or other such being who might be a willing participant, and one has a list of the religious practices of this mundane religiosity.[18]

These basic activities and interactions, tweaked in certain ways and directed toward the divine, constitute the religion of everyday social exchange. The ancient household—which was busy with economic production, human reproduction, and all the social relationships that accompany these—is a primary site, although certainly not the only site, for this mode of religion.[19] The religious practices that take place in the household relate to these activities and concerns; they are practices bound to a specific time and place. Thus household religious worship can include not only the specific gods of the head of the household and various ancestors but also gods of the storeroom, doorway, hearth, field, boundaries of property, shop, and so on.

This model of everyday social exchange is based in part on recent work in the area of cognitive science. This research identifies characteristics of the human brain that lead to basic commonalities in religious behavior. Jennifer Larson, a classicist who has used cognitive science to understand Greek religion, writes: "A fundamental insight of the cognitive approach to religion is that our mental architecture creates a susceptibility to representations of superhuman agents, a tendency to find them memorable, compelling, and plausible."[20] According to cognitive theory, human brains are wired to conceptualize "superhuman agents" (deities, spirits, ancestors, etc.) who are interested in humans and who share human traits themselves.[21] Led by intuitive cognitive processes, humans tend to interact with these divine beings in a system of exchange. Humans offer prayers, gestures, and gifts; divine beings communicate back with signs, blessings, and revelatory messages.[22]

Importantly, these basic features manifest themselves differently as they are shaped by the social and cultural influences of the societies in which they are embedded. In Stowers's religion of everyday social exchange, they emerge primarily in the form of offerings of plants and animals—first given by the gods to people and then offered back to the gods through sacrifice and other rituals. Thus daily-life religion, that which is the most intuitive and widespread according to cognitive theories of religion, is bound up in the central social features of the ancient Mediterranean world: an agricultural economy and social networks of households.[23]

The second mode of religion is what Stowers calls "the religion of the literate cultural producer" or the "literate expert."[24] While the first mode involves the mundane tasks of daily life, this second mode primarily involves textual practices: reading and interpreting written documents. Because only a fraction of the population was literate, the religion of the literate specialist was exclusive; it required skills of reading, writing, and interpreting complex ideas about the divine that were communicated primarily through texts.[25] Literate specialists were interested in ideas about gods and operated under the assumption that right belief and moral formation pleased the gods more than, for example, offerings of grain or meat. Philosophers of various stripes are a good example of this mode. Some of these specialists attempted to give meaning to the practices of everyday social exchange; others critiqued them as misguided.[26]

This mode, too, is supported by research on cognitive science and represents a different form of cognition. The first mode—everyday social exchange—is produced by intuitive cognitive processes, as mentioned above. The practices involved in this mode are learned in childhood, are connected to certain environments, and seem effortless and self-evident to participants.[27] By contrast, this second mode is related to reflective cognitive processes and requires more work. Reflective cognition involves analysis, interpretation, and abstractions, and it uses language to communicate. Participation in these practices usually requires literacy and education and thus was available to very few in the ancient world.

So the first mode involves behaviors that people "just do"; they make sense in certain contexts, like bowing your head in prayer or taking off your hat for the national anthem. Everyone does them, including at different levels of society. Your parents and grandparents do these things. So do your neighbors. The second mode involves evaluating those gestures, thinking about why people bow their heads or what is the right way to take off one's hat. It asks who divine beings are and how to interact with them. The two modes are not mutually exclusive but often interact with and influence each other in interesting ways. To give an example from early Christianity, when Paul addresses the Corinthians about their practice of the Lord's Supper in 1 Corinthians 11, he plays the role of the literate specialist, a self-proclaimed interpreter of Jewish writings who encourages the

Corinthians toward a correct perception and practice of this ritual and of the divine. The meal itself, however, is a good example of the religion of everyday social exchange. Some of the tension evident in this passage may be generated precisely because the Corinthians experience the meal in this context and Paul attempts to interfere and correct their behavior.[28] This tension between literate producers and regular followers of Christ threads through the chapters of this study.

In addition to these two modes, Stowers delineates two others, each of which is an offshoot of one of the first two. These third and fourth modes are characterized by power: each represents one of the other modes imbued with political influence. The third mode, civic religion, is essentially the civic manifestation of the religion of everyday social exchange, now imbued with political power.[29] It expands and institutionalizes daily practices for civic purposes, resulting in civic and public cults. Thus the first mode belongs to settings such as households, neighborhoods, and grave sites, and this third mode belongs to public temples and institutions. The fourth and final mode, "the religion of the literate specialists and political power," is an overlay or elaboration on the second mode, the religion of literate specialists. This last mode is exemplified by the Christian church, which, starting in the late second or third century, attempts to institutionalize and centralize the power of the literate specialists.[30] To review, the basic mode or subkind is everyday social exchange, and three others relate to this foundation: literate experts, civic religion, and literate experts with political power.

This way of conceptualizing religion in the ancient Mediterranean pushes us to think beyond the popular/official dichotomy and reimagine Christianity as a whole.[31] Scholars have long thought of the origins of Christianity as rooted within the "intellectualist" mode of religion in the ancient Mediterranean context.[32] The authors of the New Testament writings, as well as those of most early Christian texts, define religious loyalty and practice in terms of belief and right thinking. These reflective practices (second mode) have defined the Christian religion, especially since they were codified, along with communal rituals, by those who came to power in the fourth century (fourth mode). Thus Christianity is often thought of as a tradition of belief, doctrine, interpretation, teachings, and texts. Scholars have bought into the perspective of the literate specialist, whose mode of religiosity has come to represent the "official" and "authentic" version (even if literate specialists argue over *which* interpretation, teaching, or text is true). This bias has kept us from valuing, studying, or even seeing other facets of religious practice.

Implications for the History of Early Christianity (and Plan of the Book)

As I explore in the chapters that follow, understanding religion as a social kind with multiple subkinds opens up a more complex understanding of the development of early Christianity: it suggests that within what we perceive to be one religion, there can be multiple modes operating and interacting. It suggests that the first Christ followers, rather than somehow being cordoned off from others, may have honored the gods in the same ways their families and neighbors did. Furthermore, this theoretical framework prompts us to imagine that Christianity itself was not just one thing (as it certainly was not) but that it developed in a variety of ways, each of which had some relationship to how people in the ancient Mediterranean interacted with the divine. What did everyday religion look like for Christians? What is the relationship between these practices and those related to teachings, texts, and interpretations? And how did these two modes interact as church leaders gained political power in the second, third, and early fourth centuries? These are the central questions of this study.

My exploration of these questions proceeds as follows. I begin by describing daily-life religion and households in the Roman empire (chapter 1). I caution against a comprehensive, fixed understanding of this mode and present instead shared features of daily-life rituals: variability, integration into daily life, expansion beyond the physical house, and participation in power dynamics. Next, I make the case that Christians developed their own household cult practices, including prayers, gestures, and offerings (chapter 2). I show how they preserved, adapted, and tweaked traditional worship in ways consistent with everyday religious practices more broadly. This facet of Christianity is remarkably persistent over the centuries, lasting well beyond the parameters of this study, which suggests that it was important to the growth and survival of this new religion in the Roman empire.

Attention to this phenomenon suggests several insights into how we understand early Christianity, and these are taken up in the remaining three chapters. First, it complicates the way we conceptualize what "Christianity" entailed, at least for this time period. I explore this theme in chapter 3. Evidence for Christian daily-life religion suggests that Christians preserved as much as they changed of traditional practices. Indeed, bishops and other church writers very helpfully complain about the degree to which Christians carry on "heathen" rituals, especially in households, tombs, and other unofficial venues. This persistence challenges the notion that Christianity arrived fully defined, bounded, and understood by those interested in Christ and those who were not.[33]

David Frankfurter has offered a helpful way to think about this. He argues that the spread of Christianity in Egypt happened through a process of syncretism (as reclaimed and redefined by Frankfurter and other scholars), which involves an active assembling of traditional and new symbols.[34] For Frankfurter, syncretism is the means through which a religious tradition is "indigenized and rendered comprehensible in particular cultural domains," such as the household, the local shrine, or the workshop.[35] Local interests, contexts, and histories shape how this indigenization happens. The evidence discussed in chapter 3 illustrates this process nicely, suggesting that instead of thinking about people moving from traditional cults to "Christianity," we might imagine a process of integration of symbols associated with Christ into well-established practices.

This in turn raises the question of terminology. Can we use "Christianity" and "Christian" at all, or are these terms too misleading? Certainly we need to undo any notion that the term "Christian" describes some kind of stable identity or that "Christianity" existed as a well-defined entity. I hope my study contributes to dismantling these anachronistic notions. Instead we might think of those loyal to Christ as a few people gathered in someone's apartment for a simple meal, some of whom might head over to the temple down the street after dinner to participate in rituals for another god. It is perhaps more realistic to imagine that followers treated this new cult as they treated others: as one option in a panoply of ways to honor the many divine beings in the world. With these caveats in mind, I have decided not to abandon the terms "Christian" or "Christianity" (for now). As I use them, I also consistently flag that what they stand for is not necessarily stable. I also use phrases like "Christ follower," "believer," "member of the cult of Christ," and so on.

The second insight that emerges from this study of everyday religion has to do with an expanded recognition of ritual agency. Placing daily-life practices at the center of our study also allows us to place typically marginalized characters at the center as well; this is the task of chapter 4. Wives and slaves were often the ones implementing worship in the household and related contexts, even if the prevailing ideology dictated that heads of households were in charge. Frankfurter suggests that in the context of daily-life religion, ritual agents could be any number of people, including mothers protecting their children.[36] Those who are considered subordinate in society, therefore, often do the creative work of religious actors who experiment with and adapt traditional practices. Drawing on feminist and ritual theory, I argue in chapter 4 that subordinate members of households, by their participation in household religion, both facilitated and challenged patriarchal ideologies and practices. I ask what agency or influence they might have had—either with words or without, or perhaps precisely in their obedience—over the fortunes of the household or over their own interactions with the divine.

I sympathize here with Cavan Concannon, who, following Bruno Latour, seeks to "conjure as many agencies from a small amount of historical traces" as he can.[37] This requires a willingness to use one's imagination, to learn from comparison, and to be patient with scraps of evidence.[38] Chapter 4 engages in these practices and supports the idea that subordinate people were intimately involved in the development and growth of the cult of Christ. I see this historical work as political: in order to say something about marginalized people in the Roman empire, or about quotidian practices, we cannot rely solely on traditional approaches. As discussed above, the kind of evidence we all would hope for simply did not survive for the non-elite. Therefore, tactics such as imagination, comparison, and even guesswork can be useful when paired with careful work with ancient sources and when presented with transparency about what is known and what is imagined. As I hope to show, this combination can produce responsible, historical scholarship that has the huge value of making us see people, such as enslaved people or women, who are otherwise not seen or considered.

The third insight evolving out of this study relates to the ways the modes of religion interact. In chapter 5, I argue that daily-life religion influenced the development of "official" modes of Christianity in the context of burial practices. This is especially apparent in the third and very early fourth centuries, before Christianity becomes entrenched with all the changes ushered in by Constantine and his successors. Archaeological and textual evidence from this period illustrates the tensions and influences among everyday Christian mortuary rituals, the opinions of the literate producers, and the bishops and other power brokers whose political influence increases at this time. Those interested in institutionalizing recognize the vitality and popularity of rites that honor the dead and seek to appropriate and control these. Participation in the cult of the dead by Christ followers shows the continued vibrancy of traditional practices among Christians, the variety of ways Christians adapt these for their own, and the complex cooperation and tension between lay Christians and church officials as the emerging institution participates in and also constrains these practices.

I think that as scholars, perhaps under the influence of the literate producers who defined Christianity, we have been trained to see clear boundaries where they may not be so clear. We think in terms of "pagan," "Christian," "popular," "elite," and so on. These categories may serve us

INTRODUCTION 13

in some ways, but we benefit from reorganizing them; when we do, we see new things. Stowers's theory of religion as a social kind, characterized by four modes of religion (or subkinds), rearranges our understanding of how things fit together. Across the Roman empire, both before and after the rise of Christianity, the religion of everyday social exchange pulsed through people's lives in what Ramsay MacMullen calls "an unbroken flow of belief and practice across all these several manifestations of piety." These practices and beliefs, MacMullen continues, "lie within the masses and tradition" and "assert a degree—sometimes seen as an alarming degree—of lay independence, in search of an answer to everyday prayers."[39] The chapters that follow tease out these "manifestations of piety," showing how Christ followers innovated and improvised to incorporate this new cult into their daily lives.

CHAPTER 1

HONORING THE GODS IN HOUSEHOLDS

Daily-Life Religious Practice in the Ancient Mediterranean

A family gathers around a stone altar in the courtyard attached to their house. On this Kalends day (the first day of the month), they have each stopped their work for a few moments to honor the gods of the household. They bring offerings of incense and cakes to place on the altar, and parents and children recite prayers to the deities that watch over their health and their livelihoods.

A woman in her eighth month of pregnancy passes through the reception area of her house. She pauses at a niche in the wall and reaches out to touch a bronze figurine of Aphrodite, the deity who protects women in childbirth. This gesture, which she repeats daily now, serves as her petition to the goddess for a healthy delivery and her own survival of the birth.

An enslaved man steps out of the bakery where he works, headed on an errand for his owner. On the busy street corner he stops at a small niche in the wall dedicated to Silvanus. Here he leaves a few kernels of grain, whispers a quick prayer, and continues on his way.

All of these scenes—historically imagined but rooted in literary and material evidence—represent everyday devotions in the Roman period. These rituals reflect the widespread understanding of people living at this time that myriad powerful beings could influence life for good or for ill and that, therefore, it was critical to supplicate and thank the gods for their gifts related to all facets of life, including food, health, economic production, and reproduction.

As discussed in the introduction, these sorts of rituals constituted the most widespread mode of religious practice in the Roman period. Folded into daily life, sometimes no more than a gesture offered while passing through a doorway, these practices were pervasive, adaptive, and practical.

This collection of actions made up a common vocabulary for supplicating the gods and other powerful beings regarding quotidian concerns. While sharing a similar logic as civic rituals—exchanges with the gods that reinforced societal relationships—daily devotions were more mundane, more flexible, and often unsupervised.

The aim of this chapter is to offer a sense of what everyday devotions were like in the Roman period. I do not attempt to construct a comprehensive picture of this mode of religious practice across the empire; such a goal is neither attainable nor, I would argue, desirable. The nature of the evidence itself precludes such a construction: it is often the kind of material that either might not survive (such as food offerings) or that might not be recognized as religious (such as a cup or amphora). Indeed, it can be hard to know whether a jug is simply for storage, or for pouring libations, or both.[1] Scholarly attitudes have also rendered a thorough description of this mode challenging: historically, these artifacts have not been valued, so they have not been catalogued and analyzed with the same attention as other material evidence. Fortunately, attitudes have been changing in recent decades as scholars have become more interested in studying everyday life.[2]

Yet even if we had more evidence and better documentation, the variability that characterizes this mode of religious practice, as discussed below, would caution against any unifying description. I proceed, therefore, by describing several features of this mode and then by presenting archaeological evidence from sites particularly rich in domestic finds. These "snapshots" of evidence for daily worship allow us to locate these rituals in specific spaces and to see how the common features of this mode manifest themselves in a variety of ways.

Features of Daily-Life Religious Practices

One of the most pervasive traits of household worship was its variability. The literary and material evidence in this period makes clear that there was no doctrine or uniform practice for domestic rites. Instead, it seems that households improvised their own worship, depending on their particular needs and activities.[3] Assemblages of statuettes found in different locations suggest this: the assortment of deities honored differs from place to place, from house to house. One elaborate shrine in Rome includes representations (in the forms of statuettes, busts, stele, and herms) of Isis-Fortuna, Serapis, Harpocrates, Horus, Zeus, Apollo, Aphrodite, Hecate, Hercules, and a dedicant of Bacchus.[4] Others were more humble and included a combination of local and regional deities. Similarly, there might be different groups of worshipers, or perhaps individuals within a household—such as enslaved workers in the kitchen or the pregnant woman imagined above—who could adapt their worship practices to their space or responsibilities.[5] Household worship was as various as the needs of people coping with the challenges of life in the ancient Mediterranean world.

A second feature of household worship was its integration into daily life. Although there were special occasions for worship, such as the Kalends or other holidays, quotidian activities also prompted interactions with deities. For example, the gods were honored when lamps were lit at the end of the day or when a small libation was poured at the beginning of a meal. Simply entering and exiting the house could be accompanied by a gesture asking for protection or luck.[6] Pliny the Elder discusses the efficacy of gestures such as blowing, pouring an unseen libation, and clucking the tongue (*Natural History* 28.5.25–26). Thus household rituals, unlike official civic rites, could be performed by many members of the household, including not only the head of the household but also subordinates such as women, enslaved people, and children.

A third feature of household worship is that it was not confined to the concrete borders of the house. As described in the introduction, domestic worship extended into shops, tombs, and neighborhood shrines, the spaces where people made their petitions and offerings related to family, food, fertility, protection, and so on. A good example of this is care for the dead. Mortuary rituals often began in the household itself, with the preparation of the body, then proceeded to a tomb for burial, and then continued in the following days, months, and years as household members honored the deceased family member at regular intervals.[7] The tomb became the site of family gatherings, offerings, and meals, as though it were an extension of the household (see chapter 5).

A final feature of household worship is that it is implicated in power dynamics, both those internal to the household and those related to wider society. Within a given household unit, ritual activity was shaped by hierarchical relationships: just as humans honored the divine, subordinate household members, in particular, also honored the head of the household. Indeed, belonging to a household as a wife, child, slave, or dependent meant obedience and loyalty to the gods of the master/father/husband.[8] This expectation could create tension, because subordinate members such as wives and slaves were often responsible for enacting household rituals. Recognizing how this might destabilize power relationships, Cato warns slaves not to initiate their own rituals but only to do so at the request of the master (*De agricultura* 143.1); likewise, Plutarch admonishes a wife to worship only her husband's gods and to close the door to others (*Advice to the Bride and Groom* 140d). These authors recognize the patriarchal power dynamics of household worship—and worry that they might not always be followed (see chapter 4).

In the context of the wider society, household worship was both revered and treated with suspicion. In one context Cicero asks, "What is holier and more strongly fortified by all religious awe than the house of each and every citizen? . . . Here are the altars, here the hearths, here the Penates, here the sacred things, reverence, rituals are contained" (*On His House* 109).[9] Cicero casts the house as holy, the very epitome of Roman identity and piety. Yet elsewhere he warns, "Let no one have the gods separately, either new gods or foreign gods, unless publicly adopted. Privately let them worship those gods whom they have received as duly worshiped by their fathers (or ancestors: *patres*)" (*De legibus* 2.19).[10] This echoes the early concerns of Plato in his well-known abolition of domestic cult, which he perceives as a haphazard mode of worship, especially by women and the sick: "No one shall possess a shrine in his own house: when any one is moved in spirit to do sacrifice, he shall go to the public places to sacrifice, and he shall hand over his oblations to the priests and priestesses to whom belongs the consecration thereof" (*Laws* 909d–909e).[11]

As these warnings from elite writers signal, household cult practices were less contained and less subject to scrutiny than civic cult and were therefore difficult to define and to control. They might have been right to be concerned: everyday religious practices were ubiquitous, available to many, often unsupervised, and subject to adaptation and improvisation. It is not surprising that these features drew censure from civic officials and literate elites who were invested in public rituals and the power structures they supported.[12]

These four features of household worship—variety, mundanity, expansiveness, and connection to power—make this mode of religious practice both hard to document and critically important for understanding ancient life. Rooted in household concerns, these rites served as the means through which families, neighbors, and shopkeepers communicated with the powerful beings that influenced their lives. Specific examples from the material record help us further understand this mode of religious practice.

Snapshots of Household Worship: Four Archaeological Sites

To get a more concrete sense of how people interacted with the gods in their daily lives, it is helpful to look at four well-preserved sites: Karanis (Egypt), Ephesos (Turkey), Pompeii (Italy), and Sepphoris (Israel). These sites offer specific examples in four geographical regions of the Mediterranean basin and illustrate the features of household worship discussed above. I refer to the following descriptions as "snapshots" to signal their incompleteness. Even the abundance of evidence at these sites affords only glimpses of the rich variety of rituals of daily life that were ubiquitous at this time.

Karanis

The ancient village of Karanis, located fifty miles southwest of Cairo, was founded in the third century BCE and flourished as a producer of grain in the Roman period.[13] Excavations of Karanis have yielded information about domestic life there, with numerous houses having been unearthed and studied.[14] Among the finds that indicate household worship are figurines, niches, lamps, and incense burners.

A variety of deities and other beings are represented in this material, including Serapis, Isis, Aphrodite, Harpocrates, praying figures (orants), horses, and fertility figures. Isis appears in different forms, including as Thermouthis, a snake goddess responsible for harvesting grain; Isis-Thermouthis appears on two reliefs in Karanis, bearing a female torso and the tail of a snake.[15] Multiple terracotta figures in the form of praying women were found in houses in Karanis (fig. 1).[16] One seated figure is interpreted either as a worshiper bringing offerings of fruit and grain or as a deity herself (her iconography being reminiscent of Demeter).[17] Various representations of Harpocrates, standing for fertility and rebirth, were found both in houses and in civic spaces in Karanis, where he was popular in the Roman period.[18]

It is likely that these figurines representing deities were placed in niches in the walls of Karanis houses.[19] Among these finds, excavators delineate two types of niches: utilitarian spaces used for storage, characterized by a lack of decoration, and more elaborate spaces marked by fluted columns and shell motifs, among other things. These latter examples were likely used as shrines or altars.[20]

In addition, a number of clay lamps and incense burners, indicating rituals associated with lighting and offering, were found in the remains of domestic Karanis.[21] The interpretation of these objects is supported by documentary evidence from Egypt: letters written to family members mention rituals that involve these objects. For example, in one letter Apollonia and Epons ask their sisters at home, "Please light a lamp for the shrines and spread the cushions" (P.Athen. 60),[22] and Aelius Theon tells his brother that he makes an offering for his niece before Serapis (P.Oxy. LIX 3992).

The domestic finds at Karanis illustrate a household cult concerned with themes of fertility, protection, and agriculture. Indeed, in several cases, similar figures were found both in houses and in granaries, illustrating

FIG. 1 Clay (unfired) figurine, female, orants position. Karanis, Egypt. Kelsey Museum of Archaeology, University of Michigan, KM 6473.

the importance of agricultural production and the easy flow of devotion between domestic and other work spaces. Connections to civic cult are also found in this evidence, with figures in houses echoing those found in temples. One bronze statuette, featuring a mix of the characteristics of Serapis, Zeus, and Amun, is thought to imitate a monumental statue from the North Temple, now lost.[23]

Ephesos

In the heart of Ephesos, an ancient harbor city on the west coast of Asia Minor, a series of well-appointed houses were built into a hillside stretching up from the famous library and theater. Based on their location, the quality of their construction, and their decoration, it is clear that these were the domiciles of the city's elite. Called terrace houses or slope houses by excavators and scholars, these structures have yielded helpful information about household worship in elite families. In the second half of the third century CE, an earthquake leveled these houses, after which they were uninhabitable.[24] As is often the case, an ancient tragedy resulted in a treasure for modern archaeologists, who have excavated the well-preserved remains of these toppled homes. We turn our attention to a few of the finds in Terrace House 2, an area that includes seven separate living units.[25]

As in Karanis, excavators in Ephesos unearthed statuettes, niches, altars, and paintings in Terrace House 2. *Thymiateria*, multipurpose cult furnishings that served as altar, lamp, and incense burner all in one, were located in domestic entrances and in work spaces (the latter of which were often accessed by multiple residences). These were decorated with busts of deities, such as Serapis or Dionysius, who protected and cared for the occupants and their shared workshops.[26] In one case, a *thymiaterion* was found together with three bronze statuettes representing Isis Panthea, Serapis, and Athena. Based on the different dates of these pieces, archaeologists surmise that the last resident of this house had assembled this grouping,[27] most likely according to the particular needs of the family and household. A blend of Greek and Egyptian deities characterizes this collection.

In one residential unit, archaeologists have traced the renovation of an entrance hall into a small sanctuary dedicated to cult worship.[28] Two funerary reliefs decorated this room, and a third was located in the adjoining room. Each depicted the deceased (possibly ancestors) reclining at a meal surrounded by figures who were likely members of the household. By incorporating the funeral reliefs into the cult space of the house, the occupants marked their connection to past generations, deceased family members who had joined the realm of powerful beings who might influence the lives of the living.

A *thymiaterion* also occupied this room, as did a painting of a snake winding up the wall opposite the reliefs. Interpreters associate this image with protective deities, either the *Agathos Daimon* (the good spirit) from the Greek tradition or the *genius loci* (guardian of place) that we find in Vesuvian sites.[29] Strategically located so as to be seen from the entrance to the residence as well as the courtyard, the serpent likely served an apotropaic function for the household and its various activities.[30]

Evidence of domestic imperial cult also appears in the remains of Terrace House 2. In one apartment, life-sized busts of Tiberius and his mother, Livia, were found, with a bronze snake between them.[31] An altar with the eagle of Zeus was located in the courtyard, indicating that worship practices related to honoring the imperial family likely took place here.[32] In another apartment, evidence for imperial worship is indicated not by the material finds but by knowledge of the occupant, C. Vibius Salutaris.[33] He is otherwise known in Ephesos for sponsoring bimonthly processions in which statuettes of Artemis were to be carried around her temple and then placed in the theater.[34] The lengthy public inscription that outlines the parameters of this endowment indicates that an additional pair of statuettes, the imperial couple Trajan and Plotina, would be kept by Salutaris and donated to the city after his death. Scholars thus surmise that the imperial family was also honored in this apartment, although we have no material evidence left to indicate the location of a shrine or altar. This example illustrates how fluid the boundaries between domestic and civic worship could be, especially if, as some scholars assume, the imperial statuettes were moved from home to procession to theater and back. Even if they were not part of the processions during Salutaris's lifetime, he intended for them to join civic worship after his death.[35]

Pompeii

The eruption of Mount Vesuvius in 79 CE, a catastrophic event for all nearby inhabitants, has resulted in an extraordinary trove of material evidence of first-century life on the Italic peninsula. The pyroclastic flow from the volcano buried the surrounding landscape within minutes and preserved a snapshot of life on that fateful day. Excavations of houses and neighborhoods help us understand something about household worship in the Campanian town of Pompeii. In the sampling that follows, we see evidence of the worship of *lares*, *penates*, and *genii*, household deities that are typical of this region. There is some fluidity in what these beings represent: *lares* have been interpreted as spirits of ancestors and also as spirits of place; *penates* have been described as the gods of pantry and also, more generally, as the particular gods of a given household; and the *genius* is a guardian or spiritual personification of the head of the household.[36]

In the household shrine of The House of the Red Walls (VIII.5.37), we find the familiar feature of an assemblage of deities as well as paintings of *lares* and a *genius* (figs. 2 and 3).[37] This shrine took the form of an aedicula, a niche framed by columns on the side and an architrave and pediment above. This particular niche, rather than being recessed into a wall, protrudes from the wall and sits on a masonry base. Within the aedicula stood a collection of bronze figurines (see fig. 3), likely the *penates* or particular gods of the household—Apollo, Asclepius, Mercury, Hercules, and, flanking these, twin *lares* on either side—along with a bronze lamp.[38] As with the Terrace House 2 collection, the figures in this assemblage are of different sizes and quality, a characteristic consistent with the practice of householders creating their own groupings. The back of the niche features paintings of two *lares* on either side of a *genius*, who offers produce and a libation over an altar. Located in the atrium (a central room for visiting and conducting business), this shrine made a clear statement about the householders' piety.

FIG. 2 (OPPOSITE)
Aedicula shrine in atrium of House of the Red Walls (VIII.5.37 Pompeii). Photo: author.

FIG. 3 Aedicula shrine with figurines in atrium of House of the Red Walls (VIII.5.37 Pompeii). Photo from the collection of Rick Bauer. Courtesy of Jackie and Bob Dunn, https://www.pompeiinpictures.com.

A kitchen painting in another Pompeiian house helps us imagine the rituals that might have taken place at such a shrine. In the house of Sutoria Primigenia, the whole household is depicted at worship, flanked by two outsized *lares* who, by their Phrygian hats, may have offered particular protection to the enslaved and to freedpeople. The husband and wife make the offering at an altar, while enslaved members of the household stand at attention, attired in similar tunics and gesturing their prayer in unison.[39] This painting communicates the ideology of household worship: the leadership of the head of the household and his wife accompanied by the obedient worship of subservient members. The adjoining wall of this corner shrine features a painting of a snake near an altar in a garden, as well as an actual niche recessed into the wall, as though the live members of the Sutoria Primigenia household might mimic the painting by making their offerings.

We find similar features in neighborhood shrines in Pompeii, indicating that the mode of household worship extended into neighborhoods and shops as well. One altar on Via dell'Abbondanza was located in an alley next to a shop (I.11.1). The scene on the wall, which can just be made out with the paint that remains, is of two *lares* pouring wine into buckets next to an altar with a snake between them.[40] Below this scene is a stone altar, on which were discovered the charred remains of half a chicken, indicating that a sacrifice had recently been offered. Scrawled on the wall next to the painting (perhaps by a passerby?) is the phrase "by the holy *Lares*, I ask you" (*CIL* 4.8426).[41] These neighborhood shrines, although they vary greatly in size and shape, were often installed at crossroads (*compita*) and might be frequented by shopkeepers, workers, customers, and residents of that neighborhood. Sometimes an inscription or a graffito accompanied these *compita* shrines, where it was likely to be seen by many.[42]

Sepphoris

Sepphoris, in Galilee, was a thriving urban center in the Roman period. It has received attention in part because of its proximity to Nazareth (four miles), igniting the imaginations of scholars who debate whether Jesus, traditionally characterized as an uneducated carpenter, knew this city's colonnaded streets, lively commerce, and urban cultural traditions. It has been extensively excavated in the last four decades, revealing valuable information about the domestic lives of the Jews who lived in this city.[43]

In the residential quarter of the western acropolis in Sepphoris, twenty stepped pools have been excavated.[44] Although there is some disagreement about their use, many believe that these are *mikva'ot*, pools used for ritual immersion as directed by rabbinic prescriptions.[45] These pools, which fall into a date range from 100 BCE to 363 CE, vary in size depending on the available space (and likely the resources of the householder), but it seems clear that they are separate structures from those used for bathing or storage.[46] Stairs descend into the basins, allowing an adult to immerse her or his body fully in the water. The entire installation of each basin is covered in plaster, which seals in the water, prevents the stone basin from deteriorating, and preserves the quality of the water.[47]

According to the literate specialists who produced the Mishnah, ritual bathing was necessary for purification.[48] Bodily experiences such as menstruation, childbirth, contact with the dead, and nocturnal emissions rendered people ritually impure. Immersion in a *mikveh* would purify the individual so as to allow him or her to return to regular contact with others. Similar pools have been excavated in many areas in Palestine; they have been found in houses, agricultural structures, along roadsides, near graves, and outside synagogues.[49] They evince a widespread and seemingly adaptable practice of ritual immersion, a practice well integrated into daily life.[50]

One puzzling find in Sepphoris is a cache of incense shovels—ritual equipment that, at least in the context of temple service, was used to burn incense.[51] The shovels at Sepphoris, however, exhibit no evidence of exposure to fire or extreme heat: there are no burn marks to be found. One suggestion is that they did not serve any purpose except as symbolic reference to temple worship (perhaps meaningful to residents who were connected to priestly families).⁵² Another theory is that these shovels were adapted for a different use: scenting the house with fragrant plants and spices, a kind of dry fumigation with a potpourri-style mixture.⁵³ While there may well have been practical advantages to this practice (providing an alternative fragrance to those of the human and animal bodies sharing the house), it is not clear whether there was a religious component.⁵⁴ It is striking, however, that the implements resemble those used in temple service, as indicated by late antique Jewish art in synagogues and other places.⁵⁵

Trash heaps in this same residential area of Sepphoris have yielded evidence of domestic life, including a variety of decorated lamp fragments. Floral motifs, the head of Medusa, erotic scenes, menorahs, and Torah shrines are among the designs on these oil lamps, indicating both common iconography with other lamp finds around the empire as well as specifically Jewish symbols.⁵⁶ Several sherds are incised with menorahs; one in particular seems to have been executed freehand and includes other ritual objects, such as a *shofar* and a *lulav*.⁵⁷ Another example presents a highly stylized Torah shrine with closed cabinet doors next to barely visible menorah branches.⁵⁸

Like everyone else in the ancient world, inhabitants of Sepphoris lit lamps at the end of each day. For Jewish residents, however, lamp-lighting took on a special significance at the beginning of the Sabbath. The task is described in the Mishnah as belonging to women in the house (along with baking bread; Mishnah Shabbat 2:6,7).⁵⁹ This weekly observance would have also included prayers, blessings, and special meals.⁶⁰ Josephus claims that Sabbath observance, fasts, lamp-lighting, and food prohibitions are ritual traditions that are admired and imitated around the empire (*Against Apion* 2.282).

It is worth noting that the evidence found in Sepphoris is not exclusively connected to what we traditionally identify as Jewish iconography. We have already noted the Medusa image on a lamp. In this same residential deposit, archaeologists also unearthed bronze miniatures of Pan and Prometheus, figurines similar to those found at Karanis, Ephesos, and Pompeii. An elegant villa elsewhere in Sepphoris contains mosaics that depict a drinking scene with Dionysius and Hercules.⁶¹ This perceived "mixture" of cults may signal the presence of non-Jews in Sepphoris, and it also may signal the kind of blending of traditions we see in each of our other "snapshots."

Scholars have traditionally resisted this latter possibility—that Jews honored and acknowledged other powerful beings besides the god of Israel—perhaps influenced by what the literary tradition claims Jewish practice should be. Recently, however, researchers have noticed that daily-life practices do not always conform to these ideals. Ross Kraemer discusses two votive inscriptions by "Ioudaioi" in an Egyptian temple of Pan and comments that these inscriptions evince "the everyday religious behavior of two Jewish men," demonstrating "that Jews could and did honor other gods under some circumstances."[62] Karen Stern, placing these inscriptions in the context of regional travel culture, comments that they illustrate how unproblematically these self-described *Ioudaioi* "actively participated in the common devotional and social discourses of their peers."[63] This same dynamic may have occurred in Sepphoris, where, as we have seen, images of multiple gods appear among the remains of specifically Jewish symbols.[64]

Conclusion

Stern's comment illustrates the way everyday religion operates in the ancient Mediterranean world. It is a mode of religious practice that cuts across the boundaries of particular deities and peoples; it offers a common vocabulary for interacting with gods and other powerful beings. As the above snapshots evince, people offer their prayers, incense, light, food, and written words to a variety of powerful beings in ways that make sense in their daily lives. They hope for health, protection, prosperity, and fertility, things related to coping and thriving in households.

The evidence unearthed in Karanis, Ephesos, Pompeii, and Sepphoris displays features of the everyday religious practices enumerated above. The improvisational nature of this mode of religion is clear in the variety of objects, deities, and practices in these material finds. Altars and lamps show how integrated into daily life these rituals were in domestic spaces, workshops, and street corners. And hierarchies of power, so palpable at all levels of Roman society, are present here, too: women and men, enslaved and free, emperor and subject.

These archaeological sites help us begin to imagine the rituals of exchange with the gods that take place in these spaces. In chapter 2, which explores both Christian and non-Christian practices, fuller descriptions emerge with the help of textual and documentary evidence. I make the case there that followers of Christ also participated in this mode of interaction with the divine. Like their neighbors, they drew from the common pool of actions that were considered efficacious in houses and other spaces, sometimes offering their own particular twist on the rituals. Although elite writers expended a considerable amount of energy arguing that Christians are different from others, in their daily devotions, they might have looked a lot like non-Christian family members and neighbors.

CHAPTER 2

DOORWAYS, BEDROOMS, AND KITCHENS

A Sampler of Everyday Christian Practices

"Why have they no altars? No temples? No recognized images?" Thus Caecilius questions Christian practice in a dialogue written by Minucius Felix in the third century.[1] Indeed, Christians were unlike followers of many established religious cults in the ancient Mediterranean world in that they did not often worship in public, civic spaces, at least not before Constantine. Their god did not yet have a dedicated structure to receive offerings or prayers.[2] But in other ways, the cult of Christ looked a lot like other cults in the Roman world, specifically in the daily-life worship that occurred in households, neighborhoods, shops, and other places.

In focusing on these quotidian practices, I illustrate a side of Christianity that has not typically been given much attention. It is not the intellectual development of the tradition, which is debated at length in Minucius's text (and in many other texts as well), nor is it the liturgy of the institution as it grows and becomes established in the fourth century. Instead we notice the prayer uttered upon leaving the house, the sign of the cross made on the forehead before eating a meal, the amulet with a fragment of gospel text worn around the neck. These actions are subtle enough that you could miss them entirely, and indeed scholars have almost done so.[3]

The purpose of this chapter is to offer a sampler of practices. It is by no means meant to be—nor is it possible for it to be—comprehensive or to imply coherence among different populations of believers around the empire. The evidence itself is patchwork, coming from a variety of sources with different rhetorical aims and perspectives. The work of literate producers (or intellectuals) necessarily dominates, and it is important to remember throughout that this evidence is prescriptive, not descriptive, even as it offers a hint of how people were worshiping or, at a minimum, what practices were in the realm of possibility (see the introduction). Some of the evidence comes from a growing body of documentary data for everyday life; some comes from the precious few archaeological remains from this period. We must not be tempted to consider this collection of bits and pieces proof of a unified, stable set of everyday worship practices.

And it is not only the nature of the evidence that should warn against this temptation but also the nature of the practices themselves. As discussed in the introduction and in chapter 1, everyday worship, whether associated with Christ or not, is fluid, intuitive, open to innovation and adaptation. Unlike the civic or literate modes of religion, the religion of everyday exchange is not systematized; variability is one of its characteristics. By collecting evidence for Christian manifestations of this mode of worship, I hope to show the broad characteristics Christians shared with non-Christians in their interactions with the divine. At precisely the moment that literate producers and other experts were attempting to draw clear boundaries between Christ followers and others, a larger mode of religious behavior bound them together (see chapter 3).[4]

Yet inherent in this larger mode of religious practice is the notion of local, individual creativity. Christians, like others in the ancient Mediterranean world, are not simply repeating verbatim traditional prayers, gestures, and offerings; they are also weaving these into the traditions, stories, and communal rituals of their new cult. And they are doing so in ways that make sense in specific spaces they occupy in daily life. This process, as David Frankfurter describes it, is "gradual, creative assemblage, whose principal or most immediate agents might be local scribes, mothers protecting children, or artisans, not priests or monks."[5]

Thus my goals for this chapter are to acquaint readers with the range of Christian practices indicated by literary, documentary, and material evidence; to highlight connections to traditional daily worship in the Roman empire; and to hint at the innovation and creative work taking place as Christ followers construct a household cult. The chapter thus serves both as a companion to chapter 1, which explores non-Christian household worship through a series of snapshots of archaeological sites, and as a foundation for later chapters, which explore the evidence surveyed here in more depth.

Words and Postures: Prayer Practices

When Thecla falls to the ground in the house of Onesiphorus, she cries to her god in prayer, "My God and the God of this house where the light shone upon me, Jesus Christ, Son of God, my help in prison, my help before the governors, my help in the fire, my help among the wild beasts, you alone are God and to you be glory forever."[6] This second-century depiction of a Christian praying illustrates several features of ancient Mediterranean prayer practices in general. Thecla addresses the divine directly, enumerates multiple ways this god has assisted her, and offers praise to the deity. She prays with her whole body, falling down "on the place where Paul had sat" and crying before speaking. Finally, she prays in a house, addressing the god of that particular household.

Thecla here participates in one of the most basic tasks in everyday religion: communication with the divine. Through speech and gestures of thanksgiving, praise, and petition, people initiated and maintained a cycle of exchange with the powerful beings that influenced their lives.[7] Understood in this way, the term "prayer" includes a range of types of speech, writing, and movement, from those widely known and connected to liturgical settings (such as the Shema or the Lord's Prayer) to those crafted for specific people and circumstances (such as spells or incantations).[8] In the "modes of religion" model, these belong to the family of practices deployed when addressing deities and other powerful beings.[9]

Thecla's prayer is shaped by its literary context; it serves to conclude her heroic story by highlighting perilous moments and praising the god who saw her through. Other Christian prayers from our period, coming from documentary sources rather than literary, illustrate how practical prayers could be, arising from daily challenges and fears. One asks for relief from eye disease: "In the name of God and Jesus Christ and Holy Spirit, *Raba Skanomka loula amriktorathena thabytharorak*, I pray to you, O great name of *Iaô*: turn aside the afflicting ophthalmia and no longer permit any onset of ophthalmia to occur."[10] This prayer invokes both recognizable Christian names of the divine along with other names of powerful beings used in amulets and spells.[11]

Another prayer asks god to send his angels to attend the petitioner throughout the day, granting her or him success in all activities of the day or night. The words of the prayer evoke an image of the supplicant surrounded on all sides by an army of protective powers: "For I have before me Jesus Christ who attends me and accompanies me; behind me Yao Sabaoth Ado[nai]; on my right and [left] the god of Ab[raham, Isaac, and Jacob]; over [my] face [and] my heart Ga[briel, Michael], Raphael, Saruel, [Raguel], Nuriel, Anael: [Protect] me from every [demon . . .]."[12] This prayer illustrates the widespread understanding in ancient Mediterranean cultures that many powerful beings—here, angels who serve a supreme god—are potentially present and active in all moments of daily life. All of these prayers show Christ followers participating in a system of exchange with the divine, offering praise and honor and asking for help, protection, or favors. This dynamic echoes the social system of patronage, whereby gifts are exchanged between those of unequal power.[13] This notion is in keeping with the idea that in daily-life religious practices, people attribute human traits to the gods, imagining that human requests and gifts would be understood and well received.[14] In these prayers, powerful beings from Christian stories are woven into traditional petitionary formulas.[15]

In some cases, as is likely with the last two Christian prayers discussed here, there was another power broker involved: the ritual expert who produced the prayer or advised the petitioner on how to formulate it. This tends to be the case with prayers written on amulets and produced in handbooks of spells. People commissioned a practitioner—sometimes a priest or other ritual authority—to write an effective prayer tailored to their particular needs. Thus these prayers involved both the professional services of the expert and the performance, sometimes with accompanying rituals or movements, by the petitioner on his or her own.[16] The expertise of amulet producers might be comparable, in the eyes of ancient believers, to that of ritual experts who oversaw liturgical prayers in communal meetings.[17]

Other Christian prayers focus on moral standing, such as this one that asks for help, removal of sins, and saving: "God almighty, creator of the heaven, the earth, the sea and everything in them, help me, have mercy on me, expunge my sins, save me now and in the time to come by the agency of Jesus Christ, our Lord and Saviour, through whom also is (your?) glory and might in all eternity. Amen" (P.Oxy. III 407).[18] The words of this third- or fourth-century prayer, which might have been worn as an amulet,[19] reflect several familiar ideas in Christian teaching at the time, including god as the creator, the intercessory role of Christ, and the believer's need for release from sin. Scholars have noted the reference to Psalm 145:6 (in speaking about god as creator), which illustrates how Christ followers used these earlier Jewish texts—themselves a form of prayer—to construct their own communications.[20]

Jewish modes of addressing the divine, which share many of the broad characteristics of ancient Mediterranean prayer in general, fundamentally shape Christian prayer.[21] The instructions about how and what to pray in the earliest Christian texts come from Jewish contexts, and they affect how later Christian writers advise people regarding prayer, with respect to both individual and communal practices. The central place of the Lord's Prayer, found in first-century gospels, illustrates this. The *Didache* (a collection of instructions for rituals dating to the end of the first century) recommends praying the Lord's Prayer three times each day (8.3), and Tertullian asserts that the Lord's Prayer should be the model for individual prayer; specific requests beyond this should only take place once this foundation is laid (*Or.* 10).[22]

Other instructions from early letters and gospels influence later literate specialists in their advice to Christ followers on how to pray. Paul tells believers, "Pray without ceasing" (1 Thess 5:17), and the author of Ephesians encourages the audience, "Pray in the spirit at all times in every prayer and supplication. To that end keep alert and always persevere in supplication for all the saints" (Eph 6:18). Later authors consider constant prayer an ideal but also offer the more practical advice to pray at certain times of the day.[23] The third, sixth, and ninth hours are regularly mentioned as appropriate times for individual prayer throughout the day, as are morning and evening, upon waking and going to sleep.[24] Other occasions or times that call for prayer are at meals, upon the departure of a fellow believer from the house, and during the night, necessitating waking from sleep.[25] These texts indicate that prayer was not only intended as part of communal rituals but also prescribed for individual practice, meant to be incorporated into the tasks of the day.[26] The *Apostolic Tradition* (a collection of instructions for worship dating to the fourth century but likely reflecting earlier materials) makes this explicit, instructing believers to heed what they learn at communal meetings: "And you will be told also in that place the things that it is proper for you to do in your house" (41.3), and "If you are in your house, pray about the third hour and bless God" (41.5).[27]

If people are praying multiple times during the day, including early in the morning and at night, where are they praying? A natural place might be before a shrine, which was where both daily and festive offerings and prayers were often practiced (see chapter 1). A first-century poem describes such a scene on the occasion of a girl's birthday: "Juno of the birthday, receive the holy piles of incense which the accomplished maid's soft hand now offers you. Today she has bathed for you; most joyfully she has decked herself for you, to stand before your altar a sight for all to see. . . . She is making an offering to you, holy goddess, three times with cake and three times with wine, and the mother eagerly enjoins upon her child what she must pray for" (3.12.1–4, 14–15).[28] The girl's prayers follow rituals of special bathing and dressing and accompany her gifts to Juno. One can imagine the family gathered around Juno's altar, perhaps in an atrium or courtyard.

Did Christ believers do the same? Although we do not have definitive evidence that they worshiped at domestic shrines in the second, third, and early fourth centuries, two factors suggest that it is possible. One is the prevalence of such shrines (including niches, paintings, altars, etc.) in the archaeological record around the Roman empire.[29] Another is the archaeological evidence of Christian domestic shrines from the late fourth, fifth, and sixth centuries, which tells us that at least by this period such a tradition is established.[30]

Of course, a shrine or other specific location is not necessary for prayer, which, on its own, does not necessarily require furniture or props.[31] Indeed, several literate specialists, taking their cue from Matthew 6:5–6, advise that Christ believers should pray privately. Matthew's Jesus instructs his disciples thus (in a passage just preceding the directive to pray the Lord's Prayer):

> (5) And whenever you pray, do not be like the hypocrites; for they love to stand and pray in the synagogues and at the street corners, so that they may be seen by others. Truly I tell you, they have received their reward. (6) But whenever you pray, go into your room (ταμεῖόν) and shut the door and pray to your Father who is in secret; and your Father who sees in secret will reward you.

These instructions inform Tertullian's own advice to pray in the "hidden chambers" or "secret places" (*in abditum*) of the house, since god can hear petitions even there (*Or.* 1.4).[32] Likewise Origen (third century) recommends retreating to the most solemn or august place in the house (τὸ σεμνότερον), a place with no distractions (*Or.* 31.4).[33] Referring to Matthew 6, Cyprian (third century) comments that the Lord bade us pray "in secret—in hidden and remote places, in our very bed-chambers (*in cubiculis ipsis*)—which is best suited to faith, that we may know that God is everywhere present, and hears and sees all, and in the plenitude of His majesty penetrates even into hidden and secret places" (*De dominica oratione* 4.4).[34] These literate specialists, using Matthew to theologize about humility and god's omnipresence, endorse unsupervised daily prayer that could take place in private household spaces.

It seems, then, at least among those counseling others regarding this practice, that *cubicula*—typically small rooms, away from public parts of the house—were possible sites for addressing god. These rooms were used for a variety of activities, including business transactions, reception of guests, work, writing, sleep, and sex.[35] These Christian writers are not completely sanguine about this location for reasons having to do with the intimacies of marriage. Origen questions whether it is appropriate to commune with god in the same space where one has communed with a spouse (*Or.* 31.4). Tertullian worries that a Christian wife will be observed by her non-Christian husband when she rises at night to pray (*Ux.* 2.5.3).[36] The *Apostolic Tradition* advises a Christian man either to rise at night to pray with his wife or to choose another location if she is not a believer: "(11) And rising about midnight, wash your hands with water and pray. And if your wife is also present, both pray together; (12) but if she is not yet a believer, withdrawing into another room, pray and return again to your bed" (41:11–12).[37] One can trace a sense of anxiety about praying in the same room where sex occurs or in the vicinity of unbelieving spouses, perhaps both connected to concerns about proper boundaries. We do not know whether ordinary people experienced this same worry or whether it was solely the burden of intellectuals. As Kristina Sessa shows, this ambivalence continues, even as the *cubiculum* becomes a place of spiritual seclusion and intimacy with god for later Christians.[38]

Like other prayer practices in the ancient Mediterranean world, Christian prayers involved not just words but also specific postures and bodily movements.[39] Anthony Corbeill argues that Romans understood that "an effective prayer or incantation required physical as well as verbal activity."[40] Again, our literate specialists draw upon biblical examples to advise believers on what to do with their bodies in prayer. The author of 1 Timothy writes, "I desire, then, that in every place the men should pray, lifting up holy hands without anger or argument" (2:8). Tertullian (*Apol.* 30.4), Cyprian (*Ad Demetrianum* 16), Clement (*Stromateis* 7.7), and Origen (*Or.* 31.2) all comment on this posture as ideal. Origen kindly accommodates those who might be unable to hold the standing posture, allowing for those with a foot disease to sit instead and, indeed, to lie down if not well enough to sit (*Or.* 31.2). Tertullian warns that it is good to hold this prayer position in a humble way, with "not even our hands too loftily elevated, but elevated temperately and becomingly; and not even our countenance over-boldly uplifted" (*Or.* 17.1).[41] At certain times kneeling is considered appropriate: for example, when confessing sins or participating in a station or fast (Tertullian, *Or.* 23; Origen, *Or.* 31.3).[42] Thecla's character either kneels or lies prostrate when she "falls to the ground" after having returned to Onesiphorus's house.

The gesture of prayer first described in 1 Timothy, standing with hands lifted and eyes turned toward heaven, is also found in the material record in this period in early Christianity. Frescoes and reliefs of praying figures, or "orants" (*orans* is Latin for one who is praying), are found in funerary contexts (in catacombs and on sarcophagi) and constitute some of our earliest Christian art.[43] The orant, which is almost always represented by a female figure, predates Christianity, appearing on tombs and coins in a representation of *pietas* in the second and third centuries.[44] Christians, who began to use this figure on tombs in the third century, thus found a ready symbol in the figure of the orant, already understood by ancient Mediterranean cultures as a praying figure representing piety and appropriate in funerary contexts. Scholars have suggested a variety of specifically Christian interpretations of these figures, including the soul of the deceased in paradise, filial devotion, and a representation of the deceased person.[45] Given that some identified this posture as representing the shape of the cross, it is not surprising that the stance of the orant became an ideal posture for Christian prayer.[46]

Whether kneeling or standing with hands outstretched, followers of Christ may have heard that they should face east when they pray, perhaps after Paul's example just before he is executed: "Then Paul stood with his face to the east and lifting up his hands to heaven, prayed at length" (Acts of Paul, Martyrdom of Paul 5).[47] Clement notes that praying to the east is appropriate (*Stromateis* 7), and Tertullian even objects that Christians have been thought to be worshipers of the sun for this reason (*Nat.* 1.13)! Origen's comments on this practice re-create deliberation over this very issue when he imagines that someone might express a preference for praying with a view of the outdoors (so facing a door or window), even if it is not facing east. This could be perceived as much more appealing than praying to a wall, after all. Origen disagrees, arguing that what the east symbolizes—Christ's light rising—is more important than the view (*Or.* 32). This discussion conjures an amusing domestic scene of believers discussing the right place to pray in a household, standing before walls and windows to consider their options.

Signing and Blowing: Holy Gestures

When Tertullian worries about a Christian wife performing her prayers at night in the household of her non-believing husband, he mentions bodily gestures she might perform as well: signing herself or her bed and blowing on her hands (*Ux.* 2.5.3).[48] The *Apostolic Tradition* mentions these rituals, both as accompaniments to prayer (41.14) and as independent gestures (42.1, 4). As we saw with prayer above, followers of Christ communicated with the divine not only with words but also with bodily movements, like many others in the ancient Mediterranean world.[49]

In Pliny's (first century) review of various worship practices, he emphasizes the importance of bodily movements independent of speech, noting that "it is clear that scrupulous actions, even without words, have their powers" (*Natural History* 28.5.24).[50] He then offers several examples, including a spin move: "In worshipping we raise our right hand to our lips and turn round our whole body, the Gauls considering it more effective to make the turn to the left" (28.5.25).[51] He then remarks, "All peoples agree in worshipping lightning by clucking with the tongue" (28.5.25). Pliny describes a secret gesture next, in which someone surreptitiously pours a libation under the table to counteract unlucky words spoken at a banquet (28.5.26).

Each of these may have protective functions, as they attempt to avert danger.[52] The gesture of placing the hands to the lips (perhaps like blowing a kiss) serves elsewhere as a greeting to the gods, as Apuleius describes in the story of Psyche, who is mistaken by her admirers as Venus: "And moving the right hand to the face, with the first finger resting on the outstretched thumb, they venerated her with pious adoration as though she was actually the goddess Venus herself" (*Metamorphoses* 4.28).[53]

Christ followers seemed to agree with Pliny about the effectiveness of a well-placed gesture. A good example of this is signing or sealing, which is described variously as making the sign of the cross on the forehead, having Christ's or God's name written on the forehead, or simply as being sealed.[54] The numerous references to this practice refer both to the believer as the recipient of the sign or seal and as the one who makes the gesture on her or his own body. As mentioned above, Tertullian refers to signing as a gesture to accompany prayer (*Ux.* 2.5.3; see chapter 4), but he also recommends it for many moments in the day: "At every forward step and movement, at every going in and out, when we put on our clothes and shoes, when we bathe, when we sit at table, when we light the lamps, on the couch, on a seat, in all the ordinary actions of daily life, we trace upon the forehead the sign" (*Cor.* 3).[55] According to Tertullian's advice, this practice of signing marks bodies or spaces, accompanies transitions (such as entering or exiting), and takes place multiple times each day.

Like ritual gestures all over the Mediterranean world, making the sign of the cross is perceived as practical, powerful, and available to all. It invokes the aid of the divine to intervene in a variety of jams. Christian literate producers themselves, the very ones who critique traditional household cult practices, conceive of signing as belonging to that context, even as they draw distinctions between Christians and non-Christians. For example, in *Scorpiace*, Tertullian explains that signing is a treatment for a scorpion's sting. After listing other treatments (natural substances, magic, lancing, preventative drinks), he speaks of the option available to believers: "We have faith for a defense . . . in immediately making the sign (*signandi statim*) and adjuring, and besmearing the heel with the beast" (*Scorp.* 1.3). With this gesture, Tertullian explains, believers often help non-Christians as well, as the sign of the cross gives them power akin to that of Paul's when he is bitten by a snake (Acts 28:3; *Scorp.* 1.4). Thus the gesture of signing addresses the very real threat of scorpions in Tertullian's region of the world. Granted, Tertullian goes on in this text to draw an analogy between the scorpion's attack and the attacks of enemies on the church, or of those he considers heretics against those he considers true believers. Thus the cross, and all it stands for, serves as a defense against spiritual or intellectual threats as well. But in order for that parallel to work, the practice of healing scorpion wounds with the signing gesture must make sense to his readers.

The earliest references to this practice of signing and sealing associate the gesture with marking the believer as belonging to Christ. Paul explains that God has anointed believers, giving them his seal along with the spirit (1 Cor 1:22). Later Pauline tradition refers to believers as having been "marked with the seal" (ἐσφραγίσθητε; Eph 1:13; 4:30). The author of Revelation envisions a scene in which, as the events of the end time unfold, one worker angel calls to the others to wait on their destruction until "we have marked the servants of our God with a seal on their foreheads" (Rev 7:3). These are the 144,000 who were sealed (7:4) and who had the name of God and of Christ written on their foreheads (14:1), being thus protected during the apocalyptic violence taking place.

Although the sign of the cross is not always mentioned in reference to this gesture, it is clear that some authors have the shape of the cross in mind and connect this to a similar kind of protection found in Revelation. Arguing against Marcion, Tertullian refers to a tradition that links the sign of the cross with a passage from Ezekiel. He claims it was prophesied that

> his righteous ones too would have the same sufferings, first the apostles, and afterwards all the faithful, sealed (*signatos*) with that mark of which Ezekiel speaks: "The Lord said unto me, Pass through in the midst of the gate in the midst of Jerusalem, and set the mark TAU on the foreheads of the men." [6] For this same letter TAU of the Greeks, which is our T, has the appearance of the cross (*crucis*), which he foresaw we should have on our foreheads in the true and catholic Jerusalem. (*Marc.* 3.22.5–6)[56]

Two other third-century Christian writers, Cyprian and Origen, make connections between the same Ezekiel passage (9:4–6) and the Christian practice of making the sign of the cross. In his commentary on Ezekiel, Origen reports asking Jews what the significance of the letter *taw* is to them. One, who is described as a follower of Christ, reports that *taw* looks like the cross and predicts the mark that will go on the foreheads of Christians.[57] Cyprian also quotes Ezekiel 9:4–6, highlighting the protection that the sign offers and commenting that this sign "pertains to the passion and blood of Christ and that whoever is found in this sign is kept safe and unharmed." When God's judgment does arrive, Cyprian warns, only those who have been "new-born" and "signed with the sign of the cross" will survive.[58]

These witnesses attest to an understanding in these early centuries that the sign of the cross marks the believer as belonging to the god of Christ and as deserving protection. It is not surprising that these same sources associate signing with baptism, when new believers are initiated.[59] Tertullian refers to initiates being signed when they come up out of the water (*Res.* 8), and Cyprian reports a tradition of the newly baptized being "signed with the seal of the Lord."[60] Likewise, the *Apostolic Tradition* reports the practice of new initiates rising from the water and being anointed with oil in the sign of the cross, accompanied by a kiss (21.22). The Acts of Peter recounts a story of a ship captain who asks Peter to baptize him "with the sign of the Lord (*signo domini*)" and who then is found worthy of partaking in the eucharist because he has been "signed with thy holy sign (*signatus est sancto tuo signo*)."[61] Likewise, one source associated with Hippolytus refers to apostates as those who used to be marked by the cross but whose "hardness of heart" removed it.[62]

In the fourth century, John Chrysostom claims that self-signing, advised by Tertullian and the *Apostolic Tradition*, has become widespread. He praises the gesture of signing as accessible and desirable to people from all walks of life, including rulers, commoners, women, virgins, matrons, and enslaved and free people: "all impress the sign regularly on the noblest part of their bodies and daily carry the figure about on their foreheads."[63] This ubiquitous symbol offers powerful protection, the golden-mouthed bishop argues—much better than the mud salve that some apply to their children's foreheads.[64] The signed cross serves the same function, only better.

This gesture illustrates nicely the process of "creative assemblage" mentioned above. Even though the vast majority of our evidence for signing comes from literate producers, it is likely that, as with prayer, these writers are engaging (through advising and interpreting) with a widespread practice that made sense in daily life. As Pliny explains, gestures were perceived as powerful in the Roman world and served as a tool for communicating with the divine and protecting the body or space. With signing, Christians develop just such a gesture, which is perceived to activate the specific care of their god, who protects those whose foreheads are marked and who promises salvation through Jesus's crucifixion and resurrection.[65]

A similar process is at work with another version of signing associated with prayer, a kind of ritual blowing or insufflation. The *Apostolic Tradition* describes this gesture in a section on praying at night: "Through consignation with moist breath (*cum udu flatu*) and catching your spittle in your hand, your body is sanctified down to your feet. For when it is offered with a believing heart, just as from the font, the gift of the Spirit and the sprinkling of washing sanctifies him who believes" (41.14).⁶⁶ The Christian's saliva here is analogized to baptismal water and can effect a similar sanctification when signed over the body. The text offers other advice—such as hand washing (41.11) or moving to a different room from the bedroom shared with an unbelieving spouse (41.12)—indicating that purity was a concern. Tertullian, too, mentions what seems to be a similar ritual, also in the context of nocturnal praying. He calls it "blowing away some unclean thing" (*Ux.* 2.5.3) and worries over whether the unbelieving husband will discover it.⁶⁷

Insufflation is a good example of Pliny's effective, wordless devotions mentioned above. Indeed, it sounds like some of the examples he lists in this category, especially those related to saliva. He reports the recommendation that a touch of saliva behind the ear will relieve anxiety (*Natural History* 28.5.25) and that spittle can heal any number of wounds or ailments (including snakebites, epilepsy, boils, leprosy, and ophthalmia) (28.7.36–39). He describes the specific gesture of spitting into the palm as effective in making the recipient of a punch delivered by that hand less vengeful (28.7.36); it can also make one's own punch more forceful (28.7.37).

Roman-period medical writers also comment on the healing properties of saliva.⁶⁸ Aulus Cornelius Celsus, writing in the first century, explains that "a slight papule heals if it is rubbed daily with spittle before eating" (*On Medicine* 5.28, 18b).⁶⁹ Galen, in a remarkable discussion of how the body variously alters the food it ingests, explains that in the mouth food is partially altered by the properties of saliva (*On the Natural Faculties* 3.7).⁷⁰ If you chew some corn, for example, and then apply it to a boil, the paste will begin to digest and heal the sore (3.7). Saliva is simultaneously curative for skin diseases and damaging to venomous animals (like scorpions and snakes) (3.7). It was widely considered to be quite a useful and powerful substance.

Of course, Jesus himself is well known for using saliva to heal. The Gospel of Mark records two instances of this, first with a deaf and mute man ("He . . . put his fingers into his ears, and he spat and touched his tongue" [7:33]) and then with a blind man (he "put saliva on his eyes and laid his hands on him" [8:23]).⁷¹ The Gospel of John, too, recounts a story of Jesus healing a blind man ("he spat on the ground and made mud with the saliva and spread the mud on the man's eyes" [9:6]). These stories fit into the context of the healing practices mentioned above, in which contact with saliva can be curative.⁷²

Given this framework, it is no surprise that Christians incorporate the use of saliva into their own household worship. The ritual blowing of moist breath, or insufflation, as described in the *Apostolic Tradition*, implies that the spittle contained in the breath holds power like the holy water used in baptism. In a movement similar to signing, the believer can scan her body with this substance, sanctifying the body in the process.

In Tertullian's version of this gesture, he emphasizes the breath without mentioning saliva: "when you blow away some unclean thing (*cum aliquid immundum flatu explodis*)" (*Ux.* 2.5.3). The context here is nocturnal prayer; Tertullian worries that a Christian wife's non-Christian husband will witness and disapprove of her actions. Perhaps the blowing is needed to ready the space for prayer. Indeed, the breath, or *pneuma*, was considered powerful by healers and so-called magicians.[73] This interpretation is supported by another mention of blowing, this time exorcistic: Tertullian claims that believers can cast out demons by "our touch and breathing (*contactu deque afflatu nostro*)" (*Apol.* 23.16).[74] Origen, too, represents Celsus's view of Jesus's healing as on par with sorcerers who, among other things, "blow away diseases (νόσους ἀποφυσώντων)" (*Cels.* 1.68).[75] An exorcistic spell with possible connections to the Christ cult (and/or to Judaism) instructs, "Blow once, blowing air from the tips of the feet up to the face, and it will be assigned" (*PGM* IV.3083–84).[76] Similar to Tertullian's reference to insufflation, this recipe includes a full-body scan so that the power of the breath can be fully distributed. Again, the need for healing and protection motivates and shapes these gestures as Christians weave their own images, rituals, and stories into their worship practices.

Taking Eucharistic Bread Home: Meals and Offerings

Imagine a scene in a Roman-period household in which a family gathers for the evening meal. This particular meal is not a festive one, with guests and entertainment, but a regular supper at the end of the day. The head of the household pours out a little wine to honor the gods of his ancestors and places some bread on the hearth for the household gods. At the same time, the wife takes a piece of her bread and eats it, offering her own prayers to her god. These rituals complete, the meal begins.

In the ancient Mediterranean world, meals are a focal point of religious practices, both in the everyday mode and in the civic mode. Offerings of plants and animals and subsequent shared feasts among the participants honored the gods who supplied the sources of food in the first place. For Christ followers as well, a meal was the central communal ritual, evolving over the centuries from a regular dinner into a symbolic ritual of ingesting bread and wine.[77] As this ritual developed, it was interpreted variously by literate producers as a memorial of Christ's death and resurrection, a partaking of Christ's body and blood, and a festive banquet, among other things.[78] Christian writers portray the eucharist as the central communal ritual among believers, binding them to their founder and to each other as his followers.

From the second century on, Christian sources discuss an offshoot of this communal practice, which involves taking some of the eucharistic bread home to consume in the following days. In the scene imagined above, the wife performs this ritual alongside her non-Christian husband, who makes his pre-meal offerings himself. Based on the evidence, Gregory Dix hypothesizes that "the majority of acts of communion during the third century must have been made quite apart from any celebration of the liturgy by means of the reserved sacrament."[79] The "reserved sacrament" is what liturgical scholars have traditionally called this practice, based on the language used by ancient writers who speak of "reserving" the bread for later.

Several practical reasons for this portable communion are suggested, including absence from the communal ritual. Justin Martyr mentions that the bread, wine, and water were to be delivered by deacons to those who are not present (*First Apology* 65, 67). Cyprian refers to presbyters who bring communion to confessors in prison: "presbyters who also offer (*offerunt*) there among the confessors" (*Epistle 4*).[80] Tertullian suggests that reserving the bread for later solves the problem caused by fast days: Do you break your fast for communion or do you keep your fast and miss communion? Tertullian responds: "By your accepting the Lord's body and reserving (*reservato*) it, both things are safe, your partaking of the sacrifice and your performance of your duty" (*Or.* 19).[81]

This last example from Tertullian assumes that regular believers, not presbyters or deacons, will administer the bread to themselves, a situation that caused some concern among Christian writers who discuss the practice. Another example from Tertullian is illustrative. Here he is discussing the status of a man who has been married twice (of which Tertullian sternly disapproves), specifically considering whether he can still properly administer rituals at home: "Are not even we laymen priests (*sacerdotes*)? ... Accordingly, where there is no joint session of the ecclesiastical order, you offer (*offers*), and baptize (*tinguis*), and are priest, alone for yourself (*et sacerdos es tibi solus*). ... If you are twice-married, do you baptize? If you are twice-married, do you offer?" (*On Chastity* 7.3–4).[82] One issue here is the proper execution of important rituals given the morally compromised position of the twice-married householder. Other writers raise similar concerns, as we will see below. But I want to point out something that Tertullian assumes, almost without comment: in the absence of officials, the householder serves as priest to himself, and presumably to his household, baptizing, distributing communion, and perhaps other things.[83]

This domestic oversight of ritual is not controversial for Tertullian; it is merely mentioned as the example for a discussion of second marriage. That Christian household rituals are happening, even those that are typically overseen by clerics, is a given in his argument. Furthermore, as I argue in chapter 4, these rituals were likely administered not only by heads of households but also by subordinate members of the household, such as wives and enslaved people.

Tertullian's concern here about the moral fitness of householders hints at what Kim Bowes argues is a growing trend in this period: the perception of the eucharistic bread as potent material and the increasing attempts by officials to contain it.[84] Taking the bread home is both empowering and dangerous, as the instructions in the *Apostolic Tradition* show:

> (36) Let every faithful [person] take care to receive the Eucharist before he tastes anything else. For if he receives in faith, even if something deadly shall be given to him after this, it cannot harm him. (37) Let everyone take care that an unbeliever does not taste of the Eucharist, nor a mouse or any other animal, nor that any of it falls and is lost. For it is the Body of Christ, to be eaten by believers and not to be despised. (*Apostolic Tradition* 36–37; Latin: 77.32–78.2)[85]

As with Tertullian's advice above, this text recognizes that the reserved bread is appropriate for breaking a fast. Such an act will protect the believer, but the bread itself must also be protected, both from unbelievers and from critters; contact with either would be disrespectful. This assumes a scenario in which believers and unbelievers are at the table to share a meal, like that sketched at the opening of this section. And, as was likely, there were rodents scurrying about, and these, too, must be kept from the holy bread.

But unbelievers and mice are not the only threat here. The instructions continue: "(38) For blessing [the cup] in the name of God, you received [it] as the antitype of the blood of Christ. Therefore refrain from pouring out [any], as if you despised [it], so that an alien spirit may not lick it up."[86] In a rare reference to partaking of the wine at home (also see Tertullian, *Cor.* 3),[87] the *Apostolic Tradition* places the elements of the reserved eucharist in the category of powerful substances that would be recognized by other powerful beings (like an "alien spirit") who might ingest the wine as fast as a mouse might hoover up pieces of the bread. Again, we notice that Christ followers acknowledge a variety of powerful beings, both benevolent and not, in the domestic environment.

In a similar logic, but flipped the other way, the bread itself might be viewed by others as a vehicle for harm or manipulation. Tertullian worries that a non-Christian husband will view this ritual with suspicion, wondering what the Christian wife is doing and whether the bread she nibbles is really a charm or potion (*venenem*) (*Ux.* 2.5.3).[88] Thus the eucharistic bread offers protection, needs protection, and is perceived as potentially powerful over others.

If Tertullian and the *Apostolic Tradition* warn against dangers at home, another third-century text warns against the perils of transit. Novatian recounts the story of a man who, hurrying to get to a show after church, takes with him the body of Christ, as he had packed it to go as usual. Novatian derides him for carrying "the body of Christ amidst the filthy bodies of whores" (*De spectaculis* 5.5.4–5).[89] And in a series of stories about various calamities befalling unworthy people who attempt to eat the bread and wine, Cyprian tells of one woman who, "when she tried with unworthy hands to open her box, in which was the holy (body) of the Lord, was deterred by fire rising from it from daring to touch it" (*De lapsis* 26).[90] According to Cyprian's logic, "the Lord withdraws when he is denied," and the departure of sanctity leaves only a cinder (26).

Fourth- and fifth-century sources continue to recount the potency of the eucharistic bread, with stories of interventions in shipwrecks and exorcisms of evil spirits.[91] Jerome and Basil of Caesarea both mention the reserved eucharist as common, yet several church councils object to the practice, echoing the tension mentioned above.[92] The practice of eating the bread at home was clearly widespread among believers and worried over by literate producers. Thus a familiar tension emerges between two modes of religion: the everyday practices that were well established in homes, shops, and neighborhoods and the ritual practices that leaders attempted to systematize and oversee.[93] We revisit this pattern in subsequent chapters.

Wearing the Word: Gospel Amulets

In the section above on prayer, I mentioned briefly the use of amulets, objects typically worn on the body or on clothing for protection or healing. The use of amulets was widespread in the ancient Mediterranean world, and various substances were used in their manufacture, including metals, plant material, and stone.[94] Often, certain apotropaic words or images were inscribed on these materials, protecting the wearer from harm (see chapter 3). Starting in the late third and early fourth centuries, we begin to see texts associated with the Christ cult used as amulets in much the same way: papyri containing sacred texts connected to Christ were worn on the body.[95]

The majority of our evidence for Christian amulets comes from manuscripts preserved in Egypt dating to the fifth and sixth centuries and later, but we also see quite a few in the fourth century and a handful in the third.[96] Scholars have determined that these papyri were used in amulets because of the way they are folded and the position of holes perforating the papyri to attach them to necklaces.[97] Furthermore, John Chrysostom, in his critique of the practice, mentions Christian women with "gospels hanging from their necks."[98]

One of these amulet gospels comes from the late third to the early fourth century and contains four lines that include the opening of the Gospel of Mark: "Know well the beginning of the gospel and see, 'The beginning of the Gospel of Jesus Christ. As it is written in Isaiah the prophet: See, I send my angel before your face, who will prepare.'"[99] This papyrus was probably rolled into a portable shape, since there are no holes in the papyrus itself.[100]

Some have argued that gospel openings like this are intended to represent the whole gospel, thus allowing the wearer to carry the complete gospel on her body symbolically.[101] Joseph Sanzo, however, in his study of gospel *incipits* (or beginnings) on amulets, argues that this particular text does not function this way. Instead, the introductory line, "Know well the beginning of the gospel and see," specifically refers to the lines that follow, which are the first two verses of the Gospel of Mark and mention Isaiah and "my angel." Sanzo suggests that these lines could be relevant for "apotropaic or curative ritual."[102] This coheres with the view of the editors of this particular scrap of papyrus, who suggest that the line "See, I send my angel before your face" would have served an apotropaic function.[103]

Another third-century amulet cites the Lord's Prayer from Matthew 6:10–12 on a papyrus the size of half of a credit card: "Your [will be done] on earth as it is in heaven. Give us this day our daily bread. And forgive us our debt[s]."[104] This prayer is the most commonly cited New Testament text on Christian amulets.[105] Theodore de Bruyn suggests that this amulet and others that cite prayers (either the Lord's Prayer or certain psalms) were drawing upon liturgical contexts where these texts were perhaps recited.[106] Examples from later centuries are more plentiful, and these include other gospel openings, psalms, and prayers (most commonly LXX Psalm 90 and the Lord's Prayer).[107]

These amulets containing Christian scripture and liturgy illustrate how followers of Christ adapted the practice to include their own holy objects and sources of power. Both scripture and liturgy evoke the ritual context of communal worship. The liturgical references in particular, as de Bruyn argues, depend upon the "habits of prayer" that take place in churches, monasteries, and perhaps also at home.[108]

Yet these liturgical and scriptural texts are integrated into a related, but distinct, set of practices that attend the particular exchange taking place between the wearer of the amulet and the deity being called upon. These words from Christian sacred texts operate within the technology of amulet-wearing: the inscribed words themselves transmit a kind of power to those who touch them. Frankfurter calls these words a "perpetual recitation," so that wearing the amulet is a continuous ritual act of speech.[109] It is possible that the wearer of the amulet also recited all or part of the text in the amulet, perhaps upon acquiring it and perhaps at other times as well.[110] These texts, then, which might in other contexts be used for instruction, become relevant as objects themselves, analogous to relics or oil, that are imbued with an apotropaic or healing power.[111] The words themselves have power, and their physical presence, their touch upon the skin, can effect change.[112] Thus the act of wearing these gospel amulets is a devotional practice.

Belonging to Christ: Symbols of Christ on Finger Rings

Finger rings offered another way for Christ followers to wear their devotion. In the Roman period, people wore rings for a variety of reasons. Signet rings, used to impress a seal upon an object, were used in household management and commercial interactions to mark property. Some rings were used to identify specific occupations (such as physicians) or rank in the military.[113] Certain rings were worn by enslaved people.[114] Others were given to mark betrothals.[115] Some were simply worn for ornament. In each of these cases, rings could mark status in the Roman world; they said something about who you were, what you owned (or didn't), and where you stood in the complex hierarchies that determined social and economic positions in society. In some cases, ring wearing was an act of devotion, falling into the category of everyday religious practice. They might be worn for protection or to signal loyalty to a specific deity,[116] a use that is supported by a third-century ritual text that offers instructions for how to make the ring powerful (*PGM* XII.270–350).[117] Rings have been found at temples where they were given as dedications,[118] and Lucian mentions a powerful ring made of nails from a crucifixion crossbar (*Philopsuedes* 17).

The material record suggests that followers of Christ, too, wore rings, and sometimes for devotional purposes.[119] For example, several gemstones that originally belonged to rings had portraits on them (presumably of the owner) with the inscription "*Iesou Christou*" (IHCOY XPICTOY): "of Christ," or "belonging to Christ."[120] One of these portraits, with the inscription "*Christou*" (XPICTOY), has a fish carved underneath the bust.[121] A third stone, larger than most (31 mm), depicts what seems to be a family, with each person named, and the inscription "*Eutychi*" (EYTYXI), or "good luck"; "*Zoe*" (ZOH), or "life"; and "*[He]is theos*" ([E]IC ΘEOC), or "There is one god."¹²² This latter phrase might indicate a connection with the Christ cult, but this is not conclusive, in my view.¹²³

Other gems simply have the inscription "*Iesou Christou*" (IHCOY XPICTOY) or some variation on that theme with no image.¹²⁴ One striking group of third-century rings has *chi* and *rho* (the first two Greek letters of *Christos*) inscribed on the face, forming an abbreviation for Christ that became well known during Constantine's reign.¹²⁵ These earlier rings suggest that this symbol was already circulating in the third century. Another abbreviation for Christ is found on rings in our period: the Greek word for "fish," *ichthus* (IXΘYΣ), is an acrostic for "*Iesous Christos Theou Huios Soter*" (Jesus Christ Son of God, Savior).¹²⁶ One third-century inscription carved on red jasper might refer to a creedal statement: "Almighty God, Jesus Christ, Son of God" (ΘEOC ΠANTWKPATWP IHCOYC XPICTOC YIO<C> ΘEOY). "Hallelujah" (AΛΛHOYIA) is inscribed on the other side, in a different hand.¹²⁷ Another ring with a red jasper stone bears the inscription "God, son of God, guard me" (ΘEOC ΘEOY YIOC THPEI).¹²⁸ I would caution that we cannot be sure this belongs to a follower of Christ ("son of God" could be read that way), but it is still useful to see that a ring is deployed for protection and that, whether related to the cult of Christ or not, its materials, style of writing, and time period fit with the other evidence discussed here.

Sometimes rings are identified as Christian, or possibly Christian, by the image carved on the stone: fish, anchors, doves, and ships are examples. As Jeffrey Spier notes, we can be more confident that they might be related to the Christ cult when they are accompanied by an inscription.¹²⁹ One of the most popular images in early Christian art, the good shepherd, appears both with and without inscriptions on third-century finger rings.¹³⁰

In addition to the material record, we have the comments of Clement of Alexandria (150–215 CE), who thought it wise to advise followers of Christ on the appropriate images to wear on their rings: a dove, a fish, a ship, a lyre, and an anchor (*Paedagogus* 3.59).¹³¹ In general, he discourages the wearing of rings for ornament and supports only the practical use of rings for housekeeping or business. According to Clement, then, there is an established tradition of wearing rings for a variety of purposes and with a variety of styles, only a few of which align with proper Christian behavior.¹³²

Clearly there were numerous reasons to wear rings in the Roman world, from practical to ornamental. Wearing a ring with the name of a deity or cult figure, however, might also be understood as an act of devotion. The inscription mentioned above that asks "God, son of God" to guard the wearer suggests the possibility that protection was sought from rings, just as it was from amulets. The practice of engraving the name of Christ on ring gemstones, especially given the fairly widespread understanding (both by those who followed Christ and those who did not) of the power of invoking Jesus's name, is evocative.[133] Were these rings thought to keep evil away? Did they protect the wearer or perhaps signal his or her loyalty? Perhaps they were "objects with a distinct devotional and religious function," as were a couple of fourth-century rings with images of Christ's crucifixion.[134] I take up this question further in chapter 3.

Light for the Gods: Ritual Lighting of Lamps

Across the Roman empire, both in official cult settings and in domestic ones, the lighting of lamps was a daily ritual, sometimes accompanied by prayers or gestures to a divine being.[135] Archaeological evidence for lamps from our period is plentiful, much of it coming from domestic contexts.[136] Just as temple officials would mark the opening and closing of the temple each day, so, too, people in households and other spaces marked the coming of evening with the lighting of lamps.[137] Lighting the evening lamps, which were sometimes decorated with images of deities, might be accompanied by prayers or gestures to the gods who protected the house.[138] In Jewish households, lamp-lighting marked the beginning and end of the Sabbath.[139]

Followers of Christ, too, maintained this widespread practice.[140] The material record includes iconography associated with the cult of Christ.[141] Indeed, one of the earliest material remains with Christian imagery is a lamp that is likely from Rome and dates to the early third century.[142] This mold-made lamp of reddish clay features an imprint of the Good shepherd image, along with Noah's ark with a dove and Jonah being spit out of the whale. The maker's name—"FLORENT," which stands for Florentius—is stamped on the underside of the lamp. Spier notes that this workshop is also responsible for lamps with traditional deities and other images.[143] We might imagine that people in a given neighborhood would have purchased lamps from the same workshop regardless of the gods honored in their households. As Bowes comments, "The origins of the rituals, Jewish or Christian, are less important than their ubiquity, and Christian homes would have sparkled with the ritual lamps of evening alongside their pagan and Jewish neighbors."[144]

As we might guess, Christian intellectuals were not always happy about Christ followers sharing this practice with others. Tertullian bemoans the fact that Christians are enthusiastic lighters of lamps and decorators with wreaths: "But now all our shops and gates shine! These days you will find more doors of gentiles without lamps and laurel-wreaths than of Christians" (*Idol.* 15.1).[145] In the fourth century, John Chrysostom derides Christ followers for using lamps to name their newborn children (*Homily on 1 Corinthians* 12.13). In other contexts, however, written sources mention lamp-lighting as though it is an accepted practice by followers of Christ. Both the *Apostolic Tradition* and Tertullian refer to this rite in communal gatherings,[146] and Tertullian names lamp-lighting as one of the daily instances in which it is appropriate for the faithful to deploy the sign of the cross (*Cor.* 3; see above discussion).

Conclusion

The rituals documented here, those that believers performed in unofficial venues such as households, engage the body in worship. Through speech, gesture, breath, ingestion, and decoration, people could mark their bodies as belonging to Christ, and they could petition Christ or god for healing or protection. Yet these actions belong to daily life; they are woven into quotidian activities in the Roman world. As Frankfurter describes it, "the domestic sphere of religion invests a range of mundane domestic activities as the basis for ritual action and religious expressions. Ritual is layered into hearth-keeping, pot-stirring, lamp-lighting, hair-combing, sewing, and forging."[147] This is the logic of everyday religious practice, a type of interaction between humans and powerful beings that was integrated into daily life.

In this sampler of religious practices, we have glimpsed the tension over this integration in the writings of figures such as Tertullian, Chrysostom, and other Christian intellectuals. When devotion to Christ is woven into everyday rituals, it looks a lot like devotion to other deities in the household and neighborhood. As Jaclyn Maxwell comments, followers of Christ "incorporated religion into their lives in ways that originated from their own experiences and logic, rather than solely following the instructions from church authorities."[148] Indeed, the literate producers work hard to construct boundaries around the cult of Christ in the face of what seems to be an ongoing process of ritual adaptation by a variety of members of the household, including wives, enslaved people, shop workers, and so on. The tension between these two processes—the integration of symbols related to Christ into daily life and the objections by published Christians—is taken up in the next chapter.

CHAPTER 3

AMULETS, SPELLS, AND GEMS

Seeking Protection and Healing in the Name of Christ

The Acts of the Apostles tells the story of Paul and Barnabas entering the town of Lystra and encountering a man who had been crippled from birth. After a brief exchange, Paul calls upon him to stand up, and the man is healed (Acts 14:8–10). The people who witness this miraculous event, exclaiming that Paul and Barnabas are gods, bring garlands and animals for sacrifice. The two traveling teachers object strenuously, explaining that the one god they should worship is the creator of all things (and perhaps more to the point, the one who has made their crops grow), but they can barely restrain the crowd from making offerings to them (Acts 14:14–18).[1]

These scenes, which attempt to teach the audience about proper worship, play with the idea that the cult of Christ could easily be mixed up with traditional cults. The stories depict what would have been a well-understood impulse on the part of people responding to miraculous deeds: to attribute these deeds to divine powers in the apostles and to revere them for it. John scolds Lycomedes, "I see you are still living as a gentile (*ethnikōs*)!"[2] Exactly. Like a proper head of the household, Lycomedes commissions a painting and festoons it with garlands, lamps, and altars, honoring the personage responsible for restoring the lives in his household. As discussed in chapter 2, these scenes recount practices common in daily-life religion, including among those loyal to Christ.

This chapter deals with the tension raised by these stories: some people's tendency to respond to the powers associated with Christ in traditional ways met strong objections from others, who claimed that such a response was unacceptable. In what follows, I discuss what we might learn from considering the deep involvement of Christ followers in everyday religious practices, such as those evinced in what we call "magical" materials. Such an exercise, I argue, challenges traditional boundaries and encourages us to expand our understanding of what "Christianity" was at this time. As scholars, we can get tangled up in the effort to apply our own categories (such as Christian, Jewish, or pagan) to the ancient evidence.[3] And in the ancient context there were those who argued for such categories, as we will see below. But to most people who expressed an interest in the cult of Christ, the idea that their allegiance to Christ cordoned them off from their neighbors, family members, and coworkers does not seem to have made sense.[4] Indeed, what does seem to have made sense, and perhaps what gave this new cult more visibility, was to include Christ in the range of powerful beings that might be supplicated using long-standing methods.

To illustrate the need for—and the potential fruits of—reimagining ancient Christianity, I turn to a body of evidence that is typically referred to as "magic." This label, which has served as a catchall for ritual practices deemed "illegitimate" (such as spells, incantations, curses, etc.), has matured as its own rich field of study, even as scholars of these materials debate the usefulness of the category.[5] I consider this material in the same spirit as J. Z. Smith's famous characterization of the Greek Magical Papyri: they represent "something quite precious: one of the largest collections of functioning ritual texts, largely in Greek, produced by ritual specialists that has survived from late antiquity."[6] These spells and manuals, presumably prepared by ritual experts for paying customers, attest to a well-developed and professionalized technology for petitioning powerful beings in the ancient Mediterranean world. The successful execution of the recipes depends on the expertise of local scribes and ritual specialists who produced them and who likely advised clients on the proper steps to take or may have assisted in the administration of the rituals themselves.[7]

Likewise, and critically for my work, each of these texts—which include ritual instructions, prayers, recipes, curses, and figural representations—offers a glimpse of the daily needs and desires of ancient people. Their wishes, grudges, injuries, and sufferings percolate through their petitions to powerful beings. The recipes detail the props to use, the divine beings to invoke, the words to utter, the gestures to make, and the places in which to perform their rituals. Smith notes that the logic of sacrifice runs through these instructions, as people are guided in what offerings to make, how to set up small altars, how to position bodies for speaking and acting, and so on.[8] These are riches for the study of everyday religious practices.

One of the characteristics of this material, often puzzled over by scholars, is the apparent mix of deities and symbols used, creating a challenge for classification. Is it "pagan," "Christian," "Jewish," "magical"? These categories do not map neatly onto the evidence, and this is telling for my investigation. The petitions and rituals are practical and resourceful, calling upon a range of deities and powerful beings—and using unintelligible but efficacious words and syllables as well—for help in a variety of situations. Those who produced, oversaw, and used these spells do not seem concerned with the same classifications that scholars bring to their work.[9]

Indeed, as a valuable body of evidence for daily-life religious practices, these texts and artifacts illustrate a process of integration that defies the borders we typically employ. They show that symbols associated with the power of Christ get integrated into traditional ritual practices, seemingly without difficulty. As such, they complicate the way we understand "Christianity," a term that suggests that there was a discrete, stable, and coherent entity that ancient Mediterranean people would have understood as "Christian." There certainly was such an entity for the literate specialists, especially those whose writings survive to us, who expend quite a bit of energy arguing for it. But these very arguments, alongside a variety of different objects and texts from the material record, suggest that there were many ways to define the cult of Christ. And for many, it was a fluid category, perfectly available for incorporation into the larger flow of exchanges with the gods that took place in households, on street corners, and in shops.

In what follows, I turn first to Christian intellectuals—literate experts, in Stanley Stowers's theoretical framework—to show a sampling of their efforts to define Christianity. I then turn to various spells and amulets that invoke symbols connected to the cult of Christ (and that illustrate why the intellectuals had to work so hard)! These artifacts, I argue, invite us to think more creatively about what it meant to participate in the cult of Christ in this period.

Policing Boundaries: Christian Intellectuals

Christian intellectuals and leaders sought both to erect and to police the boundaries of their new cult. Theodore de Bruyn describes this phenomenon well: "In the first several centuries of the Christian church, the overwhelming preoccupation of its writers and leaders was to differentiate 'true' Christians from those who might resemble or mislead them—from Jews, pagans, 'erroneous' Christians, 'lax' Christians."[10] This is hard work given the ubiquity of everyday religious practices, especially those related to healing and protection. Arguing for devotion to a single deity is a bit like swimming upstream in a culture in which many powerful beings were perceived to control people's lives.

Tertullian spends time on this topic, writing multiple treatises in which he advises Christ followers on how to navigate a "heathen" world.[11] At times he bemoans the participation of Christians in traditional practices. For example, he complains that they are more enthusiastic lamp lighters and wreath decorators than their neighbors: "But now all our shops and gates shine! These days you will find more doors of gentiles without lamps and laurel-wreaths than of Christians" (*Idol.* 15.1).[12] Other times he describes the confusion of boundaries by others, explaining that some have thought Christ followers worship the sun because of their habit of praying toward the east (*Nat.* 1.13.1; *Apol.* 16.9–10).[13] At still other times, he sounds the alarm at the specter of evil powers claiming the innocent for their own via traditional religious practices. Here he describes these dangers at birth:

> Thus it comes to pass that all men are brought to the birth with idolatry for the midwife, whilst the very wombs that bear them, still bound with the fillets that have been wreathed before the idols, declare their offspring to be consecrated to demons: for in parturition they invoke the aid of Lucina and Diana; for a whole week a table is spread in honour of Juno; on the last day the fates of the horoscope are invoked; and then the infant's first step on the ground is sacred to the goddess Statina. After this does anyone fail to devote to idolatrous service the entire head of his son, or to take out a hair, or to shave off the whole with a razor, or to bind it up for an offering, or seal it for sacred use— in behalf of the clan, of the ancestry, or for public devotion? (*An.* 39)[14]

This passage illustrates the aid solicited from a variety of beings during the vulnerable circumstances of birth and infancy: the womb is wrapped with ribbons, various deities are invoked, offerings are made, and so on. Notice that Tertullian does not deem these practices ineffectual. Indeed, his warning is predicated upon the assumption that they will bind the newborn (and perhaps the parents) to the "demons."

Tertullian can also be remarkably flexible in his advice, recognizing the challenges of avoiding idolatry altogether. At rites of passage such as weddings and namings, and somewhat contradicting the example of birth above, Tertullian surmises that there is not much danger. One attends such events for one's friends and family, not for the gods themselves. If a sacrifice is being offered, it is acceptable to witness it but not to participate in it in any way (*Idol.* 16). The same is true for enslaved people or children who attend their non-Christian head of the household; they should do their best to fulfill their duties without contributing to the sacrifice itself.[15] Likewise, Christian men holding administrative office need to discern where they might cross the line into idolatry while performing their duties (*Idol.* 17).

Despite the flexibility of these few examples, concerns about participating in traditional ritual practices evolve into a rhetoric of censure that relies on imagery of mixing and pollution, both in Tertullian and in other writers.[16] Tertullian imagines an artisan who makes statues of the gods, raising "to God the Father hands which are the mothers of idols," touching "the Lord's body those hands which confer bodies on demons," or passing on to others "what they have contaminated" (*Idol.* 7). Such artisans are even granted clerical positions, Tertullian complains: what a scandal![17] With a similar logic of contagion, Cyprian writes of those who attend the sacrifices and then partake of the eucharist: "Returning from the altars of the devil, they draw near to the holy place of the Lord, with hands filthy and reeking with smell, still almost breathing of the plague-bearing idol-meats; and even with jaws still exhaling their crime, and reeking with the fatal contact, they intrude on the body of the Lord" (*De lapsis* 15).[18] Cyprian and Tertullian both articulate high stakes in keeping clean borders: the body of the Lord itself is in danger of being contaminated.

With respect to rituals aimed at securing protection or healing, sometimes labeled as "magic" by ancients and moderns, Christian writers generally join their intellectual peers in deriding them as deceitful and superstitious.[19] Justin represents a larger trend by associating these practices with demons.[20] Irenaeus is well known for targeting other types of believers with accusations of magic.[21] Origen's preservation of Celsus's views shows that these accusations were also made to discredit the claims that Jesus and others performed miracles.[22] Boundary-making fuels these discussions as writers sort out what is truly Christian, Jewish, or neither. Later Christian intellectuals continue this work and pay particular attention to rituals of healing and protection.[23] Athanasius articulates the stakes quite concretely when he comments that wearing an amulet changes one from a believer to an unbeliever (ἑαυτόν ἐποίησεν ἀντὶ πιστοῦ ἄπιστον), a gentile instead of a Christian (ἀντὶ δὲ Χριστιανοῦ ἐθνικὸν).[24]

But this rhetoric, in the end, does not always amount to an outright rejection of the types of exchanges with the divine that are being administered through spells and incantations. Instead, Christian intellectuals argue that Christian words and symbols can better accomplish healing and protection than others can. In doing so, they tacitly accept the system of exchange but substitute their own deity, ritual, and symbols. For example, Justin claims that exorcisms in the name of Christ are more effective than others (*Second Apology* 5[6].6). Tertullian asserts that Jesus's name is effective in driving out demons:

> All the authority and power we have over them is from our naming the name of Christ, and recalling to their memory the woes with which God threatens them at the hands of Christ as Judge, and which they

expect one day to overtake them. Fearing Christ in God, and God in Christ, they become subject to the servants of God and Christ. [16] So at our touch and breathing, overwhelmed by the thought and realization of those judgment fires, they leave at our command the bodies they have entered, unwilling, and distressed, and before your very eyes put to an open shame. (*Apol.* 23.15–16)[25]

The power of those who invoke Christ effectively enslaves the demons, who, repelled by ritual "touch and breathing," flee the bodies they have invaded.[26] Responding to an accusation of magic by Celsus, Origen agrees with Tertullian's view and even claims, "The name of Jesus is so powerful against demons that sometimes it is effective even when pronounced by bad men" (*Cels.* 1.6).[27]

This logic of superior protection provided by symbols associated with the Christ cult emerges in discussions of making the sign of the cross. Lactantius, writing in the first decade of the fourth century, conceptualizes this gesture as influencing superhuman entities. He claims that followers of Christ, using the sign of the cross, have the same power to control demons as Christ did. The proof, he explains, is that when enslaved believers with marked foreheads attend sacrifices, the expected communication with the gods does not work. The gods flee the mark of the cross, so the diviners cannot read the entrails of the animal (*Divine Institutes* 4.27).[28] Signing not only protects those who are marked but also disrupts exchanges between non-Christians and their gods. They participate in the same power grid: the signed forehead, backed by the god of the Christians, repels the other gods and disrupts the divination practices.

Reacting to similar practices some decades later, John Chrysostom argues that the cross should replace other gestures for protection and healing. He has heard of women who smear mud on children's foreheads to ward off the evil eye and other threats.[29] Chrysostom then expresses his incredulity that "worshippers of the Cross (τὸν σταυρὸν προσκυνοῦσι)" partake in these practices. He asks, "And when you should inscribe on his forehead the Cross which affords invincible security; do you forego this, and cast yourself into the madness of Satan?" He goes on to counsel, "from earliest life encompass them with spiritual armor and instruct them to seal the forehead with the hand (τῇ χειρὶ παιδεύτε σφραγίζειν τὸ μέτωπον): and before they are able to do this with their own hand, do you imprint upon them the Cross."[30]

The bishop agrees with the women that babies need to be marked; he disagrees on which mark to give. The sign of the cross on the forehead carries powerful protection, more powerful than mud. For its overall usefulness, on bodies and on spaces, Chrysostom lays out this general advice: "Therefore both on house, and walls, and windows, and upon our forehead, and upon our mind, we inscribe it with much care."[31] Chrysostom and other authors[32] do not object to the idea that people or places need protection and marking, but for them, the instruments that are used and the gods supplicated are the wrong ones. When it comes to a child's safety, Chrysostom argues, do not use amulets, bells, and thread; use the cross.[33] The basic system of everyday religion—exchanges with the gods for safety and prosperity—remains unchallenged.

Illness, marriage, birth, injury: these experiences continued to call for rituals of healing and blessing through amulets and incantations for a long time after the period of our study. Church leaders wrestled with their congregants' use of amulets, a phenomenon that persisted into later centuries perhaps because, as Ramsay MacMullen comments, the church in this period did not offer what traditional practices did: a wide variety of techniques and experts to address illnesses and difficulties of all kinds.[34] Voicing his concern over this issue, Augustine likens resistance to amulets, especially when ill, to martyrdom itself.[35] Severus of Antioch, writing in the sixth century, advises Christians to avoid amulets altogether, since it is impossible to tell the difference between a Christian one and a non-Christian one.[36]

The writer Julius Africanus (160–240 CE) offers a fascinating exception to this broad trend of censuring traditional practices. Scholars have not known how to categorize Africanus, whose loyalty to Christianity is clear in his correspondence with Origen and in his *Chronographiae*, in which he charts a time line of Christian history.[37] Africanus is also the author of *Cesti*, a kind of encyclopedia of advice and information on a wide range of topics.[38] Among the portions that survive are remedies for illnesses and wounds; they employ the traditional techniques often labeled as "magic." William Adler poses the question that has left scholars puzzled: "How could the author of the *Chronographiae* and the epistles to Origen and Aristides have also written a work so heavily invested in amulets, charms, incantations, and other occult practices, but as far as we can tell devoid of identifiably Christian content?"[39] Scholars have tried to resolve this apparent contradiction by arguing that the *Cesti* is scientific or even secular, so there is no conflict with Africanus's Christian beliefs.[40]

The contradiction, of course, only arises when we assume that the boundaries argued for by the literate producers discussed above are understood, agreed upon, and operative among ancient Christ followers. As Sanzo writes, "If we read between the lines of these proscriptive Christian texts (and take into consideration the extant material record), we quickly discover that a sizable number of Christians—if not a majority—found nothing incompatible between following Jesus and visiting local specialists to acquire curative or protective objects or to receive information about the future."[41] The texts and artifacts discussed below, ranging in date from the second century to the fourth, support this contention.

Seeking Protection in the Name of Christ

On a tiny scrap of gold leaf, someone in the second century CE inscribed the following petition: "Turn away, O Jesus, the Grim-Faced One, and on behalf of your maidservant, her headache, to (the) glory of your name, IAÒ ADÒNAI SABAÒTH, III ***, OURIÈL ***, {OURIÈL}, GABRIÈL."[42] This gold *lamella* (a thin sheet of precious metal), measuring 6.35 × 2.5 cm, was folded many times, indicating that it was worn or carried either on its own or perhaps in a capsule or case.[43] The petition addresses Jesus directly, asking for the expulsion of the "Grim-Faced One" and the headache presumably caused by this being.[44] Noteworthy here is the use of "your maidservant" (*tē paidiskē sou*) to identify the sufferer of the headache, which may be a term for a female follower of Christ.[45] The final lines contain a list of divine names often used together for the god of Israel (*Iaō, Adonai, Sabaōth*) along with names of angels (*Ouriel, Gabriel*).[46] A variety of powerful beings are acknowledged and addressed here, including Jesus, the demon that causes the headache, a number of angels, and the god of Israel.[47]

An even smaller gold *lamella* (4.2 × 2 cm), this one dating from the third century (based on letter forms), adjures a variety of divine beings to protect "Aurelia" from seizure.[48] This phylactery, too, was intended to be worn on the body: it was rolled up to fit inside a (now lost) container. The spell opens with "The God of Abraham, the God of Isaac, the God of Jacob, our God, deliver Aurelia from every evil spirit and from every epileptic fit and seizure."[49] Names of deities and angels follow, as well as names used in other spells, Greek vowels (also common in spells), and a variety of symbols.

While we cannot be sure that this spell was made or practiced by followers of Christ, there are several hints that it was, or that symbols and texts connected with the cult of Christ were considered powerful by others. For example, in line 16 there is a *chi-rho* (a symbol made from the first two letters of *Christos*), and immediately following there is what looks like a *rho* with a horizontal line across the stem. These indicate that Christ is invoked in the list of powerful beings called upon in this petition.[50] Roy Kotansky notes that the opening line echoes Acts 3:13 ("The God of Abraham, the God of Isaac, and the God of Jacob, the God of our ancestors"), and the verb used for "deliver" (*rhuomai*) is the same as that in Matthew 6:13 (the

Lord's Prayer). Likewise, the phrase "evil spirit" (*pneuma poneron*) is found several times in Luke and Acts (and is uncommon in the *PGM*).[51] These careful observations suggest the possibility that the creators and users of these spells might have been familiar with these texts.

Other features of this *lamella*, however, are right at home in the collection of spells in the *PGM*. It names powerful beings that show up frequently in this corpus (angels and deities; lines 9–12), lists Greek vowels (lines 13–15), and deploys *charakteres* (signs, often in shapes that resemble letters; lines 19–22). Each of these was thought to be effective in securing the aid requested. This spell also uses *diaphulasse* (lines 17–18, 22, and on the left margin next to the lines with the *charakteres*), a typical verb in the *PGM* for protection from harm and disease.[52]

Aurelia's *lamella* illustrates how someone, whether affiliated with the Christ cult directly or aware of the power of this figure, collected symbols, words, and possibly references to texts that were perceived to work together toward the goal of protecting her from seizures. Both this spell and the first one discussed (for a headache) understand Christ to be an effective agent in healing and protection. Symbols from the Christ cult are incorporated into traditional practices to respond to practical needs related to illness and possession. This kind of assimilation may have triggered the objections of the literate producers described above.

Another *lamella*, this time on a silver sheet (9.3 × 3.3 cm) that was found inside a bronze capsule, also seeks protection, in this case from "evil spirits": "For (evil) spirits: 'Phoathphro, depart from Basilius, by the right hand of God, and the blood of Christ, and by her [*sic*] angels and (the) Church.'"[53] Kotansky argues that this exorcism text, which dates to the third or fourth century, is linked to a tradition of baptismal liturgies, many of which use the verb *anachorein* (the verb here for "depart"); he even suggests that this could be the text of one such liturgy, which often included exorcisms before or after the baptism.[54]

A striking feature of this spell is that it calls upon the "blood of Christ" to exorcise the demon. Elena Chepel argues that this is the earliest in a cluster of amulets (with dates ranging from the third century to the eighth) that use the "blood of Christ" not in eucharistic contexts but for other purposes.[55] Here, Chepel argues, "the blood is invoked as a tool of exorcism together with the hand of God, angels, and the church."[56] Christian intellectuals and leaders, too, understood the blood of Christ as apotropaic, able to scare away evil spirits and drive out demons.[57] As I discuss in the next section, it is possible that people understood Christ's death itself, and the suffering that attended it, as powerful. Perhaps the reference to his blood here represents a similar attitude.

A final example may also have baptismal connections. Rather than being enclosed in an amulet worn around the neck, this papyrus seems to have been intended to be wrapped around a portion of the body or perhaps affixed to a wall; it is larger than our other examples, measuring 17.4 × 26.6 cm.[58] It is generally thought to belong to the fourth century, possibly the first half (based on similarities in the lettering between this and other papyri).[59]

A visual representation creates the focus of this artifact: a snake arranged in a circle (an *ouroboros*) frames a bookroll with blocks of Greek vowels inscribed in it. A dove perches on top of the bookroll, holding a Christogram (a *chi-rho*) in its mouth; the dove's stick legs also look like letters, perhaps another monogram for Christ.[60] Phrases occupy spaces outside the *ouroboros*: "*Iēl*" (short for Israel), "finger of Solomon" (or possibly "ring of Solomon"), and "seal of the living god."[61] Names of angels and other powerful beings also surround the bookroll.

Yvona Trnka-Amrhein points out that this papyrus is unusual in that it seems to be producing its meaning "through the juxtaposition of images, symbols, words, and phrases" rather than through text.[62] And in this way, it has more in common with ritual gemstones, which I discuss in the next section, than with spells on papyri. Trnka-Amrhein summarizes the symbols, including those connected to the cult of Christ, arguing that baptism is central: "In creating its design, the papyrus combines the idea of the seal with the powerful tradition of Solomon's ring. It harnesses a nexus of concepts surrounding the rite of baptism and the expectation of the apocalypse to craft a powerful message through word and image: Israel, the sign of the cross, and the dove of the Holy Spirit which is closely tied to Jesus' own baptism."[63] On this papyrus, these symbols work in tandem with the more traditional features of spells and other petitions for aid from across the Mediterranean basin (such as the Greek vowels and the *ouroboros*).

In chapters 2 and 4 I discuss the ways that everyday religious practices interact with the communal rituals of Christ followers. One of these rituals involved blowing on the hands, such that the moisture from the breath was captured by the hands, which then could scan the body, delivering the protection and cleansing from one's baptism to one's current bodily state.[64] These last two amulets, each with a possible reference to baptism, could be doing the same thing. As such, they offer an extension of the benefits of the communal ritual in daily life, weaving together long-standing technologies with their new cult.[65] Indeed, Cyril of Jerusalem complains about exactly this in his treatise on baptism, urging the faithful to flee from using amulets and inscriptions on *lamellae*—along with several other practices that belong to everyday rituals—because they serve the devil (*Catechesis*

19, *Mystagogica* 1.8). Like his boundary-making colleagues discussed above, he does not like the fact that followers of Christ participate in such traditional forms of worship. Yet we can imagine that this would have been an instinctive impulse for believers who sought to integrate the powers associated with Christ into their daily lives, seeking ways to mark their bodies with protection, healing, and belonging.

Two insights emerge from studying this material. One is that in response to the widespread and ongoing need for protection and healing, ancient Mediterranean people utilized techniques for enlisting and manipulating powerful beings, not only at the civic or empire level but also as a part of daily life. This evidence—which belongs to the religion of everyday social exchange—offers abundant confirmation that these techniques permeate many of the religious "traditions," as we label them. Some scholars have called this a "transcultural magical lingo"[66] or "shared magical culture."[67] People devoted to a wide variety of cults from around the empire participated in this culture, including those loyal to Christ.

A second insight is prompted by the first: we need to develop a more flexible understanding—or understandings—of what might count as "Christian." Followers of Christ may have been attracted to this cult because of the healing and apotropaic powers of Jesus; they likely viewed local ritual experts who could produce the spell (with similar loyalties to Christ, or not) as their access to this power. They acknowledged multiple gods, demons, and other beings as powerful, too, and sought their protection—or asked that they be kept away. In keeping with practices across the empire, they incorporated elements of communal worship into their daily-life worship, wearing amulets or posting papyri over doorways. They trusted widely used technologies to be effective.

One way to read the collection of different symbols on amulets, such as those discussed above, is as a deliberate mixture, as though various categories are clear to all and are strategically combined for powerful effect. Such disregard for boundaries stands in stark contrast with the literate experts' position, as I have shown above. I think it is entirely possible that followers of Christ in this period were open to this kind of syncretism, as David Frankfurter describes it.[68]

A second way to interpret these materials, not necessarily exclusive of the first, is that this seeming "mix" of symbols was not perceived as any kind of boundary erasure. It might conflict with our sense of Christianity to have Christ side by side with multiple other powers on the same amulet, but to ancient practitioners and their clients, this may have simply been a true representation of their loyalty to Christ. This interpretation is in keeping with the work of Ra'anan Boustan and Joseph Sanzo, who have studied the perceived mix of Jewish and Christian symbols in amulets. They argue that we should focus not so much on the origins of symbols on amulets (whether a name originates in Judaism, for example) but on their reception and use.[69] When we do, we notice that ancient people do recognize boundaries—but different ones from those employed by the literate producers (and modern scholars). In some ways like the literate experts, practitioners of Christian "magic" were constructing their own versions of the tradition.

Important to both interpretive possibilities is the notion that the category of "Christianity" was in play. If it was perceived as a distinct entity by some, it was not necessarily stable or uniform. This encourages us to be open to a more expansive, flexible understanding of what it meant to follow Christ at this time.

A "Different Orthodoxy": The Bloodstone Gem

To explore this idea further, I consider an intriguing gem housed in the British Museum (figs. 4 and 5).[70] Like the papyrus with the *ouroboros*, a focal point of this gem is a figural representation: a crucified figure underneath the words "Son, Father, Jesus Christ."[71] Other lettering, both intelligible and unintelligible, suggests an association with traditional protective spells. Like the examples discussed above, the gem offers a rich site for thinking further about boundaries and the integration of the Christ cult into wider society in this early period. This green and reddish-brown gem is carved from jasper and measures 3 cm tall, 2.5 cm wide, and 0.6 cm thick. It is inscribed on both sides, with the crucified figure on the front/obverse. According to the most recent scholarly consensus, the gem dates to the second or third century CE.[72] It belongs to a group of similar pieces, all semiprecious stones of similar size, shape, and decoration; they contain words and signs intended to protect the wearer.[73] In keeping with these second- and third-century intaglios, the bloodstone gem features unintelligible lettering (*voces magicae*) along with some Greek letters.[74]

On the front/obverse there are nine lines inscribed, beginning with "Son, Father, Jesus Christ," followed by so-called magical names, including "*soam noam*" (others are unintelligible), and seven Greek vowels. Then there are letters that the original publisher suggested might be the word "hung up" (ἀρτάνη),[75] but this has been amended to refer to the crossbeam or the T-shaped cross itself.[76]

FIG. 4 Bloodstone gem, obverse. The British Museum, BM 1986,0501.1. © The Trustees of the British Museum. All rights reserved.

YIE / ΠΑΤΗΡΙΗ / COY XPICTE / COAM NWA / M WAWIA / CHIOYW / APTANNA / YC IOY / I

Υἱέ, / πατήρ, Ἰη / σοῦ χριστέ, / σοαμ νωα / μ, ωαωι, α /εηιουω, / ἀρτάννα / υσ ίου / ι.

O Son, Father, O Jesus Christ, *soam nōam, ōaōi, AEĒIOYŌ*, O, suspension beam/rope, (??)[77]

On the reverse, we again find nine inscribed lines, possibly by a different hand.[78] We recognize two names from Greek Magical Papyri and other ritual gems.[79] There is also the name Emmanuel (*E/psmanauêl*), which Kotansky identifies as a "common epithet of Jesus ('God is with us') in Christian magic."[80]

IWE / EYAEYII / IOYICYE [or NOYICYE] / [I]IAΔHTOΦΩ / ΘIECCBTCKHE / ΨMANAYHΛA / CTPAΠEPKMH / ΦMEIΘΩAP / MEMΠE / [.] . . . [.]

Ἰωε / ευα ευη / [. . .]ιουι, σὺ ε/[ἶ] Ιαδητοφω/θ Ἰεσεβτεκη
Ἐ/<μ>μανauηλ Ἀ/στραπερκμη/φ Μειθω Αρ/μεμπε/ . . .

Iōe eua euē(?) [1–3] *ioui,* you a[re] *Iadētophōth Iesebtekē E<m>manauēl Astraperkmēph Meithō Armempe* . . .

AMULETS, SPELLS, AND GEMS

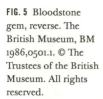

FIG. 5 Bloodstone gem, reverse. The British Museum, BM 1986,0501.1. © The Trustees of the British Museum. All rights reserved.

The image of the crucified figure is striking. It is presented as nude, long-haired and bearded, with the body facing front and the head turned to the side. He hangs on a *tau* cross (in the shape of a "T") with bent legs splayed open, and his arms droop loosely from the crossbar, to which they seem to be tied at the wrists.[81] The position of the body suggests that it might be resting on a seat or bar, but this is not visible in the carving. Such a device was used in crucifixions to prolong the life—and the suffering—of the victim.[82]

Most scholars agree that the bloodstone gem, too, is an amulet, possibly originally intended to be worn as a pendant or set in a ring.[83] As discussed in chapter 2 and above, amulets were used for any number of reasons, but most often for protection and healing. There probably would have been several people involved with the production and use of the gem: the ritual expert who designed it, the engraver who carved it, and the customer who purchased and wore it.[84]

Interpretation of the Bloodstone Gem

Not surprisingly, this intriguing gem has drawn a lot of attention from scholars, and its interpretation has been a puzzle. Similar questions as

FIG. 6 Constanza gem. The British Museum, BM 1895,1113.1. © The Trustees of the British Museum. All rights reserved.

those discussed above echo through the scholarship: Is it Christian? Is it magical? Is it pagan? Is it some mix of these? If it is Christian, what do we make of this disturbing crucifixion image?

Interpretation is made trickier by the fact that we have only a few parallels for comparison. One possible candidate is a later stone, dated to the mid-fourth century, that shows a nude Christ on a *tau* cross, head turned to the side and arms dangling loosely from the crossbar. This gem, called the Constanza (for where it was found in Romania), includes six figures on either side of the cross who look as though they are processing toward it (fig. 6). The theory is that these are the twelve apostles, so the image is not a biblical scene but representative of later developments in Christian symbol and self-understanding.[85] This is an important difference, however. The presence of the apostles, plus the presentation of the body (these legs are straight, not splayed open), gives more dignity to the scene, such that it is possible to read this Christ as authoritative and worthy of honor even in his crucifixion. In our earlier gem, there is little to find in the image that does not point to the humiliation and violence of his execution.

A second parallel is the famous Alexamenos graffito, which was sketched on a wall in the slaves' residence of the imperial palace in Rome in the early third century (fig. 7). A figure that is half human and half donkey hangs

AMULETS, SPELLS, AND GEMS

FIG. 7 Line drawing of Alexamenos graffito. Photo: Wikimedia Commons.

on the cross, with the donkey head turned to the side and possibly looking down at a man on the ground who looks up at the half-ass/half-man. The inscription reads, "Alexamenos, worship god" or "Alexamenos worships god" (*Alexamenos sebete theon*).[86] The position of the body on the cross echoes that of the two gems we have discussed so far. It hangs on a *tau* cross; the arms are limply hanging (as though attached to the crossbar at the wrists); the head is turned to the side. The graffito has a clear footrest, which is not obvious in the two gems. This image scratched into a plaster wall mocks those who might worship a crucified man, such as those who followed Christ.[87]

These two examples present us with very different interpretive possibilities. Does our gem convey themes of triumph, authority, redemption, and power, in keeping with later depictions of the crucifixion (such as the Constanza gem or other depictions of apostles processing toward the cross that belong to the fourth century and later)?[88] Or, like the Alexamenos graffito, does it aim to mock the worship of this crucified man?[89]

Our interpretive difficulties with this gem are further complicated by the same issues discussed above: the categories we use in our analysis. The bloodstone gem presents the same ostensible mix of deities, symbols, and imagery that we see in many "magical" pieces, and scholars debate whether it is Christian, pagan, or magical. Felicity Harley-McGowan, who has treated this gem in a number of publications over two decades, points out that the gem encompasses the "apparently disparate spiritual elements of Christianity and magic."[90] Her use of the word "apparently" signals her own hesitation regarding a neat division between the terms "magic" and "Christianity." This collection of deities, symbols, and powerful figures on the gem, Harley-McGowan remarks, generates "religious ambiguity"; we cannot ascertain from this jumble the religious loyalties of the producers or wearers of the gem.[91]

Furthermore, the image of the crucified figure has puzzled scholars because it does not conform to traditional understandings of the crucifixion as a victory over death. Harley-McGowan acknowledges the brutality of the positioning of the crucified figure, explaining that it emphasizes "vulnerability rather than victory on the cross" and reflects the reality of crucifixion in general, which is an "intensely physical and humiliating death."[92]

One way to understand this representation of Christ is to imagine that the gem was used by outsiders: it "may . . . have been employed by a pagan magician who borrowed what he perceived as a symbol of great power."[93] This hypothesis, which I agree is quite possible, assumes that Christian symbols and deities are imported into "pagan" or "magical" practices. In this view, the gem oversteps the boundaries of the Christ cult, representing "a perception of the crucified Jesus' power that extends beyond the parameters of Christianity."[94] Traditional views of Christianity remain intact.

Another way to understand this image is to assume that people associated Christ's resurrection, and therefore victory, with his crucifixion. Bruce Longenecker, for example, comments on the image of Christ on the gem: "Notice that there is no sense here that the crucifixion must have been a shameful symbol to be avoided at all costs. Just the opposite is postulated. The Christian claim that Jesus overcame death shifted the cross from being a symbol of shame to being a symbol of apotropaic power for use even by those whose religious allegiance was not restricted to a monotheistic form of Christianity."[95] Longenecker's comment builds on an interpretation from Harley-McGowan and Spier about the nudity of the figure: "Here it [Christ's nudity] may be regarded as affirming Jesus's spiritual power, witnessed in the fact that he overcame the brutality of the cross and thereby defeated evil powers."[96] All of these scholars see the potential for the brutal portrayal of Christ's execution to be read as victorious, an interpretive move that assumes knowledge of the resurrection. There is nothing on the gem itself that hints at this part of the story, but it is perhaps reasonable to assume that its users knew about it and believed in its power.[97]

Kotansky offers yet another interpretation. He has reconstructed lines 8–9 on the obverse as "redeeming Son" and therefore suggests that the stone represents redemption offered by Christ's death.[98] While not all scholars are convinced,[99] Harley-McGowan cites Kotansky in her description of the gem as a "means of seeking redemption" for the wearer in that it "explicitly exults in the death of Jesus as the Son of God."[100] Thus in addition to the jarring image of the humiliated body on the cross and the unfamiliar words in the inscription, according to this interpretation, the gem also offers a reference to a theme we traditionally associate with Christianity: that of Christ's death as redemptive for humanity.

Reimagining Christianity

Attributions for this gem thus run the gamut from pagan to magical to Christian to some mix of these. Each of these scholars has hinted at intriguing possibilities suggested by the bloodstone gem: a non-monotheistic Christianity,[101] the use of the technology of "magic" by Christ followers,[102] the reputation of Christ as powerful among others,[103] and the possibility that some Christians were willing to acknowledge Christ's brutal death.[104] These ideas, which challenge the claims and definitions promoted by the literate producers discussed earlier in this chapter, suggest different possibilities for how people understood participation in the cult of Christ. They also call into question our own categories, such as "Christian" or "magic."

Perhaps it is time to rethink how we imagine the religious landscape—and our categories along with it. Taking a stab at this, I would like to take the interpretation of the gem in another direction, one in which we allow the ambiguities to simmer a bit. In so doing, we find other opportunities opening up: instead of figuring out where to place the evidence, we allow the evidence to suggest new boundaries and definitions.

In what follows, I imagine the production and use of this gem by a follower of Christ. I agree with others (mentioned above) that it is quite possible that this gem was used by people not associated with the Christ cult. This in itself is interesting and important, in that it shows how symbols associated with this cult began to enter the larger vocabulary of protective supplication in the ancient Mediterranean world. But let us consider for the moment that it belongs to those we might call "Christian." Instead of asking *whether the gem matches* our understanding of Christianity at the time, we might ask *what the gem tells us* about Christianity at the time. Does it ask us to change what we think we know? I suggest that instead of extending beyond the parameters of Christianity, the gem itself might extend those parameters.

Reimagining "Mixing"
We might begin simply with what we perceive to be a mix of traditions represented on the gem. As discussed above, this amulet uses symbols and

lettering typically identified as "magic," including recognizable deities and unintelligible letters, things we usually associate with practices outside of Christianity. Yet it also invokes Christ, both in word and image.

Building on Frankfurter's nuanced notion of syncretism, I would suggest that the gem was not necessarily perceived as a mix of traditions by those familiar with it; instead, these elements would have been understood to operate as a whole unit.[105] Harley-McGowan articulates succinctly how the gem functioned as its own entity: "The protective or apotropaic function of the stone itself is resident in the interaction, rather than the individual presence, of the cryptic words with the imagery."[106] I would imagine that this is closer to how ancient people would have viewed this amulet: not as a collection of separate things but as its own cohesive whole—an expression of Christianity, even—that is created in the stone itself.[107] Arguing along similar lines regarding the alleged mix of Jewish and Christian symbols, Boustan and Sanzo claim that "the co-presence of these elements should not be viewed by scholars as the juxtaposition of Jewish and Christian elements, but instead as an internally coherent idiom that reflected and gave expression to the practitioner's version of Christianity."[108]

Let us keep in mind that the production of the gem was likely collaborative, including the labor of gem carvers and the expertise of local ritual authorities, who would have offered guidance on the symbols used in the design and overseen any necessary ritual actions.[109] This team of experts was resourceful and strategic, using traditional symbols to contribute to the effectiveness of the amulet. Sanzo comments that this kind of collaborative process "opened up spaces for believers to reimagine the boundaries between the Christian and the non-Christian, perhaps under the direct influence of the local expert."[110] Thus the local context of production and use of this amulet, whether for healing or protection or some other supplication, potentially establishes a holistic understanding of the gem as belonging to a legitimate Christian practice even as it "mixes" elements we associate with non-Christian rituals. Thus we might entertain the idea that Christianity was not in fact uniform but rather fluid, collaborative, and adaptive.

Reimagining Christ's Death

Another way we might be challenged to rethink Christianity relates to the interpretation of Christ's death. The body of Christ pictured on the obverse of the gem does not look like a victorious, authoritative, or redemptive figure. Instead, it bears the features of someone executed by crucifixion. Nude and front facing, its legs are splayed open and the vertical shaft of the cross splits the body, recalling, as Allyson Sheckler and Mary Joan Leith describe it, "emasculation by impalement."[111] Indeed, crucifixion was widely perceived as a violent, shameful death that elicited horror and revulsion.[112] And as mentioned above, here on the stone there is no hint of the resurrection, of the crucial next steps in the Christian story.[113] It depicts just the moment of degradation and defeat.

Sanzo has offered a reading of this crucifixion image that accounts for both the possible power of the gem and the negative associations with crucifixion. He argues that rather than harnessing the power of Christ's triumph, the image on this gem captures a sense of his violent and premature death, after which Christ took his place in the category of the "restless dead."[114] In the ancient Mediterranean world, ritual practitioners believed that there was power in those who had not experienced a good death. These restive corpses were vulnerable to manipulation in rituals of protection, healing, and divination.

The evidence for this practice and the ideas associated with it are scattered throughout the literary and documentary record. Sarah Iles Johnston documents this tradition in ancient Greece, where she traces the role of the *goēs*, the ritual expert who specializes in communicating with and manipulating the dead.[115] We find references to this category of deceased in the *PGM*, the large collection of ritual texts documenting prayers, cures, illnesses, requests for aid, and the like, discussed above.[116] In Roman-period literary sources, crucifixion itself is associated with ritual power. Authors recount how ritual experts use nails from crucifixions or the flesh of victims in their spells.[117] Two of these sources specifically refer to the healing power of crucifixion materials. Pliny the Elder recounts that healers treat malaria either with a "nail taken from a cross" wrapped in wool around the neck of the patient or a "cord taken from a crucifixion."[118] The rabbis seem to have been aware of the association between crucifixion and healing, as one remarks to another that "the nail of the cross for the sake of healing" might be taken out on the Sabbath.[119] Christian authors, too, refer to the restless dead tradition: the author of the Pseudo-Clementine *Recognitions* (2.13) and Tertullian (*Apol.* 23.1) both mention the death of young boys used for divination and other ends.

At the same time that this interpretation accounts for the brutality of the iconography, it also invites us to rethink how Christian users of this gem viewed Jesus's death. It raises the prospect that believers might have found the executed body of Christ efficacious. Pressing needs for healing and protection are met through the ritual manipulation of the powerful and vulnerable corpse of Christ. As in the gospels, Christ is associated with healing. Unlike in the gospels, his own authority, agency, and dignity are removed; control lies in the hands of the ritual expert and in the stone itself.

In some ways this is not surprising. Those who followed Christ must have shared the larger society's revulsion at crucifixion. But when compared to the intellectual tradition developing at this time, which associates Christ's death with victory over death, and to later iconographic depictions of the crucifixion as triumphant and Christ as authoritative, the image on this gem is striking. There is no hint of victory in this iconography. The restless dead interpretation does not require this; in using this gem, people are drawn not to a victory over death or salvation from sin but to the power made available through Christ's gruesome demise.

Conclusion

The bloodstone gem, invoking power from multiple sources and showcasing Christ as a member of the "restless dead," offers an opportunity to imagine a different "Christianity." Christ's death is still central, but for different reasons. It might be hard for scholars to see this gem as a legitimate expression of Christianity, especially if the intellectuals and leaders of the tradition have told us otherwise. Indeed, we have bought into literary and theological definitions and categories more deeply than we realize. Recognizing this, I think we can make room for a more fluid understanding of the cult of Christ in this period, one that allows for substantially different beliefs and practices.

But let us note that these interpretations seem radical only when our starting point is the normative literary tradition. The symbols and practices associated with the evidence presented in this chapter are right at home in the religious practices of everyday life. Inherently inclusive, resourceful, innovative, and tactical, these are the rituals that respond to practical needs related to health and protection. This is where I find Stowers's theorizing helpful: it offers a framework for thinking about how these everyday practices operate, with a logic and set of expectations about how humans interact with the gods and other powerful beings.[120] The religion of everyday social exchange is a category that can include what we call "Christian," "Jewish," "pagan," and "magic"; it accounts for the substantial amount of material, including the texts and objects discussed above, that shows how they overlap. Furthermore, this material showcases the creative work of those who turned to Christ for protection or healing, those who contributed their own versions of "Christianity" through their petitions and prayers. This process illustrates one way that Christian symbols entered into the larger web of everyday exchanges with the gods, a phenomenon I suggest was critical to the growth of what becomes Christianity.

Thinking in this way about the development of the cult of Christ, it becomes increasingly difficult to imagine conversion in any traditional sense. Indeed, conversion requires discrete boundaries and a well-defined "something" to which to convert. The literate producers discussed at the beginning of the chapter worked hard to construct and defend just such a thing. But we need to account for what others were doing, those who created and used these spells and amulets. Integration seems to be a better description: people integrated symbols and texts from the Christ cult into authoritative, traditional practices, and instructions.

I am influenced here by the work of Frankfurter, who argues that this integration of the Christ cult into traditional practices is critical to its growth and survival. These small, local acts of syncretism—offerings and prayers by mothers, shopkeepers, artisans—are themselves the "building blocks in the process of Christianization."[121] The result, as we have seen above, is not the construction of a coherent, comprehensive, singular cult but a variety of iterations in different places and contexts. Indeed, Christianity itself is not "a state of cultural or religious accomplishment or 'identity' but an ongoing process of negotiation."[122] As we have seen in previous chapters, everyday religious practices, being flexible and practical, lend themselves to this kind of negotiation, this "experimental assemblage."[123]

AnneMarie Luijendijk, describing a fifth-century gospel amulet, makes a helpful observation for my argument in this chapter: "Joannia's amulet, with its use of canonical scripture, liturgical allusions, Christian scribal practices, and in its invocation of local saints, gives us a different view of 'orthodoxy' than a church authority like John Chrysostom promoted. This orthodoxy could include practices like wearing amulets."[124] Indeed, the evidence considered in this chapter illustrates that there were multiple understandings of what it meant to follow Christ, including those that deployed traditional practices, tried and trusted rituals for healing, blessing, and protection.

In this way the Christ cult was like other successful new cults in the Roman empire. Douglas Boin comments, "Roman religion was never a static affair. It was characterized by pluralism, syncretism, and above all, by flexibility and constant reinvention."[125] New cults found ways to "hybridize" with Roman ones, and this was critical to their success.[126] I suggest that the evidence discussed in this chapter illustrates this same process, happening not at the level of public cult (which was not in place yet before Constantine) but at the level of everyday contexts of households, neighborhoods, and shops. Those who became interested in the cult of Christ wove components of this new cult into their practices, combining innovation and respect for what works, a pattern illustrated by many across the empire. In this context, Christianity does not take hold because of something new it provides, but because it can be harnessed in a well-established exchange with the gods.

As scholars, we need to become more aware of the categories we assume and impose on our evidence and think creatively about how to reframe these. As Sanzo has pointed out, researchers have critically evaluated the label "magic," but we have largely continued to use the label "Christian" without a similar assessment.[127] I think this challenge will help us gain perspective on at least one aspect of how the cult of Christ took hold: by offering resources for exchanges with the divine that people sought in their daily lives.[128]

My larger argument in this book is that a focus on daily-life religion, on the ways that Christ followers incorporated symbols into their daily devotions, has implications for how we understand the development of Christianity. In this chapter I have argued that it challenges us to rethink what "Christian" even means. In the following chapters, I take up two further insights, both of which were touched on here as well. The first is the concept of agency: ritual agency does not belong solely to the lettered or to the experts. As the material in this chapter has shown, ritual agents might include a wide range of people, including mothers who care for their children.[129] I explore this notion specifically with respect to subordinate members of the household in chapter 4. How do wives and enslaved people engage in the cult of Christ, especially if their master does not? Is the process of integration available to them?

The second is the interaction between ecclesial officials and laypeople. The creation and administration of the spells and gems discussed earlier involved experts—scribes, gem carvers, and ritual experts—to render the symbols and gestures effective. These experts were themselves sometimes monks, priests, or scribes with positions in local churches. In a collection of Phrygian canons from the late fourth or early fifth century, we find the following declaration: "They who are of the priesthood, or of the clergy, shall not be magicians, enchanters, mathematicians, or astrologers; nor shall they make what are called amulets, which are chains for their own souls. And those who wear such, we command to be cast out of the Church."[130] As we have discussed above, the objections of the authorities help us imagine what was likely taking place: Christian clergy were using the tools and techniques of traditional religious experts. The production of amulets and spells thus suggests a fascinating cooperation and interchange between regular laypeople and clerics, all of whom participate in the process of integrating Christian symbols into authoritative, traditional rites. Chapter 5 explores this interaction further in the context of burial practices.

CHAPTER 4

FOREIGN GODS AND UNSUPERVISED WORSHIP

Wives, Slaves, and Power

In his *Advice to the Bride and Groom*, Plutarch famously pronounces: "A married woman should therefore worship and recognize the gods whom her husband holds dear, and these alone. The door must be closed to strange cults and foreign superstitions. No god takes pleasure in cult performed furtively and in secret by a woman."[1] These comments represent a patriarchal ideology that the wife (along with the whole household) should follow the worship practices of the husband. It also suggests the possibility that this counsel was not always followed and that wives might bring their own gods into a marriage, attempting to maintain ritual practices in their honor, perhaps secretly.

In this chapter I explore the power dynamics at work in texts like Plutarch's. I want to focus on the position of the wife in Plutarch's warning, specifically as someone subordinate to her husband in the household but also as someone who has access to household rituals. The metaphor of shutting the door against outsider deities illustrates the assumption of an inherent connection between the status of the household and the gods who are worshiped there. It matters to householders that the right gods are honored. The wife is portrayed here as a vulnerable part of the husband's household; she is somewhat of an outsider herself, having joined this household from another one.[2] Therefore, in Plutarch's thinking, she is someone who might "open the door" to foreign gods.

As we will see below, similar worries surface about household slaves. Indeed, wives and enslaved people share a common position in the household: as part of their subservience to the head of the household, they are responsible for implementing many components of the household rituals.[3]

This shared position prompts the central question I explore in this chapter: To what extent did religious practices give power to subordinate people in the household?

It is important to recognize, however, that wives and slaves did not have the same power in ancient households. Intersectional analysis, by recognizing multiple lines of domination in a patriarchal structure, offers a framework for understanding this dynamic.[4] It suggests that a wife and a slave would have overlapping, interlocking, yet still discrete "intersections" of power relationships in their lives, which place them in different situations in the household, even as they share a position of subordination.[5] In the discussion that follows, we will see examples of these differences as we follow the thread of their potential influence over household worship.

Anxiety over what scholars have called the "intimate outsider" position of both wives and slaves is illustrated by the *Controversiae* (fictional court cases designed to give students practice in delivering arguments), where wives and slaves often conspire against the husband and master.[6] Both are portrayed as conniving, untrustworthy, and avaricious; it is necessary to trust them because of their responsibilities in the household, but they are not in fact trustworthy.[7] That same anxiety underlies the Plutarch passage above as well as many of the texts discussed below. Those who rule worry about access to religious practices and powerful beings on the part of those who are ruled.

In this chapter, these concerns serve as our entry point to thinking about how wives and slaves might have had agency or power through their participation in—or even oversight of—domestic rituals. The context that often triggers these discussions is what I call "mixed households," by which I mean households in which there is potential tension created by a mixture of gods, some sanctioned by the head of the household and some not. Elite writers, including Christians, address these issues. Typically, these warnings are issued to householders who, like Plutarch's addressee, must be concerned with keeping the invading cult out.

In the Christian texts under consideration here, however, the focus is not on protecting the house from foreign cults but on protecting the foreign cult—centered on Christ—from outsiders. Paul, the author of 1 Peter, and Tertullian all address Christ-following wives married to non-Christian husbands, and Paul and 1 Peter also address enslaved believers. The comments of these writers reflect a situation in which the wife—or perhaps a slave—has not shut the door against foreign cults but has instead brought one into the household.

These three Christ-following authors are all literate producers: they participate in the intellectual practices of interpretation, making claims about right thinking, and they are invested in guiding believers in their daily lives. In previous chapters I have outlined how the intellectual output of these writers constitutes one mode of religious practice in the ancient world, and this mode is by far the one most associated with Christianity. The more widespread mode of religious practice belongs to daily life, the rituals people perform in households and neighborhoods throughout their day (see the introduction). In the passages discussed below, we find a familiar theme: the tension between these two modes as published Christians comment on, advise, correct, promote, and interpret the daily-life practices in households.

For the most part, these Christian intellectuals respect the power of the head of the household (even if he is not a believer) and the importance of religious ritual in maintaining that power. Indeed, this is what leads some of our Christian authors to fret over mixed households, as they recognize that their own cult is potentially disruptive to the patriarchal authority of the household. I argue that the work of these literate specialists is suggestive for thinking about how power operates in the case of subordinate members bringing new gods into the household.

The argument unfolds in the following steps. First, I lay out theoretical frameworks—including ritual and feminist theories and modern slave studies—for thinking about the power of subordinates in the household. Second, I turn to the ideologies articulated in non-Christian household management literature to show how societal power is mapped onto household relationships. Third, I turn to Christian literate specialists who comment on mixed households; they, too, use household relationships to promote a certain moral order. Finally, I analyze a specific set of rituals mentioned by Tertullian, arguing that these might afford power or agency, even if limited, for subordinate members of the household.

Theoretical Frameworks for Subordinated Power

To think through how this might work, I first outline several theories of power that I have found useful for teasing out complex hierarchies in ancient households. I begin with Catherine Bell's notion of "ritualization" (a term she prefers over "ritual") as an arena in which power is asserted, accepted, and resisted.[8] Building upon Michel Foucault's concept of bodies as sites of power, Bell argues that ritualization, as action mediated by the body, becomes a process of power negotiation: "Ritualization is a strategic play of power, of domination and resistance, within the arena of the social body."[9] As such, ritualization can both reinforce social order and destabilize it. A key factor in the latter is the distinction between self and society, or between "private and social selves," which ritualization can promote.[10]

In this model, power does not operate in a one-dimensional fashion, exercised upon those of lower status by those of higher status (by the head of the household on subordinate members, for example).[11] Instead, power is consensual and tensive, and, as Bell argues, ritualization allows those of the lowest status to enact some power, even as their subordination is reinscribed by the ritual itself.[12]

Another way to conceptualize Bell's multiple selves is by distinguishing between structural positions and subject positions as articulated in feminist theory. One's structural positions are determined by circumstances largely out of one's control. Elisabeth Schüssler Fiorenza writes, "Every individual is *structurally* positioned within social, cultural, economic, political, and religious systems by virtue of birth."[13] Subject positions, by contrast, attempt to describe the ways that individuals might respond or act in their specific constellation of structural positions. Subject positions are malleable, yet also constrained: "A *subject position* is variable, open to intervention and changeable, but also limited by hegemonic structures of domination."[14] Like structural positions, subject positions are multiple, and they help us think about how wives and enslaved people might react to their situations. Schüssler Fiorenza holds that "an individual becomes a social agent insofar as she lives her structural positions through an ensemble of subject positions."[15] The idea of multiple possible subject positions motivating social actors is potentially fruitful for thinking through options for wives and slaves in households: it suggests a kind of flexibility in defining the self in certain moments, enacting different roles in different contexts.[16] Religious ritual offers a venue for activating various subject positions, some of which are in line with the expectations of the subordinate roles argued for by writers like Plutarch, and some, like worshiping a foreign deity, may not be.

At the same time that I am interested in highlighting how ritual can be potentially empowering for women and slaves, I also want to caution against an overly simplistic reading of this phenomenon. As appealing as it might be to imagine that wives and slaves were uplifted by their new faith, I think a more subtle and more powerful dynamic is at work here. I have already mentioned that the religion of everyday social exchange is grounded in practice theory, which suggests that people operate out of a set of learned practices that become instinctive rather than premeditated (see the introduction). People in a given culture might agree that certain gestures in specific situations seem to just make sense in those moments without much analysis regarding why this is so. I suggest that it is the same with power in ancient households; it can operate among members unassisted by their intentions or even awareness. The dynamics of ritualization are that deeply woven into the dynamics of human interaction.

Judith Butler theorizes this phenomenon of limited or unpremeditated agency. Butler argues that societal norms—such as the expectations for hierarchical relationships in the Roman household—cannot exist on their own. In order to be sustained, they need to be performed and thus reiterated by social actors. She calls this process "performativity," describing it as "a process of iterability, a regularized and constrained repetition of norms."[17] A similar distinction between structural position and subject position operates here: individuals (as subjects) participate in the power structure by reiterating or performing the norms that place them in that structure. These iterations, however, do not necessarily neatly replicate the norms. They can also offer tweaks and shifts to these norms, which Butler calls "citations." She notes that "a citation will be at once an interpretation of the norm and an occasion to expose the norm itself as privileged interpretation."[18] The reiteration of one's structural position can both reify the norm and complicate it by exposing the power dynamic at play. The complexities of power, the fact that the structure needs to be continually reiterated but can never be done so in exactly the same way, "opens up the space for citations or iterations that subvert precisely those norms they are supposed to reinforce."[19]

I contend that wives and slaves, perhaps even unwittingly, contribute to a dynamic of maintaining and shifting power in the household through everyday rituals.[20] We are invited to think about power not in a purely binary way—as an opposition between the slaveholder and the enslaved person—but as operating in a network of interactions that occur not only among humans but also between humans and deities.

Scholarship on modern slavery supports the case I am building. Vincent Brown, arguing against Orlando Patterson's notion of "social death," suggests that when people are faced with the coercion and violence of a slave system, agency becomes more of a "politics of survival" than a revolt against the system.[21] Brown builds on Walter Johnson's notion that we should assume agency on the part of enslaved people rather than treating it as though it is an exceptional thing to be discovered.[22] Brown illustrates his argument with the example of ritual mourning practices that took place on board a slave ship in the late eighteenth century. When one of their number died, the first on that passage, the other captives gathered to mourn, offering a kind of funeral, marking her death.[23] Their keening and whispers to the spirit of the deceased were not intended as a revolt against slavery but served to construct a new community among those who remained, to define for the mourners "their place among ancestors, kin, friends, and future progeny."[24] As such, these rites are political and constructive; they generate the terms through which people will survive enslavement.[25]

This analysis of ritual among enslaved people of a different historical era evokes the kind of empowerment I am suggesting for subordinate people in ancient households. Through daily-life rituals—such as signing the body with the cross, blowing on the hands, or nibbling on holy bread, as I discuss below—wives and enslaved people had access to a kind of agency, one that was both constrained and made possible by the larger system of power at play in the household. These rituals imitate and modify traditional, non-Christian practices in ways that allow Christians to participate in the household and signal their loyalty to their god simultaneously.

Mapping Power Through Household Cult

To understand these smaller moments of ritual agency for subordinates, it is important to recognize that the household itself is perceived and constructed in the Roman period as an arena of power negotiation. Recent work on Roman-period households has called attention to this phenomenon.[26] Kate Cooper discusses the "spatial grammar" of the *domus* and calls it a "stage for the performance of authority by the *dominus*."[27] Kristina Sessa argues that the household was an "index of an individual's public status" and was therefore subject to public scrutiny.[28] These power dynamics might play out in a variety of ways, including the domestic cult.

The connection between the authority of the head of the household and the power of the gods was widespread in the Roman world. Indeed, the very notion of belonging to a household, whether as a slave or as a family member, meant precisely that you tended to the gods who protected it, the gods of the head of the household. In patrilocal marriages, which were common in the Roman world, the bride moved into her husband's household and took up the responsibility for worship of its gods.[29] Plutarch's advice quoted above illustrates this patriarchal ideology, as he admonishes wives to shun any gods but those of her husband. Not doing so amounts to a kind of "religious infidelity" not tolerated by Roman moralists.[30] Plutarch invokes a spatial image of closing the door of the household against "foreign" gods, drawing a boundary between the physical space of the household, the wife's obedience to her husband, and religious fidelity to his gods on one side and foreign superstitions on the other. The same logic applied to enslaved members of the household, who also expressed their obedience to the head of the household through participation in domestic cult.

An explicit example of this ideology put into practice is the cult of the *genius*, which might be described as the guardian spirit of the male head of the household. On his birthday, his *genius* was honored by the household members, an action that signaled allegiance to him.[31] Augustus himself recognized the potential of this tradition when he reorganized the city of Rome around wards and neighborhoods that honored the *genius Augusti* and the *lares Augusti*.[32] These changes transferred Augustus's household cult to the city, fitting for an emperor who was cast as the ultimate *paterfamilias* or *dominus* of the Roman empire. This strategic use of cult practices to secure power illustrates how ritualization (in Bell's schema outlined above) can reinforce social order.

Just as the model of the household was useful to Augustus in the political arena, it was also useful to moralists and philosophers as a moral compass by which to talk about a variety of issues: economic production and wealth-getting; proper comportment of men, women, and slaves; health and healing; agriculture; leadership and management skills; and politics, with the household as the model for the state. Authors of these discourses on "household management" are preoccupied with the proper distribution of power and status. Order, efficiency, productivity, and virtue depend upon each person knowing and occupying a specific position in a larger hierarchy: some are meant to rule and some to be ruled.[33] The household thus becomes a site for mapping out various levels of superiority and subordination, and discourses about households serve as a means of deploying elite values.

There are several recurring and intersecting themes in discourses on household management, such as the unity of the husband and wife; the subordination of the wife to the husband and the enslaved to the free; order and stability; and the reverence of all members to the household gods, resulting in the divine sanction of the marriage and the prosperity of the household. We find this cluster of themes expressed by Xenophon, a fifth-century BCE Greek philosopher whose work on this topic, *Oeconomicus*, became the model for Roman-period writers such as Cicero, Philodemus, and Columella.[34] The model head of household in this text is Ischomachus, who explains to Socrates that when he married his wife, she knew hardly anything about managing the household, and it was his job to teach her (she was only fourteen, after all). Before doing so, Ischomachus describes how he sacrificed to the gods and prayed for his success as a teacher and for her ability to learn (7.6–7). When asked if his wife sacrificed with him and offered prayers, Ischomachus replies, "Oh yes, very much so, and she vowed and prayed fervently to the gods that she might become the sort of woman that she ought to be" (7.8).[35] In this view, the husband and head of household is a teacher and the wife a student. She eagerly follows his lead in honoring the gods and submitting to his instruction, which includes the supervision of enslaved workers (7.35). As a counter to the *Controversiae* literature, which associates wives and slaves with betrayal, authors of household management discourses call for a cooperative, friendly, and orderly obedience from all subordinate members of the household. They consistently link the proper hierarchies and functioning of a unified household with devotion to the gods, a rhetorical move that claims divine sanction for their version of a proper household.[36]

We find an extension of this theme in Cato's second-century BCE farming manual, *De agricultura*, a treatise written for aristocratic men who might acquire a country estate. Cato views religious practices as a way of distributing power and maintaining control of slaves in an elite household. Brendon Reay argues that Cato treats enslaved workers as prosthetic extensions of the estate owner, such that their actions and words become those of the master.[37] As Cato recognizes, this positioning of enslaved people—as representatives of the estate owner but also under that person's control—requires management. Here Cato addresses the head male slave (*vilicus*) of the household and farm. One of his duties is to supervise the head female slave (*vilica*), who may be given to him (by their owner) as a wife (143). She must clean the hearth daily and decorate it on holidays: "On the Kalends, Ides, and Nones, and whenever a holy day comes, she must hang a garland over the hearth, and on those days pray to the household gods (*Lari familiari*) as opportunity offers" (143.2).[38] Decorating the hearth and offering prayers to the *lares* on specific holy days are among the duties the slave performs.

Cato is careful to point out, however, that the slave's role in religious rituals is limited and distinct from the roles of the *dominus* and *domina*: "She must not engage in worship (*rem divinam facere*) herself or get others to engage in it for her without the orders of the *dominus* or *domina*. Let her remember that the *dominus* attends to the worship (*rem divinam facere*) for the whole household" (143.1). Anxiety over unsupervised worship emerges here as Cato outlines the limitations on the slave woman's freedom to perform religious practices.[39] She must perform these rituals only as a prosthetic extension of the *dominus*.

This passage offers a glimpse of the role of both a slave woman and a free wife, at least as Cato sees it: the slave woman performs religious duties connected to the hearth, which she tends daily, and the *domina* is responsible for ordering and overseeing these duties. Cato's careful delineation of who has power over whom alerts us to important differences between wives and slave women, at least in this context of the rural estate. The *vilica* is ruled over by both the *vilicus* (who supervises her) and the *domina*, who can order worship. The *dominus*, though, the male head of household, is in charge of the rituals of the whole household; his authority trumps that of everyone else. According to Cato, autonomy with respect to religious practices reflects the power structure of the household, which is shaped by gender and status. Cato's instructions echo the prevailing ideology of patriarchal power in the Roman household as well as the intertwined gender and status hierarchies that order its subordinate members.

Yet his instructions also betray a recognition of the potential for destabilizing this structure. Cato seems to recognize the possibility that the slave woman might initiate religious practices herself, or get others to do so, acts that mimic and undermine the authority of the head male slave over her or the *domina* and *dominus* over both of them.[40] As I discuss below, several scholars have suggested that slaves did have access to their own shrines in kitchens and service areas and may therefore have been able to exercise at least a limited autonomy in their worship practices. We can thus imagine in households a tension similar to what we see in Cato's instructions to the *vilicus* and in Plutarch's warning to wives about foreign gods: power was imposed on others by the head of the household, but subordinate members could both assent to and resist their place in the social hierarchy through religious rituals.[41]

We might read household rituals, ancient households in general, and the literature prescribing household behavior (including those Christian ones described below) in this context; power relationships are mapped out in each. When we imagine wives and slaves (whether Christian or not) in mixed households, a complex picture emerges—illustrating Bell's notion of ritualization—in which daily religious practices reinforce their subordination and also offer moments of limited agency and empowerment, even simultaneously.

Christ Followers in Mixed Households: Christian Intellectuals Weigh In

We have seen that Plutarch and Cato are both concerned about the potential for foreign or unsupervised religious practices to disrupt the traditional power structures of proper households. They worry about rogue subordinate members of the household interacting with deities in ways that are not prescribed by those in power. In the texts that follow, we find Christ-following authors—literate producers like Plutarch and Cato—addressing the same issue, but as proponents of the objectionable, invading cult. Instead of addressing householders, they address the subordinate member, the wife or enslaved believer. These authors—Paul, the author of 1 Peter, and Tertullian—all participate in the discourse of household management. Their comments help us think about the possible agency of subordinate Christ followers in this situation.

1 Corinthians

1 Corinthians represents our earliest witness to the phenomenon of mixed households, where Christ followers and others share familial and household relationships.[42] Paul's text stands out as quite different, both from those we have just discussed and from those Christian texts whose authors use him as a model for their own opinions.[43] Having just addressed married believers and counseled them not to divorce, he writes:

> (12) To the rest I say (I and not the Lord): if a brother has an unbelieving wife and she agrees to live with him, let him not leave her. (13) And if a woman has an unbelieving husband and he agrees to live with her, let her not leave her husband. (14) For the unbelieving husband is made holy by the wife and the unbelieving wife is made holy by the brother. Otherwise your children are unclean; but now they are holy. (1 Cor 7:12–14)

One striking feature of this passage, and a sharp contrast to Plutarch and Cato, is that Paul offers reciprocal advice to men and women; he does not acknowledge the asymmetrical power relationships of the patriarchal household. Furthermore, instead of counseling adherence to the husband's gods and rejection of "foreign" gods, Paul advises both spouses to stay with their unbelieving partners as long as the latter are willing, advice that implies a certain amount of toleration for the situation. Indeed, Paul seems to envision that this sort of mixed marriage could work, at least for the short term (which is the only time frame Paul is considering).

Another striking feature of this passage, and one that has garnered much discussion among scholars, is the implication that the believer somehow makes the rest of the family members holy.[44] Here the potentially unharmonious issue of mixed households has been raised, perhaps initially by the Corinthians themselves, and Paul suggests that a kind of contagious holiness is at work. In contrast to 1 Corinthians 6, in which Paul raises the possibility that *porneia* can pollute the body of Christ (6:15–16), this mixed-marriage passage suggests that the status of the believer's body—a member of Christ (6:15), a holy temple (3:16–17; 6:19)—overrules the status of the unbeliever's. The holiness of the believer somehow transfers to the unbelieving spouse, at least enough to render their children not unclean but holy (v. 14).

One way to understand this intriguing passage is in the larger context of Paul's advice throughout 1 Corinthians 7. He urges people in different status positions (married, unmarried, enslaved, uncircumcised) to stay as they are. Paul's idea of contagious holiness, by transforming the unbelieving spouse, attempts to dispense with conflict that might arise from this situation and, for the sake of stability, secures the holy status of the whole family. Thus the holiness language here is intended to operate almost as a quick fix, serving the larger goal of encouraging inertia and preserving the status quo.

Yet the passage is slippery, for it leaves open the possibility of other readings that undermine Paul's advice to "stay as you are." In Paul's writings, the language of "being made holy" or "being sanctified" marks the change that occurs at baptism (1 Cor 6:11, for example). It identifies members of the *ekklesia* over and against outsiders, or what the gentile audience members were before. Thus the notion of one spouse sanctifying another has implications for the boundaries of the group: Was baptism by an established leader necessary, or could one become a member of the *ekklesia* through marriage to a believer? Or through birth to believing parents (or even one believing parent)? Does the believer, regardless of status in the household, serve as a kind of portal for other members to the community of believers?

This scenario becomes especially remarkable if the believer is a wife. The passage could be read as an acknowledgment of the power of wives to influence and transform other family members, including their husbands. Such a reading subverts traditional household ideologies, including the expectation that women and other subordinates will follow the loyalties of the male head of the household. Perhaps even more striking is that it also undermines Paul's own efforts elsewhere in the letter to rein in the practices of female bodies (e.g., 1 Cor 11:2–16; 14:34–36). As many scholars have discussed, this is a chief concern in this letter.[45]

Paul's quick fix also leaves us wondering about how such a household might operate. Does he—or do the Corinthians—imagine that all the household gods would continue to be worshiped in this mixed marriage? How would the god of the Christ cult be worshiped? Paul's overarching advice is to keep peace with non-believing neighbors and spouses. What does that look like in daily life? In chapter 3, I suggest that many Christ believers were not necessarily exclusive in their worship practices; the unanswered questions raised by this passage hint at this possibility as well.

Furthermore, would this same principle of contagious holiness apply to enslaved believers, who were not even legally allowed to marry?[46] Paul does not address enslaved believers on this particular topic, but he does turn to them a few verses later, continuing his "stay as you were called" theme (7:21–24). His comment to enslaved believers is notoriously difficult to interpret: "Let each one remain in the condition in which he or she was called. Were you a slave when called? Do not be concerned. But even if you are able to become free, make use of it" (7:20–21).[47] Both modern and ancient readers have debated over what exactly Paul admonishes believers to make use of: their potential freedom or their enslaved state?[48] If the former, it would be an exception to the overall theme of the chapter. He does not specify whether he speaks to enslaved people of believing slaveholders or unbelieving ones; we can imagine that both heard his advice.[49] As with his passage on mixed marriage, here he mentions no tensions related to enslaved believers worshiping a different god, nor does he explicitly address their obedience to their owners, as later Christian writers will do. He does offer an extended metaphor of their status before their new god (as freedpersons) as compared to the status of free believers (as slaves of Christ) (v. 22), and he concludes with a reminder that they were "bought with a price" (v. 23). Any notion of contagious holiness is absent, but the slave market language—applied here to both enslaved and free believers—might be read as a leveling of the two status positions.[50]

Whereas Plutarch constructs a threat posed by wives who might allow unsanctioned gods into the household, Paul's rhetoric (with other goals in view) ignores the power structures of ancient households and the importance of exchange with the gods in maintaining those structures. Plutarch expects a wife to conform to the worship practices of her husband's household; Paul's counsel implies that both husbands and wives should tolerate each other's gods. We do not know if Paul would apply the same advice to enslaved and slave-owning believers. As I mention above, it is possible that subordinate believers might have read 1 Corinthians as a confirmation of their own influence in the household, whether through religious practices or otherwise. Paul's sanguine attitude about household hierarchies in this passage stands out among Christian writers. Later authors, even as they use 1 Corinthians to support their arguments, take a different tack: they allow traditional hierarchies to guide their counsel to believing wives and slaves.[51]

1 Peter

In 1 Peter we encounter a strikingly different attitude about believers in unbelieving households, one that is closer to Plutarch and Cato than to Paul. Whereas Paul does not engage with the complications of mixed households, the author of this late first-century letter presents them as quite concerning, especially for subordinate Christian members. Both wives and slaves are vulnerable to censure or violence for their disobedience to the head of the household.[52]

Slaves and wives are addressed in two adjacent passages (2:18–25 and 3:1–6), following a broader admonition to believers to "be subordinate to

('Υποτάγητε) every human institution," including the emperor and those who enforce his rule (2:13). Just before launching into a passage that addresses slaves directly, the author commands: "Fear God. Honor the emperor" (2:17).

Our two passages, one addressing slaves and one addressing wives, follow this broad mandate and open with parallel phrases: "Slaves, be subordinate to (ὑποτασσόμενοι) your masters with all deference" (2:18) and "Likewise you wives: be subordinate to (ὑποτασσόμεναι) your husbands" (3:1). Similar verbs have been used three times in close succession: be subordinate (ὑποτάγητε) to human institutions (2:13); be subordinate to masters (ὑποτασσόμενοι) (2:18); and be subordinate to husbands (ὑποτασσόμεναι) (3:1), linking the passages.[53] Wives and slaves also share vulnerability, as the author seems to recognize some danger associated with being subordinate believers in an unbelieving household.

Yet there are also important differences between the two passages, which help us see how enslaved people and free wives are positioned differently—in distinct intersections of power—in households. The author tells slaves to obey even harsh masters, adding that the violence inflicted upon them is more valuable when it is unjust: God approves of this kind of suffering most (1 Pet 2:18–21). Indeed, undeserved suffering imitates Christ's experience, the author argues, which should be a model for all believers. In this way, the enslaved believer being abused by his or her master becomes an analogy for the Christian living in a hostile world.

The author makes a different set of moves in the advice to wives. First, there is only the hint of the danger of their situation; the author says that, like Sarah, wives do what is right, "not fearing any terror" (3:6).[54] Second, religious conflict is made explicit in this set of instructions, in which wives are implored to obey their husbands "even if some disobey the word" (3:1). But the author does not merely advise obedience in these instructions. He also encourages wives to "win over" their husbands through their "reverent and chaste conduct" (vv. 1–2). Think about the position of the wives: they are to be obedient to their husbands, like good Roman wives, yet they are also told that they might yield some persuasive influence, not with words but with actions. According to this author, Christian wives are potentially evangelists through action rather than speech.[55] 1 Peter 3:1–6 simultaneously reinforces the control of the non-Christian husband *and* empowers (albeit in a limited way) the Christian wife in her submission.

What choices did wives and slaves have to "fear God" and "honor the emperor" (2:17), or, here, to "fear God" and "be subordinate to" the head of the household? Each of these mandates requires religious devotion to different entities. This scenario raises intriguing questions about the relationship between power and religious practices and the ways that people of lower status might have exercised some sort of agency or influence in spite of, or perhaps even because of, their servile position. Butler's theorization of the subject—as one who acts within a larger power structure in ways that replicate, shift, and possibly subvert the norms of that structure—provides fertile ground for thinking about what it would mean for believing wives and slaves, as they "reiterate" their loyalty to the head of the household through religious practices, to insert their own modification to the system. The author of 1 Peter suggests that through her very obedience and *silence* (reiterating the norm of the obedient wife), the wife might still influence her husband. This advice could be read as an example of Butler's concept of citation, showing how the wife's iterations of the norm (her obedience and silence) has the potential "to subvert precisely those norms they are supposed to reinforce."[56] Although 1 Peter's rhetoric supports the structure of the patriarchal household, it also expresses the hope that it might be challenged by allegiance to a different god. Enslaved believers, too, might be able to participate in a similar dynamic. I return to this suggestion below.

Tertullian

So far, I have examined two literate specialists who address household arrangements of believers living in mixed households. 1 Corinthians and 1 Peter express starkly different attitudes, one nonchalant and the other concerned. Both hint at the power of wives in this situation: Paul suggests that a wife might make her unbelieving spouse holy, and the author of 1 Peter imagines that she can influence her husband through mute action. Our next author, Tertullian, lines up more with 1 Peter, as he vociferously objects to marriages between Christian women and non-Christian men.

One of Tertullian's objections derives from an argument related to purity: mixed marriages constitute an unholy mixing akin to fornication or adultery (*Ux.* 2.3.1). This assessment is nearly the opposite of Paul's, who claims that the holiness of the believer will prevail. Indeed, to make this claim Tertullian has to appeal to a different part of 1 Corinthians (chapter 6) and basically ignore Paul's direct comments on mixed marriages.[57] For Tertullian, the union of believers and unbelievers is corrupt from the start.

Another of his objections relates directly to power in the household. He offers this succinct assessment of the Christian wife's dilemma when he asks how the Christian wife can "obey two masters, the Lord and her husband" (*Ux.* 2.3.4).[58] This question acknowledges the close link between the patriarchal structure of the household and the religious practices of the participants. As a subordinate member of the household, the wife would have been expected to worship her husband's gods; yet, as Tertullian explains, she is also required to obey the Christian god (2.3.3).[59] We can see how the different modes of religion interact in Tertullian's observation. He agrees with other literate specialists in the ancient world, including those discussed above, who promote a certain household ideology that required good management from the head of the household and subservience from other members. Precisely because these hierarchies were also operative in household practices, Tertullian has identified what could be a potential conflict in the spouse's daily life: being a good wife (and carrying out devotions to the gods of the household) and being a good Christian (and carrying out devotions to the Christian god). Although Tertullian does not address this issue, we can imagine how his formulation of the Christian's predicament—as obligated to obey two masters—is even more acute when applied to people who are enslaved, whose servitude to masters is not metaphorical.

Tertullian identifies not only with the Christian wife in his argument but also with the non-Christian husband. A mixed marriage potentially challenges this husband's authority, which Tertullian respects, even as he calls him an agent of Satan (2.4.1). *Ad uxorem* is thus a censure of Christian women who might marry "heathen" husbands but also a warning to these women that they might be censured by their husbands for disobedience, and rightfully so.[60] The authority of the head of the household, even if he is not a Christian, is not to be compromised. Tertullian's solution is that a Christian woman should marry a Christian man so that she can perform her household devotions without hiding or censure (*Ux.* 2.8.7). In this way, she can be properly obedient to the head of the household.

Signing, Spitting, Eating: Empowering Gestures

The comments of these Christian literate producers signal that something was at stake in the situation of mixed households. Believing slaves and wives were perceived as vulnerable but also potentially influential in their subservient roles. To explore this dynamic further, I examine several rituals mentioned by Tertullian as those a wife might perform at home. We have already been introduced to the variety of Christian and non-Christian household practices in Tertullian's *Ad uxorem* in chapter 2; here I return to a few of them to illustrate how these practices potentially wield power in the household.[61]

In *Ad uxorem*, as we have seen, Tertullian has many reasons to dislike the notion of Christian wives marrying non-Christian husbands. He particularly objects to "heathen" husbands witnessing certain rituals performed by their Christian wives, rituals that might look like disreputable practices. The list of rituals is framed, therefore, by his concern over disrupting the authority of the husband, as discussed above. He asks, "Will you escape notice when you sign your bed or your body; when you blow away some impurity, when you rise at night to pray? Will you not be thought to be engaged in some form of magic? Will your husband know what it is that you secretly taste before taking any food? If he recognizes it as bread, will he not believe it to be that bread which it is said to be? Will a husband really endure this, whether it be bread or a magic potion?" (2.5.3–4).[62] In chapter 2 I argue that these rituals—signing, blowing, praying, and eating eucharistic bread at home—are all part of a loosely connected, improvised Christian household cult. They could be imagined as individual acts as opposed to the collective rites of official household (or church) rituals. Christ-following wives (or, as I suggest below, slaves) might easily perform these gestures on their own in their mixed households.[63] And in so doing, as I argue here, these believers attain some agency or power for themselves.

Each of the rituals mentioned in this passage is portable and requires few or no props. Most are low profile, relying only on the body to enact them, and might be done in any space. Given the flexibility of household practices, we can imagine that the wives addressed here had the opportunity to enact these rituals, perhaps even without the detection of others (despite Tertullian's skepticism) to the extent that this was useful. Only the reserved eucharist would require access to the bread brought home from the communal ritual.[64] Simply in practical terms, then, these gestures are amenable to private practice, available at any hour, and quickly performed. Even people with few resources and little time could do them.

Furthermore, as I discussed in chapter 2, several of these gestures echo the rituals of communal gatherings. The phrase "when you blow away some unclean thing (*cum aliquid immundum flatu explodis*)" likely refers to insufflation, described in the *Apostolic Tradition* as blowing "moist breath" into the hand to catch some of the saliva, which replicates baptismal water.[65] This action sanctifies the whole body, down to the feet.[66] In chapter 2 I note that saliva was considered a powerful healing agent in the Roman world. With this blowing gesture, Christians combined the efficacy of saliva with the powers associated with baptismal water.[67] Unlike baptism, which occurs one time and might be performed by an official, Tertullian suggests that a wife can administer this mini-baptism to herself when the need arises.[68]

Like ritual blowing, eating bread brought home from the eucharistic meal reenacts—on an individual scale and in a different context—the eucharist, an important communal ritual.[69] Tertullian refers to the wife's taking the bread before "tasting any food," which suggests the possibility that this ritual took place before a meal, perhaps alongside other rituals that accompanied meals, such as offerings to the gods. The eating of the bread is thus recontextualized from Christian communal ritual to one of several domestic devotional acts in honor of a variety of beings and deities that watch over the household. Again, the wife here acts like the Christian ritual expert as she administers the bread to herself at home.

Finally, these gestures might be viewed as a way of protecting or marking the body or the space, which, for some believers, might have been relevant in a context in which many gods are worshiped.[70] As discussed in chapter 2, the sign of the cross on someone's forehead was understood by Christians to signal that that person belonged to and was protected by the Christian god. Church manuals indicate that it accompanied baptisms, sealing initiates into the new cult (*Apostolic Tradition* 21.22). Like insufflation, however, it can also be practiced by individuals as needed, independent of communal gatherings or church authorities. Tertullian recommends signing liberally throughout the day (*Cor.* 3).

In more dire circumstances, believers might sign themselves for protection. In the second-century Acts of Thecla, the heroine is about to be burned at the stake for her rebellious decision to leave her family, including her betrothed, and follow Paul. She makes the sign of the cross (τὸν τύπον τοῦ σταυροῦ) before ascending the pyre and, miraculously, the fire does not touch her because God causes a burst of rain to squelch the flames (Acts of Thecla 22).[71] This story nicely illustrates the protective quality associated with this gesture, as Thecla's vulnerable body is marked and then protected from her persecutors by her god, triggered by her own autonomous gesture.[72] The protective quality of self-signing is echoed in the *Apostolic Tradition*, which, in addition to discussing this gesture as part of the rite of baptism, also offers instructions for individual signing, including "sign your forehead with reverence. For this sign of the Passion is clear and approved against the devil" (42.1) and "signing the forehead and eyes with the hand, let us escape him who is trying to destroy us" (42.4).[73]

Tertullian imagines this kind of autonomous gesture on the part of the wife in her mixed household. To the extent that Christ followers agreed with Tertullian about the potential pollution of living with non-believers, signing the bed (if it is the bed the believing wife will share with her husband) might be perceived as protection from the impurities of intercourse with her non-believing husband.[74] Or, to the extent that Christ followers shared the widespread notion that harmful beings lurked everywhere, signing the body or space is useful protection. Likewise, the ritual blowing away of impurities or other threats is a highly convenient gesture for Christians interested in defining their bodies in relation to others, as it reactivates the sanctifying effects of baptism.

Eucharistic bread, too, was perceived by some as protective and healing. Ignatius of Antioch, writing to the Ephesians, calls the bread "the medicine of immortality, and the antidote that we should not die."[75] The *Apostolic Tradition* advises that if eaten with faith, the reserved bread will protect the believer from "something deadly" (36).[76] The power of the eucharistic bread is emphasized by Cyprian in a series of stories about the fates of those who are unworthy to eat it. One example in particular, also discussed in chapter 2, seems to refer to a domestic context: "And another woman, when she tried with unworthy hands to open her box, in which was the holy (body) of the Lord, was deterred by fire rising from it from daring to touch it" (*De lapsis* 26).[77] The "box" mentioned here refers to the container one would use to carry the bread home.[78] A dramatic story told by Gregory of Nazianzus about his sister, Gorgonia, shows that this protective and healing power of the bread still resonated in the fourth century. He recounts how she healed herself by creating a salve by mixing together eucharistic bread, wine, and her tears and then rubbing this on her body.[79] The historical veracity of these stories is less important than the rhetorical aims of the writers, which depend on an acceptance of the power of the eucharistic bread and on the ability to self-administer it.[80]

Given the ideology of patriarchal marriage in the Roman period, in which wives were subject to husbands, this ability to mark and protect one's own body and space is potentially empowering to wives (and even more so to enslaved people, to whom I turn below). These daily gestures illustrate Bell's notion of ritualization. In particular, gestures such as signing or blowing, which mark the body or space, fit with Bell's notion that ritual can produce "schemes for the differentiation of private and social selves."[81] If wives and slaves are managing multiple allegiances, then these gestures—as "sequences of repetitive movements of the body that simultaneously constitute the body"[82]—serve to identify the practitioner as dedicated to a particular deity, even as she or he continues to show allegiance to the household through worship of its gods. Tertullian himself presents multiple allegiances as a problem; he objects that they will be perceived by the husband as "magic," which is powerful and not to be trusted. Such secretive actions potentially pose a challenge to his authority because they direct loyalty and obedience to a different "master." His comment may be prompted by the fact that the wives (or maybe even the husbands) did not see it that way.

Imagining Slaves

Tertullian does not list domestic rituals that enslaved believers might perform. Indeed, our evidence for the practices of Christian slaves is sparse. We must, therefore, use our informed imaginations to reconstruct the possibilities. I follow the lead of scholars of Greek and Roman slavery who insist that we assume the presence and engagement of enslaved people in the historical record, rather than accepting the invisibility promoted by the "master story" and the material and literary record.[83]

As we saw above in 1 Corinthians and 1 Peter, enslaved believers have been acknowledged by Christian writers since the earliest Christian literature. Outsiders, too, noted the presence of enslaved people in Christianity, even if to disparage it.[84] As is typical of most evidence for slaves at this time, we have no evidence produced by enslaved believers. Instead, they are largely represented by elite writers who have an agenda. These authors, like the author of 1 Peter, advise enslaved believers to obey their masters without complaint, whether they are believers or not.[85]

Third- and fourth-century church manuals, which may preserve earlier traditions, suggest that enslaved believers were also beholden to their masters when it came to initiation into the community of believers. The *Apostolic Tradition*, for example, states that someone seeking teaching should be asked if he is a slave and, if so, whether the slave owner approves of this petition. The instructions continue: "If his master does not testify on his behalf, that he is good, let him be cast out. If his master is a heathen (ἐθνικός), teach him to please his master so that there shall be no scandal" (15.3–5).[86] This advice reflects what we have seen in 1 Peter and Tertullian: a concern to preserve the authority of the slave owner, Christian or not.[87] Christian authors illustrate that they thought in much the same way as non-Christian authors about the propriety of hierarchical relationships: Christian slaves, like all slaves, were expected to conform to the wishes of their owners.[88]

Whether this always happened is another question, one that scholars still debate, prompted in part by Franz Bömer's groundbreaking study that sought to determine whether slaves' ritual activity ever occurred independently or was always tied to institutions run by slaveholders.[89] Although he concluded the latter, his question was narrow enough that the evidence is worth reconsidering. I agree with those who have argued that our evidence for the ritual activity of enslaved people—such as funerary inscriptions, vows, and certain household and neighborhood cults, such as the *lares compitales* and the cult of Silvanus—represents religious initiative, even if it depends in some part on patrons or owners.[90] Niall McKeown notes that the activities involving contact with people outside of the household, such as association meetings, afford enslaved people the opportunity to have some semblance of independence.[91]

Furthermore, the archaeological record suggests the possibility of ritual agency for enslaved members of the household. Several large houses in Pompeii have multiple shrines, some in service areas like kitchens (which theoretically would have been occupied by enslaved workers) and others in the more public spaces of *atria* or gardens (areas used primarily by the free members of the household and their visitors). Some scholars argue that this arrangement of the space itself suggests the possibility of autonomous—perhaps even separate—worship by enslaved members of the household.[92] Pedar Foss points out that the best supporting evidence for this theory is limited to the largest houses, such as *casa grande* VII.14.5, I.7.10–12 (Casa del' Efebo), and I.10.4 (Casa del Menandro).[93] John Bodel comments on this spatial arrangement: "What evidently mattered in the articulation of domestic space was the social differentiation of the freeborn kin, with their household gods related somehow to the spirits of the ancestors, and the slave household, considered collectively but in fact comprising (at least potentially) elements of multiple slave 'families,' with its separate but parallel set of household deities."[94] Again we see how the very expression of social hierarchy through religious practice (with enslaved members of the household as separate and lower) simultaneously affords religious agency for those enslaved members.

We have to be careful with these interpretations. They are based on a narrow slice of the population living in large houses, and they depend on assumptions about spatial boundaries in households (e.g., that slaves occupied kitchens and free people occupied other rooms) that may not hold.[95] I do not think, however, that we need clear evidence of separate group worship to imagine slaves as ritual agents in households. We have already seen how domestic ritual practices lend themselves to innovation and individual appropriation. Vincent Brown's modern example of enslaved mourners, mentioned earlier in this chapter, supports this idea: enslaved people ritualized their grief by adapting mourning practices to very difficult circumstances.[96]

Shifting away from the collective model of ancient religiosity can be fruitful for thinking about the agency of subordinates. As Stephen Hodkinson and Dick Geary note, the collective or "'civic model' leaves little scope for personal religiosity or for the possibility that subordinate individuals or groups, especially slaves, might fashion their own religious behaviours."[97] From gestures to prayers to offerings, individuals, including enslaved people, had access to devotional practices.[98]

Given the number of enslaved people who were war captives in the Roman imperial period, it is not difficult to imagine a scenario in which they would want to maintain their ancestral worship traditions in some way.[99] Tacitus seems to have this in mind when he reports a senatorial speech about slave punishments. His character portrays slaves as outsiders and casts their religious activity as a threat: "But now that we have in our households nations (*nationes*) with different customs to our own, with a foreign worship (*externa sacra*) or none at all, it is only by terror you can hold in such a motley rabble" (*Annals* 14.44).[100] This statement echoes the "intimate outsider" idea discussed earlier, casting enslaved members of the household as completely "other": they are a different people (*nationes*) worshiping in a foreign manner. Recall that Cato warns against the slave woman initiating her own rituals, unauthorized by the *dominus*. Her role is critical to the maintenance of the household cult: she must garland the hearth and pray to the *lares*. Perhaps she also maintains a separate shrine for her own ancestral gods—negotiating and enacting multiple selves, as theorized by Bell and others above—a practice Cato would not endorse.

We find similar anxieties among Christian writers whose slaves honor other gods. Tertullian recounts the story of a Christian "brother" who returned home to find that his slaves had wreathed the gates upon having heard an announcement of a public celebration. At issue seems to be whether the Christian head of the household should be held accountable for this behavior, which Tertullian refers to as a matter of "our household discipline (*disciplina familiae nostrae*)" (*Idol.* 15).[101] A church council from the early fourth century warns the faithful against keeping "idols" in their homes: "If, however, they fear violence from their slaves (*si vero vim metuunt servorum*), they must at least keep themselves pure. If they do not do this, they are considered to be outside the Church" (Synod of Elvira, canon 41).[102] These texts indicate that slaveholders, both non-Christian and Christian, believed that enslaved people could be religious agents, incorporating their own gods into their households.[103]

Might enslaved Christians do the same? What options might be available to those addressed in 1 Peter, for example?[104] Perhaps some had access to their own niche in the kitchen where they might offer prayers to their gods. Many may have had no space to themselves. Imagine Tertullian's gestures—signing, blowing, eating—being performed by an enslaved believer in a non-Christian household. The bodies of slaves were considered the property of their owners, to be used for work, pleasure, or reproduction. A common term for a slave was simply *sōma*, or "body," to be used as needed by the slaveholder.[105] If an enslaved woman were to cross her body or eat a bit of the eucharistic bread, we might read these gestures as making an alternative claim on her body; in a private moment she marks her body as belonging to her god, or perhaps to herself, rather than to her master.[106]

Again, studies of other slave cultures are useful in thinking about this possibility. In a volume that brings together research on ancient Mediterranean slavery and modern Brazil, the editors report studies of enslaved people from the continent of Africa who were imported in great numbers to Brazil between the sixteenth century and the nineteenth.[107] In this context of extreme displacement, people from various cultures and backgrounds on the continent of Africa came to learn one another's languages and form new kinship groups.[108] New religious traditions—for example, candomblé—emerged from this process, bringing together elements from Africa, from the Indigenous peoples in Brazil, and from the official religion of the ruling colonizers, Roman Catholicism. Existing in a variety of local forms, candomblé was largely a product of the creativity of the enslaved population and could be a hybrid mix of traditions, or it could manifest as a "bi-religious" phenomenon (with people attending both candomblé services and Catholic Mass).[109] Sometimes the religion of the ruling class was used to mask native traditions among enslaved people.[110]

I suggest that we assume a similar kind of creativity and resourcefulness on the part of enslaved believers in the Roman period. As I have argued, precisely because of their servile role in the household, enslaved people were involved with domestic rituals. The variety of daily practices discussed above could be incorporated into their duties—either openly, at separate kitchen shrines, or perhaps masked by devotions to the household gods. Such agency does not necessarily amount to a revolt against slavery or against specific slaveholders, but it could constitute a subtle form of empowerment within the confines of the power dynamics of the household.[111]

Conclusion

Most of the intellectuals discussed in this chapter express their sympathy for the larger cultural construct of patriarchal power in households. If Christian wives would just marry Christian men, Tertullian pleads, then there would be no conflict between "masters": wives could be fully obedient. His ideal is the Christian household, which he describes as harmonious and industrious in its daily devotions (*Ux.* 2.8.7). This ideal is shared by the Acts of the Apostles, which recounts stories of whole households being baptized together. Typically this follows an encounter between a head of the household and a traveling teacher, who convinces him (or her) to follow Christ (Acts 11:14; 16:14–15, 31–34; 18:8). A counter to this pattern is offered by Celsus, who accuses Christian teachers of preying upon women, children, slaves, and the foolish, encouraging them to flout the authority of the head of the household.[112] He lines up with other literate producers, both non-Christian and Christian, who frame Christianity as problematic for the way it disrupts household hierarchies.

In this chapter, I have taken Celsus's worry seriously. Looking at early Christian responses to mixed households and using ritual and feminist theory, archaeology, and studies of modern slavery, I have reconstructed how believing wives and slaves might incorporate, even in small ways, their new cult into their mixed households. I have suggested that the daily exchanges with the gods that took place there might afford wives and slaves a means of both sustaining and complicating the power dynamics in the household.

One danger in framing this study with intellectuals like Plutarch, Cato, Paul, the author of 1 Peter, and Tertullian is that it can be difficult not to be led by their interpretation of mixed households. Almost all of them share the notion that wives and slaves worshiping their own gods pose a threat to the authority of the head of the household. Even if rituals were perceived as rebellious at times, a different model was likely more pervasive in daily-life religious practice, one that involved less antagonism. The ancient evidence considered here, along with feminist theory and work on modern slavery, points to moments of limited agency, moments that empower through their ability simply to mark and protect the body.

In previous chapters, I have argued that Christ followers shared spaces and rituals with non-followers much more often than we are led to believe by the published representatives of the cult of Christ. Everyday rituals provided a common vocabulary for interacting with the divine, one that was shared by members of a variety of other categories, including "Christian," "Jewish," "Greek," and "Roman." Indeed, the goal of Christian intellectuals was to create these very categories and to draw boundaries between Christians and others.

But my argument does not depend on a model of rebellion of subordinates against household or other patriarchal structures. Empowerment through ritualization can be at once more subtle and more complex than a binary model allows. As the texts above have indicated, power dynamics in households—which involve relationships among humans and between humans and a variety of divine beings—are fueled in part by religious practices. Through a quick gesture or bite of bread, perhaps even without awareness, Christ-following wives and slaves participate in those power dynamics, perhaps in ways that resist, appropriate, or consent to the larger structure in place. This might cause disruption, as some fear, but it also might cause social cohesion, as Christ followers incorporate their devotions into the daily life of the household, simultaneously blending in with non-believers and marking themselves as loyal to a particular god. Given the ubiquity and flexibility of the everyday mode of religion, this addition of a new deity would likely have been received with less concern or interest than Christian intellectuals claim.

CHAPTER 5

"PETER AND PAUL, KEEP US IN MIND"

The Cult of the Dead Among Pre-Constantinian Christ Followers

In the previous chapter I argued for the individual agency or power that might be accessed through daily-life religious practices. This final chapter also takes up the issue of power—but in this case, political power. I show that everyday religion, specifically in the form of burial practices, influences the complex process of shaping the cult of Christ into an official institution (a mode of religion Stanley Stowers calls "the religion of the literate specialists and political power").[1] Mortuary rituals, both for the recently deceased and for those long dead, serve an important function in household continuity, as they bridge the gap between generations. Graveside rites establish an exchange between the living, who bring offerings to the dead, and the dead, who confer favors on the living. These rituals, which expanded from family groups to larger networks, proved attractive to those in power, who saw opportunity in their popularity.

The traditions and rites involved with honoring the dead are a little different from the rituals we have discussed so far. Although they are very much a part of the household structure, they are performed away from households, outside of city limits, at tombs and shrines, both aboveground and underground. And unlike signing, praying, or amulet-wearing, these rites can take place individually or communally, either in household groups or, in the case of festivals for the dead, in larger groups involving whole villages, neighborhoods, or cities. At least by the third century, the shrines of martyrs began to draw crowds of Christ followers who came to make offerings, to feast, and to petition the martyr for favor. These practices of everyday exchange, now with the holy dead, brought devotees together to honor the martyr, who was sometimes treated as a deceased and honored ancestor.[2]

The title of this chapter, "'Peter and Paul, Keep Us in Mind,'" taken from a graffito etched on a third-century shrine just outside Rome, illustrates this interaction between the living and the holy dead. As I discuss further below, this petition is one of many asking these two beloved martyrs (and eventual patron saints of Rome) for ongoing care. This particular site drew pilgrims to its sacred space, as did the large funerary basilica that was eventually built on top of it.

The cult of the dead, even as it was based in daily-life rituals, was ubiquitous, public, and powerful in the ancient Mediterranean world. For this reason, as I argue in what follows, burial practices became a focal point of competition among a variety of power brokers vying for recognition, recruits, and influence. These power brokers included (but were not limited to) elite writers, local sponsors, ritual experts, imperial patrons, confessors, and clergy. As the Christ cult grew in the second and third centuries, these various experts—whose roles regularly overlapped—jostled for power in a process that would eventually contribute to a public, imperially backed church in the fourth century. Peter Brown has argued that late fourth-century bishops understood the strategic value of the cult of the dead. He describes how Ambrose, in his translation of martyr relics into his own church, did not destroy old practices or create entirely new ones but merely (and brilliantly) "rewired" the flow of the martyrs' power to pass through the bishop.[3] I argue that similar impulses motivated earlier bishops and other power brokers, all of whom recognized the advantages of patronizing, celebrating, and controlling the cult of the dead among Christ believers.[4]

I begin by describing Roman-period mortuary rites as practiced both by non-Christians and by Christians; we will see below that there is little difference. These discussions prepare the way for three case studies of archaeological sites from our period, all of which involve an early tomb and a later building project related to that tomb. Following the discussion of these sites, I reflect on how these built environments and their attending rituals attracted power brokers who invested their resources in efforts to appropriate and control them.

Burial Practices in the Roman World: A Shared Religious Vocabulary

In the Roman period, funeral practices centered around—and were primarily organized by—the family.[5] Rituals began in the household itself, with the cleaning and the dressing of the body for burial. In elite families, there followed a procession to the site of burial or cremation outside the city walls. Bodies were interred in a variety of types of tombs, from family monuments to sarcophagi to ash chests (depending on wealth, status, and popular trends). The bodies of the poor might end up in large pit graves.

Grave offerings might be placed in the tomb; sometimes a coin was placed in the mouth of the deceased.[6]

After interment, rites for the dead continued, and they echoed those of the domestic cult: eating, drinking, and making offerings. Gatherings at burial sites took place not only immediately after death but also on anniversaries of the death in subsequent days and years, providing an opportunity for the household to affirm its continuity by connecting across generations. These tombs, as resting places for deceased family members and sites of shared meals for living family members, served as an extension of the household itself.[7]

A variety of practices made up funeral rites in this period. We have both textual and archaeological evidence for offerings of various types: grain, wine, oil, and incense, for example.[8] Ovid encourages small gifts, such as a "few grains of salt" or a "tile wreathed with votive garlands" (*Fasti* 2.533–42).[9] Singing and dancing are also attested, especially at communal festivals honoring the dead, such as the Parentalia.[10] Perhaps the most ubiquitous practice is that of shared meals at tombs.[11] The archaeological record affords a good picture of this, with dining benches, tables, dishes, cookware, and remains of animal bones discovered at many burial sites.[12] Tubes for libations to be poured into the chamber holding the body are common, which supports the idea that people not only made offerings to the dead but also shared the repast with them.[13] Lucian, a sarcastic critic of such practices, remarks, "They get their nourishment, naturally, from the libations that are poured in our world and the burnt-offerings at the tomb; so that if anyone has not left a friend or kinsman behind him on earth, he goes about his business there as an unfed corpse, in a state of famine."[14] These comments, even as they ridicule the notion of hungry corpses, illustrate the practice of graveside offerings.

The following inscription from 299 CE nicely sets the scene of a graveside gathering in honor of a deceased mother, Aelia Secundula:

> We all have already spent much, as is right, on the burial, but we have decided furthermore to put up a stone dining chamber where Mother Secundula rests, wherein we may recall the many wonderful things she did, while the loaves, the cups, the cushions are set out, so as to assuage the sharp hurt that eats at our hearts. While the hour grows late, gladly will we revisit our tales about our virtuous mother, and our praises of her, while the old lady sleeps, she who nourished us and lies forever here in sober peace. She lived 72 years. Year 260 of the province. Statulenia Iulia set up [the memorial][15]

The donor recounts many of the features involved with honoring the dead: they dine and drink late into the night, telling stories about the departed. Aelia Secundula's tomb was likely covered with a *mensa*, a stone slab that served as a table. We have evidence of such *mensae*, as well as the remains of food, including animal bones, in tombs in various places around the empire.[16]

One of the striking characteristics of Christian burial practices, when the evidence begins to emerge, is how little they seem to have changed from those of their non-Christian counterparts.[17] That is, Christians, despite many efforts on the part of literate experts to draw clear boundaries, looked an awful lot like their non-Christian neighbors in death rituals.[18]

The Roman catacombs are perhaps the most famous examples of such evidence.[19] Here, in spaces traditionally thought to belong primarily to Christ followers,[20] we find paintings of people gathered for meals.[21] Typical menu items are depicted on the table: bread, fish, and wine.[22] The postures and gestures of the participants indicate that these scenes represent the traditional meal for the dead, including raising glasses for toasts (such as "Drink, live!" [*Pie zeses*] or "Peace!" [*Irene*]).[23] While the scenes of banqueting are represented on the walls, archaeological remains indicate that meals were eaten and offerings were made in the spaces that housed the paintings: we find stone couches, *mensae*, fragments of dishware, and cups.[24] In one sarcophagus in the catacombs under San Sebastiano, a libation tube from the mid- to late fourth century was excavated.[25]

All of these practices belong to daily-life religion, whereby the primary task is to interact with the gods and other powerful beings by giving thanks and asking for future gifts and blessings. Funerals mark a moment when a family member becomes a member of the beloved dead, belonging to that category of powerful beings who can influence the fate of the living. The various grave offerings found in tombs (coins, shells, lambs, necklaces, dolls)[26] make sense in this context, as do the libation tubes and *mensae* that indicate offerings of wine and food.[27] As divine beings, the dead were referred to as *manes*,[28] and we have ample evidence that Christ followers used this same vocabulary: Christians, like their neighbors, inscribed "DM" (for *Dis Manibus*, "for the gods-*manes*") on their gravestones.[29]

In keeping with the practices ridiculed by Lucian above, Christ followers also enjoined their departed to participate in the meal, often called the *refrigerium*. This term literally means "refreshment" or "cooling off," but in a funerary context it can mean "rest" or it can refer to the funerary feast.[30] In an inscription dating to 291 CE, Virginius invites his dead wife to "eat the *refrigerium* with a holy spirit."[31] A similar wish attends another inscription, in which the departed is also petitioned for help: "Januaria, enjoy the meal and pray for us (*Ianuaria bene refrigera et roga pro nos*)."[32] This inscription occurs on a *loculus* (grave covering) in the Callistus catacomb and is accompanied by a pitcher, a goblet, and a lamp.[33] We see similar sentiments directed at Peter and Paul in our discussion below.

Christian literary sources, too, confirm this picture of offerings and meals at grave sites. Speaking of the duties a wife would perform for her deceased husband, Tertullian explains, "Indeed, she prays for his soul, and requests *refrigerium* for him meanwhile, and fellowship (with him) in the first resurrection; and she makes offerings on the anniversaries of his falling asleep" (*Mon.* 10.4).[34] I am leaving *refrigerium* untranslated here to account for its multiple possible meanings, as mentioned above: refreshment, rest, or the funeral meal. Again in the context of marital duties, and in service of the argument to marry only once, Tertullian raises the issue of the rituals a widower owes his deceased wife: making requests for her spirit, rendering annual oblations, commemorating in prayer, offering, and sacrificing (*Exh. cast.* 11). Referring to communal practices (such as baptism and the eucharist), Tertullian remarks, "As often as the anniversary comes round, we make offerings for the dead as birthday honours (*Oblationes pro defunctis, pro nataliciis, annua die facimus*)" (*Cor.* 3.3).[35]

In none of these examples does Tertullian explain what is being offered or where. Robin Jensen suggests that these could be food and drink brought to the grave, or they could be gifts brought to the church.[36] Éric Rebillard argues that the terms *facere*, *oblationes reddere*, and *offere* refer specifically to the bread and wine Christ followers would bring for the eucharist.[37] If this is the case, then Tertullian refers to the integration of the cult of the dead into communal worship, an important development, which I discuss below. In each of these examples, Tertullian seems either to approve of these rituals or at least acknowledge them as a given; they are part of the duties of a spouse and believer.

It is puzzling, therefore, although perhaps not so surprising, that Tertullian represents a very different opinion of these practices in another text. In a discussion of idolatry, Tertullian refers to the belief that the dead become divine and asserts that Christ believers do not participate:

> On this account, therefore, because they have a common source—for their dead and their deities are one—we abstain from both idolatries. [4] Nor do we dislike the temples less than the monuments: we have nothing to do with either altar, we adore neither image; we do not offer sacrifices to the gods, and we make no funeral oblations to the departed (*sed neque de sacrificio et parentato edimus*); nay, we do not partake of what is offered either in the one case or the other, for we cannot partake of God's feast and the feast of devils. (*Spect.* 13.3–4)[38]

Here Tertullian equates the offerings made to the dead with idolatry (since the dead are thought to be deities) and claims that Christ followers do not participate in these, contradicting the passages cited above. Elsewhere, he derides people for their own contradictory views of the dead, who are perceived at times as worthy of pity and at other times as fellow revelers, such as when family members venture out to the tombs, bringing their "dainties and delicacies,"[39] reclining and carousing with them and finally staggering home drunk (*Test.* 4.4).[40] Tertullian's complaint addresses the belief discussed above and shared by many in the ancient world: that the dead participate in the funeral feasts.

We glimpse in Tertullian's various opinions a multilayered view of burial practices that will be a theme throughout our discussion: he approves of and accepts these practices and he also critiques them. Notice that his critique arises in the context of separating "us" from "them," which is characteristic of Christian intellectuals of this time, as I have discussed in earlier chapters. Daily-life religion serves as fodder for marking boundaries around this relatively new cult.

Communal Mortuary Worship: Cult of the Martyrs

When Tertullian speaks of Christ followers participating in the cult of the dead, he refers to practices that might be understood as individual or family rituals (such as a spouse making offerings for a deceased husband or wife) as well as practices performed by a group, such as the annual offerings made for the dead on the anniversaries of their death (which he lists after baptism and the eucharist) (*Cor.* 3.3, mentioned above).[41] This suggests that mortuary practices were incorporated into communal worship at least by the early third century, perhaps at grave sites or at other meeting places. Like their friends and neighbors, members of the Christ cult also venerated their dead, especially their honored dead, with festivals and communal gatherings.

Sources describing this period mention Christians visiting graves. An edict of Valerian from 257 CE, recorded by Eusebius, restricts Christ followers from "gathering in or entering so-called cemeteries (κοιμητήρια)."[42] Shortly after, in 260 CE, Gallienus removed these restrictions, granting Christ followers permission to return to the "cemeteries" (κοιμητηρίων).[43] Christians, too, attempted to regulate other believers. The early fourth-century church council in Elvira, Spain, issued two canons that warn against practices in "cemeteries." One warns that "candles should not be lit in a cemetery (*in coemeterio*) during the day, for the spirits of the saints are not to be disturbed."[44] Here is another reference to the idea that the dead are present and sentient at their tombs, potentially disturbed by candles. The second canon bans women from staying overnight in a cemetery (*in coemeterio*) for fear that their prayers will cover other illicit deeds.[45] This second comment may refer to festivals for the dead, which perhaps started with the evening meal and continued from there.

Rebillard has shown that the term translated as "cemetery" in these texts—*koimeterion* in Greek and *coemeterium* in Latin—is used by Christians to designate specific, special tombs rather than a general burial ground. These references, therefore, may be to Christians visiting tombs of the special dead, specifically those of the martyrs.[46] Second- and third-century stories of martyrs hint that a cult focused on these particular special dead was developing at this time. In the Martyrdom of Polycarp (d. 155 CE), for example, the author describes the reaction of the faithful after Polycarp's execution: "And so later on we took up his bones . . . and deposited them in a suitable place. (3) There gathering together, as we are able, with joy and gladness, the Lord will permit us to celebrate the birthday of his martyrdom."[47] This "suitable place," where Polycarp's bones are buried and the faithful return annually (perhaps with offerings and food for a picnic), is the kind of *koimeterion* Rebillard identifies. The Acts of John (chap. 72) and the Acts of Thecla (chaps. 23–25) both refer to communal meals at tombs. Other stories of martyrs during our period recount similar attention to the bodies of the deceased and concerns over the cult that might develop around their tombs.[48]

In the third century, Origen refers to the tradition of the whole assembly coming together from the tombs (ἀπό τῶν κοιμητηρίων) of the martyrs (*Homily on Jeremiah* 4.3.2).[49] In what seems to be a similar tradition, Eusebius, speaking of those departed who were "beloved of God," remarks in the early fourth century: "Hence comes also our custom of visiting their tombs, and offering our prayers beside them, and honouring their blessed souls, believing that we do this with good reason."[50] The tomb thus allows for communion between the holy body of the martyr and those who commemorate his or her death annually.[51]

The correspondence of the third-century bishop Cyprian is particularly noteworthy for this discussion. It not only offers evidence of a growing cult of martyrs but also illustrates a bishop's administrative maneuvers to incorporate funerary practices into his church in Carthage, a dynamic that helps us understand the archaeological evidence discussed below. In one letter, Cyprian writes about the community's devotion to the martyrs: "As you recall, we never fail to offer sacrifices on their behalf every time we celebrate in commemoration of the anniversary dates of the sufferings of these martyrs" (*Epistle 39.3.1*).[52] And in another missive, Cyprian instructs presbyters and deacons to track the death dates of those confessors who perish in prison; these, too, he argues, should be counted among the martyrs. He writes, "Accordingly, you should keep note of the days on which they depart this life; we will then be able to include the celebration of their memories in our commemoration of the martyrs" (*Epistle 12.2.1*).[53] In the specific context of persecution in Carthage, Cyprian encourages the incorporation of the martyrs' deaths into the calendar of his church. He praises a certain Tertullus for tending to the bodies of the deceased and for informing Cyprian of the dates of their passing. These dates, then, determine the "offerings and sacrifices" (*oblationes et sacrificia*) performed in their honor (*Epistle 12.2.1*).

As with Tertullian's comments discussed above, it is not entirely clear where these commemorations take place or what, exactly, the rituals entail. Scholars have suggested festive meals, prayers with the recitation of the names of the departed, and the eucharist.[54] Another letter might offer a clue as to the location. Here Cyprian reprimands a bishop for appointing a presbyter as a guardian (which violated a local ecclesiastical order) and proclaims that the punishment will be that neither the "offering" nor "the sacrifice for his repose" will be performed, for he does not deserve to have his name read at the "altar of God" (*Epistle 12.2.1*).[55] Rebillard argues that the location of these rites was likely in the church itself because of the reference to the "altar of God."[56] The term "offerings" that we have seen throughout these texts could indicate either. We know that families brought food and drink to grave sites; they also brought bread and wine to the church for the eucharist.[57]

Cyprian seems to have been keenly aware of the power of martyrs, confessors, and the cult that followed their deaths. With the resources of his own wealth at his disposal, which in turn had helped him establish his role as patron of both the clergy and the laity, Cyprian fashions himself as the keeper of this cult and folds it into the calendar of his church, so that the death-day anniversaries determine the gatherings of the faithful.[58] These rituals became powerful enough as honors for the dead that their removal is considered punishment. Families may still be involved, but, at least from Cyprian's perspective, oversight has passed to the clergy, with the bishop in charge.[59]

Two related trends emerge in this evidence. One is that as early as the second and third centuries, followers of Christ were meeting at special graves. Similar to traditional festivals for the dead, such as the Parentalia, mortuary practices among Christ followers found expression in a public, communal format as believers honored their special dead. This is critical in the history of Christianity, as we see daily-life practices of honoring

"PETER AND PAUL, KEEP US IN MIND"

the dead, traditionally initiated and enacted by families, taking on a more visible role. The second trend emerges, I would argue, in response to the first: those in power, such as Cyprian, began to assert their authority over these practices. With a variety of interests in mind, certain "power brokers" in the Roman empire—whether clerics or patrons or other interested parties—sought to attach themselves to, appropriate, control, and tamp down the popular devotion taking place at tombs. Cyprian's missives offer literary evidence for this process. I argue that the case studies discussed below offer material evidence of the same trend.

Archaeological Case Studies

As mentioned above, it is not always easy to tell where the rituals referred to by Tertullian and Cyprian took place. Traditionally these would be at the tombs, perhaps at special shrines, but Cyprian's efforts to incorporate rites for the martyrs into his church calendar imply that they might have moved into the regular meeting space of the *ekklesia*. The evidence we turn to now takes up this critical issue of space. Archaeological evidence, along with the textual evidence discussed above, offers glimpses of the interactions between those seeking power and the mortuary cult. These three case studies illustrate the ubiquitous burial practices we have discussed and how these practices draw attention from various power brokers and experts.

"Drink Up! Live Long!" The Mensa of the Martyr Januarius
The first of our examples is the *mensa*, or table-top covering, of the grave of a certain Januarius, called here a martyr, in northern Africa (fig. 8). It is located in the Roman province of Mauretania Caesariensis, near the modern city of Altava, and was found in what was likely a cemetery.[60] In addition to Januarius, the inscription commemorates several structures built by the bishop L. Tannonius Rogatus:

> [—] DOM [—] / [——] / Me(n)sa Ian- / uari Mar- / 5 tyris. P[i]- / e Zeses. / [Confe]ssione sancti et / basilica dominica / [et] memoria b(eatorum) v(irorum), Honorati / Ep(iscopi), Ta[n- / n]oni/Victori Z(aconi), et Tannoni R[ufini]- / 10 ani Ep(iscopi), fecit L. Tannonius Rog[atus] / [Epi]s(copus) IIII ab Honorato, a(nno) p(ro- / vinciae) CCLXX[. . .][61]

> [——the Lord (?)——]. (This is) the *mensa* of the martyr Januarius. Drink and you shall live. The *confessio* of the saint, the dominical basilica, and the *memoria* of the(se) blessed men—Honoratus the bishop, Tannonius

Victor the deacon, and Tannonius Rufinianus the bishop—L. Tannonius Rogatus, the fourth bishop from Honoratus made in the year of the province 270 (?).[62]

The "year of the province 270" translates to 309 CE in our calendar, but there is some uncertainty over whether "CCLXX" is the full date listed on the stone slab. The end of the line where the date is written is damaged (see the lower right corner of the slab in fig. 8), and it is hard to tell whether further numerals might have followed those we can see. Scholars have calculated a number of options and come up with 309–34 CE as a possible range.[63]

Both the *mensa* (with the inscription) and the donor's advice to "drink" signal the typical burial practices discussed above. I have seen two interpretations of the line "Drink and you shall live." Ramsay MacMullen translates it as "Drink up! Live long!" and reads it as an indication of the "party atmosphere" of gatherings at tombs.[64] Others have taken it in more theological terms, referring perhaps to the cup of martyrdom that brings life.[65] The former seems more in keeping with funerary traditions,[66] but I am not sure we can rule out the other interpretation; it could be a Christian twist on a familiar statement. Perhaps it was available to be read either way.

One of the structures mentioned in the inscription is a *memoria* for three people, a deacon[67] (Tannonius Victor) and two bishops[68] (Honoratus and Tannonius Rufinianus). We do not know anything more about these people, nor do we know more about the donor, L. Tannonius Rogatus, but there are a couple of intriguing possibilities to consider. One is that there might be a family relationship among these men who carry similar names.[69] A second relates to the phrase "L. Tannonius Rogatus, the fourth bishop from Honoratus." L. Michael White claims that this phrase "places him in a clear succession of local bishops going back into the third century"[70] (though when in the third century depends on whether we date this inscription to the early or late part of our date range of 309–34). White's suggestion is compelling, but we need to be careful about assuming "successions" of bishops and whether the term denotes sequential terms or something else. Still, I think we can tentatively register this as evidence for church clerics having—or at least claiming—some connection to the martyr Januarius, with the donor-bishop also serving as a patron for what might be a building complex connected to the martyr.

We are not sure of the relationship of the structures mentioned (*confessio*, basilica, *memoria*) in the inscription to the martyr Januarius and his *mensa*, but it seems likely that they are all part of the same building project or that the *mensa* now being dedicated is being added to these structures.[71]

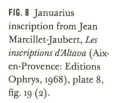

FIG. 8 Januarius inscription from Jean Marcillet-Jaubert, *Les inscriptions d'Altava* (Aix-en-Provence: Editions Ophrys, 1968), plate 8, fig. 19 (2).

The "*confessio* of the saint" likely refers to a marker of Januarius's tomb or perhaps a container of his relics; the basilica represents a church building;[72] and the *memoria* is a space or architectural feature honoring the three "blessed men" named (perhaps the *confessio* and *memoria* are part of the basilica).[73]

The Januarius inscription illustrates a number of themes considered above. It offers material evidence for the practice of tomb-side eating and drinking, here connected to one honored as a martyr. The *mensa* of Januarius is somehow related to (incorporated into, perhaps?) what seems to be a building complex or several architectural features of a church building (basilica). People with clerical titles (bishops and deacon) are honored, and a bishop is the donor of these buildings. We know so little about the circumstances here, but given the other evidence discussed, we can imagine that the donor sought to connect the martyr and his cult to the clergy named in the inscription (who are possibly family members) as well as to himself. The building complex to honor Januarius and the other clergy members offered new space for the cult practices that took place in this cemetery. Perhaps the patron-bishop, L. Tannonius Rogatus, like Cyprian, sought to incorporate the cult of the martyr into the communal practices of his church.

Tomb G in the Kapljuč Basilica

Our second example comes from Salona, in the Roman province of Dalmatia, in modern-day Croatia. Several late antique sites in this area—Manastirine,

FIG. 9 Photo of *mensa* slab on top of Tomb G with depressions and rectangular hole. From Johannes Brøndsted, "La basilique des cinq martyrs à Kapljuč," in *Recherches à Salone*, edited by Ejnar Dyggve (Copenhagen: J. H. Schultz, 1928), 138.

Marusinac, and Kapljuč—offer rich evidence for the phenomenon that might be described in the Januarius inscription: churches built in cemeteries. We turn our attention to the site of the oldest basilica in the region, Kapljuč, and the cemetery in which it was built. The relationship between the two—burial ground and basilica—illustrates how the cult of the dead influenced later built expressions of Christianity.

The cemetery itself was active from the first century CE and held a variety of types of graves, including amphorae burials, chamber tombs, and sarcophagi.[74] Of interest to us is one particular tomb, Tomb G, which is identified as preceding the fourth-century basilica. Freestanding and built of stone, Tomb G enclosed a rectangular cavity measuring 1.7 m long by 1.1 m wide and 0.6 m deep.[75] This area was enclosed on top with a stone *mensa*, or table-top, such as those discussed above. Cut into this slab are circular depressions and an approximately rectangular hole, presumably for making offerings and sharing food at the tomb (fig. 9).[76] Early excavators have suggested that the unusually thick walls surrounding the tomb might have provided benches for reclining around the *mensa* on three sides (see fig. 12, phase I).[77]

The original excavators assumed that Tomb G belonged to four "martyr-soldiers," men who, according to later sources, were imperial guards under Diocletian and were executed for refusing to persecute fellow Christians.[78] This identification was made not through an inscription but by associating the four carved indentations on the slab with the tradition of the four martyrs.[79] In addition, the placement of the indentations seemed to the excavators to make the sign of the cross, perhaps signifying an important Christian burial.[80] Since the tomb was empty when it was excavated (and an opening was found in the corner through which grave

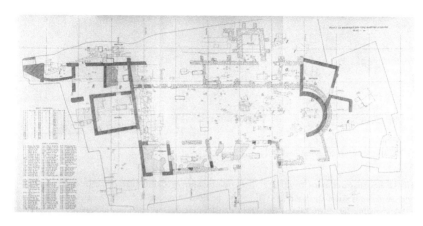

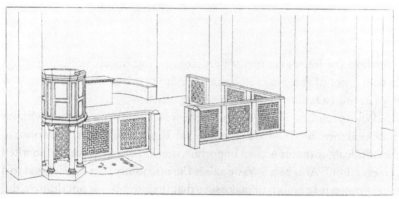

FIG. 10 Aerial view of Tomb G in basilica and earlier cemetery; Tomb G marked "G." From Johannes Brøndsted, "La basilique des cinq martyrs à Kapljuč," in *Recherches à Salone*, edited by Ejnar Dyggve (Copenhagen: J. H. Schultz, 1928), plan 1.

FIG. 11 Reconstruction of Tomb G on floor of fourth-century basilica, below pulpit. From Johannes Brøndsted, "La basilique des cinq martyrs à Kapljuč," in *Recherches à Salone*, edited by Ejnar Dyggve (Copenhagen: J. H. Schultz, 1928), 182.

goods and remains could have been removed), there were no further clues to help identify the original, or any, occupant.[81]

The remarkable thing about this tomb, especially when compared to others around it, is that it was preserved when the basilica was built, kept *in situ* and incorporated into the church floor as the new basilica was constructed around it (fig. 10). In the new configuration, the *mensa* of Tomb G lined up with the floor level of the church (fig. 11).[82] Emilio Marin emphasizes the importance of this preservation. While the vast majority of graves at Kapljuč and at the other church/cemetery sites in Salona were destroyed by later building projects, this grave constitutes a "privileged burial," signaling someone important to those involved with the construction of the

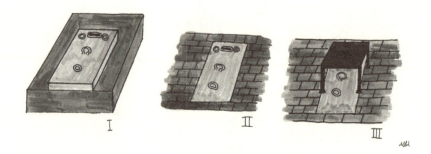

FIG. 12 Reconstruction of Tomb G in three phases: aboveground and freestanding (I); preserved in the floor of the basilica (II); and in the floor of the basilica with an altar over it (III). Drawing by Marty Martinage after Ejnar Dyggve, *History of Salonitan Christianity* (Oslo: H. Aschehoug, 1951), 27, fig. V.

church in the fourth century.[83] Furthermore, excavators noticed tracings in the corner of the *mensa* slab that indicate that legs were attached, perhaps to hold a table or altar above it (fig. 12).[84]

Whose tomb is this? Unfortunately, we cannot know for sure without more evidence. Some have suggested that Tomb G belonged to a donor of the basilica[85] or that it was an important non-Christian grave that merited preservation.[86] Ann Marie Yasin raises the possibility that it belonged to a family powerful enough to make sure that their tomb was not destroyed.[87] Yasin also, however, suggests the possibility that Tomb G was associated with a martyr, but a different one from the four soldier-martyrs. His name is Asterius, identified as a presbyter by tradition, and his tomb was thought by the excavators to lie under the altar of the basilica.[88] Yasin's support for this suggestion is a fifth-century votive inscription to Asterius that is located near Tomb G.[89] She points out that it is not a funerary inscription, so it is not intended to mark or accompany a grave; rather, it is a votive inscription, a dedication to the presbyter-martyr Asterius. Its proximity to Tomb G is suggestive of an association between the martyr and the tomb. At a minimum, it tells us that in the early fifth century, the martyr Asterius was honored by a donor at the Kapljuč basilica.[90]

Given what we know, and proceeding with caution given how much we do not know, I summarize a possible reconstruction for the Kapljuč basilica and Tomb G. Sometime before the basilica's construction in the fourth century,[91] Tomb G was erected for an honored person. If the tomb was meant to honor a Christian martyr, then perhaps this could have been in the wake of the Diocletianic persecutions of the early fourth century,[92] although an earlier date is also possible.[93] We have to leave open the possibility as well that this was not necessarily a holy person but an important church patron or donor (or possibly even a non-Christian).

In its original context, Tomb G was an aboveground structure located in an area with many other graves around it. People brought offerings to the tomb and perhaps ate meals there, given the markings on the slab and the possible use of the surrounding stone as dining benches. We can imagine family members visiting the tomb and maybe others as well, especially if the person or people commemorated here were considered "special dead," perhaps martyrs or others worthy of veneration. Perhaps on special days honoring the dead, crowds would come to the cemetery, bringing offerings, food, and drink.

We have in this example some possible parallels with the Januarius inscription: an earlier honored tomb, possibly of a martyr, that gets preserved in a later architectural elaboration. We are less sure in the Kapljuč site who the patrons are, either of the original tomb or of the fourth-century basilica. It is striking here, though, that Tomb G is so carefully incorporated into the basilica, where it would presumably still be honored but now in the context of official rituals, overseen by clergy. One wonders what rituals took place on the altar positioned over the *mensa* inside the basilica.

Memoria Apostolorum

One of our most famous sources for third-century Christian burial practices lies under the Roman church of San Sebastiano. This complex—often referred to by its later name, the Memoria Apostolorum—was a site for the veneration of two foundational figures for Christian Rome, Peter and Paul.[94] It lay along the Via Appia, one of the consular roads leading into (or out of) the city. Like the previous two examples, it was located in a cemetery.

In the Roman period this site was known simply as "the catacombs" (*ad catacumbas*, or "near the caves"), so called because of the tombs that were dug into a quarry in the first century CE.[95] This area grew into one of the largest cemeteries in Rome in the imperial period, with the majority of the early tombs belonging to imperial slaves and freedmen.[96] In the middle of the second century, a roof of the quarry collapsed, creating an open-air lower level with vertical "walls" of soft rock, perfect for creating mausolea. Three were excavated here, all originally non-Christian. Eventually there seems to have been a mix of Christian and pagan tombs at this site.[97]

In the mid-third century, the cemetery was renovated to create a paved open area connected to a covered dining room, creating a complex measuring 18 m × 23 m.[98] This project required filling in and covering older graves that had been dug into the walls of the mine. The dining area, which the excavator named the *triclia*, had benches on three sides and painting on

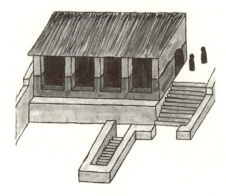

FIG. 13 Reconstruction of *triclia* at the *ad catacumbas* site, under San Sebastiano. Drawing by Marty Martinage after instructional materials at https://www.catacombe.org.

the walls (fig. 13).[99] There was room for twenty-five to thirty people to sit in this *triclia* area. Resources for water—a well and a fountain—were also found at the site. As at other cemeteries, these supported the commemorative meals that took place there.[100]

The treasure for those of us seeking evidence of third-century Christian practices is on the walls of the *triclia*. Here we find, scratched into the plaster, the petitions of hundreds of pilgrims, often offered directly to Peter and Paul (fig. 14).[101] These are critical both because they help us date the structure (it was in use in 260 CE) and because they tell us something about how the space was used.[102]

Here is just a sampling of the petitions.

"Peter and Paul / (keep) / in mind."[103]
"Paul and Peter pray / for Victor."[104]
"Peter and / Paul pro- / tect / (your) servants; / holy / spirits, protect / a *refrigerium* [ΑΝΑΓΙCΜΟΙC]."[105]
"Thirteen days before the Kalends of April, / a *refrigerium* was held / Parthenius in God and all of us in God."[106]
"Peter and Paul / keep us in mind / . . . sinus during the / *refrigerium*."[107]
"Peter and Paul, / protect your servants. / Protect the holy souls. / With offerings for the dead [. . .]."[108]

These inscriptions offer wonderful evidence of Christian daily-life religious practices. The exchanges that are characteristic of this mode of religion are evident in the petitions and prayers, which were accompanied by meals (*refrigeria*) and likely offerings as well. This is early evidence that members of the Christ cult congregated at the site of the "special dead," in this case

FIG. 14 Fragments of graffiti from *triclia* at the *ad catacumbas* site, under San Sebastiano. © foto Archivio PCAS.

the honored martyrs Peter and Paul. As with our other sites, we can imagine people gathering at this complex on festival days to honor the dead, perhaps with families, perhaps along with non-Christians who were visiting graves, doing what most people did to honor the departed: eat, drink, offer, pray, and perhaps sing and dance.[109] And some of them left their prayers written on the walls.[110]

These scratched prayers tell us something about how the devotees viewed the martyrs. They asked for protection, for intercession, for prayers and blessings. In exchange, the pilgrims and diners left their offerings of food and drink. David Eastman argues that this echoes a patron-client relationship; the holy dead were viewed as powerful intercessors and healers.[111]

While the graffiti help us imagine the scene, there are a number of things they leave mysterious. They do not tell us, for example, why this spot became the site of veneration for these two saints. There have been many theories related to relics (remains of Peter and Paul), but none of these has found solid support.[112] Nor do they tell us who constructed this site. Someone—or some group—funded the rather significant construction project of filling in the lower graves, creating a courtyard space, and building several structures around it. I suppose it is safe to assume that the donor was a member of the Christ cult, or at least was sympathetic to it; perhaps the donors had a specific loyalty to the two figures honored here (and perhaps an interest in connecting them with Rome). I am less satisfied with the explanation offered by some scholars that "the church" is responsible for the development of this cult site, given the lack of evidence we have for a unified and coordinated institution at this point in history.[113] A wealthy patron, whether a cleric or not, is more likely.

Based on her study of the non-Christian mausolea in the *piazzola* (which gets covered over by the courtyard/*triclia* complex), Barbara Borg suggests that this site was managed and funded by imperial administrators. As mentioned above, the early graves belong to imperial slaves and freedpeople and, Borg argues, such a large area is best explained as having a single owner.[114] She further documents the theory that by the early third century, one of these mausolea was used by people "connected by their service to the emperor," perhaps a funerary college of praetorians.[115] The imperial connections of the larger site, as well as its location on a major consular road, signal that this was a busy, "well-watched" public space.[116]

Another fascinating but hard-to-pin-down characteristic of this site is the mix of traditional and Christian cult activity. That non-Christians and Christians are buried together or near each other is not unusual.[117] And here we have clear evidence of non-Christian graves from the first to the early third century (as outlined above) and clear evidence of Christian cult activity related to Peter and Paul in the second half of the third century. We also have what have been interpreted as Christian symbols inscribed on earlier, non-Christian hypogea (or those that have been identified with non-Christian families and groups).[118] Whether non-Christian cult activity was happening here at the same time that Christians were visiting the *triclia* is not entirely clear, but Lucrezia Spera refers to three altars in the "immediate area," two to Attis and one to Jupiter, dedicated around 295 CE by Lucius Cornelius Scipio Orphitus.[119]

Like our first two sites, the Memoria Apostolorum on the Via Appia evinces third-century veneration of martyrs through typical practices of the cult of the dead (meals, offerings, prayers). Unlike the other two sites, however, this veneration does not seem to be associated with a tomb. (Although the space contains tombs, none is clearly for Peter or Paul.) Regardless, the graffiti on the wall of the *triclia* is rather spectacular evidence of a cult dedicated to these two "special dead" who would take their place as the twin patron saints of Rome. Finally, the Memoria Apostolorum does have a fourth-century architectural change, like the other two, but it is much more drastic than what we have seen so far. And whereas the other two examples preserve or mark the tomb, here the site of veneration seems to have been destroyed.[120]

FIG. 15 Reconstruction of the Basilica Apostolorum. Drawing by Marty Martinage after instructional materials at https://www.catacombe.org.

How and why this architectural change occurred is not clear, but we do know that by the mid-fourth century (see below), an enormous basilica-like structure stood on this site (fig. 15), with the *triclia* complex filled in and covered over, now positioned directly underneath the central part of the central aisle (or nave).[121] Tombs lined the dirt floor of this new structure, hundreds of them, organized in a fairly orderly fashion.[122] The scale of the building is impressive, measuring 70 m × 35 m, and Spera notes that it was built for visual effect.[123] Unlike churches inside the walls of Rome, the Basilica Apostolorum, as this place came to be known, had no clergy assigned to it, no altar, and no martyr's tomb.

Furthermore, this edifice was one of six similar structures erected in this period, all following a similar pattern: they were circiform basilicas (so called because they resembled a circus where imperially sponsored races took place); they were built over cemeteries and located outside the city walls on consular roads; and they housed hundreds of tombs.[124] These buildings were intended for large gatherings, for people to pass easily through the many doors around the structure, and for relatively easy access from the roads.[125] As a comparison, I imagine modern structures at large fairgrounds. But these were cemeteries: people came here to honor the dead, to share food, and to make offerings, just as people did at tombs all over the empire. For the relatively brief period in which these buildings stood,[126] they offered generous space for these practices of tending to the departed.[127]

How scholars understand these buildings is in flux; any definitive interpretation is made difficult by the scant remains. The traditional view is that they are martyr-churches constructed in a wave of enthusiasm by the newly converted emperor, Constantine, in the fourth century.[128] As mentioned above, their status as churches is open to question, although perhaps that depends on how well defined "churches" were at the time. They were not set up with the usual accoutrements, such as clergy, altars, and equipment for rituals such as the eucharist.[129] Their specific association with martyrs has recently been challenged by scholars who have pointed out the tenuous connection between martyr tombs or relics and these buildings.[130] And this particular structure, the Basilica Apostolorum, does not appear on the list of benefactions from Constantine.[131]

So how might we interpret this rather drastic architectural change that takes place on the Via Appia site? In both of our previous examples, Januarius in Altava and Tomb G in Kapljuč, the earlier tomb (whether martyr or patron) was preserved in the later manifestation, whether basilica (Tomb G) or inscription (Januarius). Are Peter and Paul—their memories if not their remains—thought to be preserved here in this enormous, covered cemetery?

According to some, the answer is yes: the new structure sits squarely over the *triclia* complex. Borg notes that the one component that survived demolition when the basilica was constructed was a staircase and shallow basin; if these were associated with Peter and Paul, then this signals a continuation of their cults here.[132] According to others, the answer is no: there is nothing in the new structure that commemorates the cult activity to Peter and Paul, and a fragment of the *triclia* complex was found to have been used in the construction of the basilica, suggesting that it was considered scrap.[133] Others have suggested that the *triclia* was already destroyed by the time the basilica went up, having fallen victim to the Diocletian persecution in the first decade of the fourth century.[134] In this case, perhaps it made good sense simply to fill in the area in order to build the basilica.

How we decide this question depends on another uncertainty or two. Who built the large structure? And when? The traditional answer holds that Constantine or one of his sons built it, a view supported by material evidence: a marble tile in the atrium has a monogram that refers to these emperors,[135] and an epitaph on one of the graves dates to 349 CE.[136] This line of thinking coheres with the traditional view that these are among the first bursts of Christian building in the fourth century.

These material finds certainly tell us that the building was in use in the mid-fourth century, but an earlier construction date is possible, even prior to 313 CE. The reasoning for this has to do in part with a lack of evidence: it is not mentioned in Constantinian donation lists or in the *Liber Pontificalis*, both of which would help connect it to patronage of Constantine (or a later emperor).[137] There is also existing evidence to support the possibility of an early date: the large basilica and the Maxentian villa in the near vicinity share identical building techniques.[138] Furthermore, this basilica is not the only one that might be early. There is stronger evidence that the funerary basilica on the Via Praenestina—similar in proportion and location on the third mile—dates to the late Tetrarchy.[139] After weighing these factors, Monica Hellström states, regarding the date of the Via Appia basilica, "The issue of chronology is thus far from settled, but a year not much later or earlier than 312 must be reckoned with."[140]

As for who built them, there is a good case to be made that these buildings had imperial sponsors. Who else could have mobilized the enormous resources necessary to prepare the land (which included some serious leveling of uneven terrain) and build these massive structures that changed the landscape of their neighborhoods?[141] The land occupied by the Basilica Apostolorum had most likely been imperially owned for centuries, as evinced by the graves of people linked to imperial service since the first century CE.[142]

Hellström offers a compelling argument, especially with respect to the two earliest basilicas, Praenestina and Appia (= Basilica Apostolorum): they were built at times of "transformations of power," and their purpose was to "make manifest the power, legitimacy, and continuity of the new imperial family."[143] They would have been perceived by the public as tombs, as gathering spaces, and as places to honor imperial patrons buried in the mausolea erected along the walls of these great halls. These basilicas represented a meeting of imperial power and munificence with the masses and a reiteration of the patronal relationship between these two entities.[144] It was a strategic move on the part of the emperor, whom we might designate as the ultimate power broker in the empire—a strategy that, Hellström argues, works well for either Maxentius or Constantine.[145]

There are some fascinating possibilities raised by this proposal. One coheres more or less with the traditional view (minus the martyrs, at least): Constantine built this structure as a part of his coming to power. With this benefaction of a place to honor the dead, he attempted to win over the populace and solidify his relationship to them as their new imperial patron. This effort was perhaps even more urgent in the years before his victory over Licinius in 324 CE. I would imagine that this would be deemed effective even if, or perhaps especially if, the basilica were not exclusively for Christians.

Another possibility is that the structure predates Constantine's rise to power in Rome, originating perhaps as part of the building campaign sponsored by Maxentius across the Via Appia. This would suggest that the massive basilica was not originally intended as a Christian structure at all. The similarities in building features between Maxentius's complex and the basilica, mentioned above, might indicate a common patron and building crew.[146] Maxentius's motives would have been the same: to consolidate power and recruit a loyal following from his subjects. In this case, it seems that the structure was taken over by Constantine, perhaps for similar purposes, after which it evolved into a site primarily associated with Christian burials. Indeed, as imperial power became aligned with ecclesial power, these structures served the development of the institution of the church in the fourth century.[147]

One might think that the building's placement over the earlier cult site for Peter and Paul would help us decide which emperor was responsible. But it is unclear whether Christians (or anyone) visiting the basilica would have associated it with Peter and Paul. It is hard to know what to make of the placement of the *triclia* complex in relation to the basilica over it: lying underneath the middle of the nave, it occupies a central, but seemingly invisible, space in the new building. Might the new structure have been placed haphazardly, or at least with no consideration of the site occupied by the earlier tombs and the Christian cult site? It is difficult to decide. One possibility is that this large funerary basilica served as a space for everyone, regardless of their loyalty to or knowledge of the cult of Christ and its martyrs: a strategic offering by an imperial patron. After all, the basilica occupied the site of a centuries-old cemetery. Perhaps this ground carried the status of a "holy hot spot" for Christians and non-Christians.[148] In this case, the specific cults of Peter and Paul could have been incorporated into the wider range of commemorations taking place in this space, or perhaps they were no longer associated with it.[149] Over the course of the succeeding centuries, however, the space was claimed for Christian worship, with the basilica of the apostles (Basilica Apostolorum), and in the eighth century, it was dedicated to Saint Sebastian and renamed for him.[150]

Reflecting on the Case Studies: Power Brokers and Ritual Space

The example of the development of the Via Appia site, from a cemetery to a cult site for Peter and Paul to a funerary basilica, sets up nicely the point I want to make about daily-life religion, here represented by burial rituals: the cult of the dead, whether practiced by non-Christians or Christians, was perceived by those in power as potent and worth harnessing for their own benefit. The Januarius inscription, Tomb G, and the Memoria Apostolorum all represent an older burial ground or tomb being repurposed for a building program in honor of the special dead. Even though we do not know who the patrons were in each case (just the name of the bishop who commissioned the Januarius complex), we can imagine a variety of characters who might have been interested in such investments. They might include bishops and other clergy (who seek to oversee these rites as part of the church), local elites (who support graveside rituals outside of church contexts, whether members of the Christ cult or not), and imperial sponsors (with the political goal of winning popular support). These architectural projects recontextualize the mortuary rites with new spaces, sometimes magnifying and sometimes channeling or constraining popular ritual practices for the dead.

One way to interpret the pattern represented by these archaeological sites is as the steady march of the institutionalization of "the church" in the third and early fourth centuries. In my view, the evidence suggests a much more complicated picture than this. In the third century we do see local church authority growing in some places, but theories about an empire-wide church at this time have not held up.[151] I would like to suggest instead a more complex model, in which multiple people attempt to claim power or establish influence in the cult of Christ. I call these figures "power brokers" to highlight what I am arguing is their main interest: to capitalize on the cult of the dead for their own purposes.

My argument builds on work that conceptualizes ancient Mediterranean religious practices in terms of competition among various experts.[152] In keeping with Stowers's theorizing of religion as a social kind (with various modes or subkinds), this scholarship invites us to categorize our ancient evidence not solely in terms of what is "Christian," "Jewish," or some other religious tradition but also in terms of what particular skills, services, and practices are being promoted.[153] Recontextualizing Christian practices in this way reveals the complex ways that the Christ cult belongs to larger cultural phenomena in the Roman world, a shift away from seeing it as unique and new.

As scholars have shown, in the third and early fourth centuries, we find among followers of Christ a range of experts—many of whom jockey for position and influence in the same way as the power brokers described above—who compete with each other for influence, including intellectuals, patrons, charismatics, and clergy.[154] This phenomenon is similar to what Michele Salzman calls "status culture" in her description of the late fourth-century senatorial aristocracy: a collection of practices aimed at displaying, asserting, and defining one's elite social status.[155] Making use of this same phrase, Daniel Ullucci explains the widespread use of these strategies: "These practices and discourses were variously recognized, resisted, and adopted competitively by various socioeconomic groups."[156] In the context of religious experts, a category that expands beyond the Roman aristocracy that Salzman addresses, the status being negotiated relates to interacting with powerful beings: claims of knowledge, ritual expertise, access to resources.[157] Individuals often occupy more than one of these categories, as flexibility and maneuverability are integral to how experts work. Indeed, the eventual success of bishops is in part due to their ability to multitask in this way. As discussed above, Cyprian embodies this multitasking. As a bishop, he is a ritual expert, an intellectual producer, and a patron. As his letters demonstrate, he recognized the potential of mortuary rituals and used the resources at his disposal to incorporate martyr celebrations into the church structure that he oversaw.

We can read the case studies above as the result of similar impulses by power brokers seeking to capitalize on these widespread practices, and I would suggest three related reasons for this. One is that the dead, whether special or ordinary (but perhaps particularly those honored above others), commanded power themselves. According to widespread understanding at the time, the deceased joined the company of supernatural beings along with deities of various sorts, demons, spirits, and so on. As such, they joined the system of exchange between humans and the beings they honored, receiving offerings and bestowing favors in a kind of "spiritual patronage," as Carolyn Osiek calls it.[158] Dayna Kalleres has shown that fourth-century bishops understood this well, and Heidi Marx-Wolf has argued the same for third-century Christian intellectuals: spirit or demon management was a critical skill, one that garnered prestige and power.[159] Influence over the dead, especially the special dead (such as the martyrs we have seen in our case studies), was a valuable asset.

A second reason, directly related to the first, is the popularity of these practices. As noted above, the practices that change the *least* when Christians come on the scene involve the care of the dead. I suggest that the enthusiasm and dedication of the populace for these practices, and the numbers of believers gathering at tombs, were noticed by bishops and other patrons. Kendra Eshleman discusses this phenomenon with respect to Hippolytus's rivalry with Callistus: the crowds, whose loyalty the bishops needed, voted with their feet.[160] In this case, Hippolytus was watching the numbers attracted to Callistus. I argue that the numbers were flocking to the cemeteries—perhaps instead of to the churches.[161] So it makes sense that in Rome an emperor, in a time of solidifying power, would construct spaces for the public to honor the dead. The enduring enthusiasm for these rites operated as a powerful engine that could be steered in the direction of loyalty to an emperor (or another power broker) and to the institutions he supported.

The third reason power brokers make moves to harness the cult of the dead flows from the previous two: the ability to control ritual space. In an article that explores Christianization in Roman Egypt, David Frankfurter argues that local shrines were critical to this process.[162] These shrines, because they attracted a variety of spirits, became sites of negotiating with these powers, including employing Christian expertise to drive unsavory ones away. Frankfurter explains that "with the decline of traditional cult centers, the development of an autochthonous Christian local piety, and the struggle of an institutional church for hegemony, much attention came to be directed to the locations and powers of holy places as sites that embraced local experience and that situated the new pantheon of Christian 'spirits' in the landscape."[163] The shrines holding the remains of the martyrs attract other spirits and, in turn, become sites of possession and exorcism. In these mortuary spaces, then, Christianity wrestles its way into local practices and landscapes. I would argue that a similar phenomenon could be at work in our examples: power brokers erect monuments in potent spaces, spaces where throngs of spirits and humans congregate and interact. In doing so, they often cover up earlier graves (either for destruction or memorialization), as Ullucci nicely describes it: "Churches were often built directly over, and literally around, popular shrines, entombing the saint or martyr in a second, ecclesiastical, sarcophagus."[164] Like householders supervising their domestic space, ecclesiastical authorities attempt to oversee burial spaces, especially those of the martyrs.

We might read our three case studies in the context of this interpretation. With Tomb G in the Kapljuč Basilica and the Januarius inscription, both of which involve Christian structures built in cemeteries, there is a relationship between an earlier special grave and the buildings that follow. In the case of Tomb G in Kapljuč, the builders of the fourth-century basilica were intent on preserving the tomb, whether this belonged to a martyr-presbyter, a donor of the church, or a prominent family. The latter two options suggest the possibility that patronage played a role in its preservation. Regardless, the veneration that took place at this particular grave, originally in the open air, was honored, remembered, and perhaps continued by its accommodation in the basilica, its *mensa* now on the floor, with an altar above it. The builders of the church were willing, it seems, to destroy multiple graves for construction, but they carefully incorporated this tomb into the structure, privileging the cult practices that took place here over others.

The Januarius inscription is also connected to patronage: the patronage of one bishop who continues a line of leaders, perhaps in the same family. Tannonius Rogatus honors the martyr, Januarius, and associates this hero with a list of clergy (as well as himself) through his benefaction of the *confessio, memoria*, and basilica.

The various phases of the site of the Memoria Apostolorum (and then the Basilica Apostolorum) likely manifest a similar pattern. Resourceful patrons build and rebuild on the site of an older cemetery, first creating a memorial for Peter and Paul and then a large public structure for funerary commemorations. This particular "holy hot spot" maintains its status through the centuries, serving different cults and audiences and benefiting from different patrons.

Conclusion

In drawing these connections among these three sites, I do not mean to assert a universal pattern that can be applied everywhere. Indeed, my work here is indebted to several scholars who have argued *against* universal models that governed the growth of Christianity.[165] They have pointed out the ways that adherence to these models has blinded us to local influences and to the complexity of factors influencing each site. For example, Nicola Denzey Lewis describes the Vatican *tropaion* as "a complex dynamic between civic patronage, authority, and imperial interests."[166] Each of the sites discussed here represents a similar dynamic: an intersection of the public's persistent burial practices on the one hand, and on the other, growing, locally inflected iterations of ecclesial institutions.

But I do want to name a thread that runs through these third-century sites and their fourth-century transitions: the recognition of the power of the cult of the dead by the various power brokers of the third and early fourth centuries. As I have discussed throughout this study, daily-life religion tends to be decentralized. It has no institutional center or supervision by officials. Yet here it enters the current in a larger movement toward institutionalizing.

This interaction creates a tensive dynamic. Mortuary practices are appealing to power brokers in part because of the crowds that gather on festival days or at special tombs of martyrs or other revered figures. Unlike most daily-life practices, these gain a public presence, which invites the collaboration and participation of bishops and other patrons. The tombs of these "special dead" attract the patronage of the wealthy for architectural elaboration, as we have seen with all three sites discussed. Yet these practices are also perceived by some experts as dangerous and in need of control. They do not originate from any official societal structure, and they maintain an organic, unsupervised character.

Stowers describes the larger trend here: "Christianity during the third century crystallized a religion that institutionalized a relation between the religion of everyday social exchange and the religion of literate specialists, with the latter attempting to control the former according to its principles."[167] I have tried to show that with respect to burial practices, we see a similar but more complex tension. It was not just the literate specialists co-opting daily-life practices but a variety of power brokers, many with overlapping areas of expertise, who gravitated toward the cult of the dead as a means to shore up or legitimize their own claims.[168] They do so through persuasive writing, publishing inscriptions, issuing rulings, and sponsoring construction of buildings.

It is worth noting that the evidence for the dynamic I have argued for here explodes in the late fourth and fifth centuries, as Peter Brown's work has shown. I return to the example of Ambrose, mentioned in the introduction to this chapter. During his tenure as bishop in Milan, festivals at the tombs of the martyrs were forbidden, and Augustine famously recounts how Ambrose prevented his mother from bringing her offerings to the graves of the departed.[169] Yet at the same time, Ambrose saw devotion to martyrs as advantageous, as is clear in his antics with relics. He understood that the martyrs' relics would afford authority to his church—and himself.[170] Other clerics, too, move to both appropriate and curb the Christian cult of the dead.[171]

This later evidence demonstrates the enduring attraction of mortuary practices. They continue to be sought after and reined in.[172] The same characteristics that made them initially appealing to third-century power brokers—that they are widespread, woven into daily life, and connected to powerful beings—are precisely those things that make them hard to control as the church develops. As scholars of the fourth century to the sixth have documented, this is a familiar pattern with everyday practices; domestic worship thrives in these later centuries and comes under regular scrutiny by authorities.[173] My argument in this chapter expands our arc of understanding of Christian history by showing the third- and early fourth-century interactions between the lived-religion practices at the graveside and the various power brokers who attempt both to mobilize and to curb them. In this early period and after, cemeteries and their attendant rituals serve as sites for creating, defining, and challenging the institution of the church.

CONCLUSION

Sitting around a seminar table at the College of the Holy Cross in Worcester, Massachusetts, I recounted for my students—the majority of whom are Catholic—some of the rituals performed by early followers of Christ. I then asked them to share what kinds of religious rituals they perform at home and in other settings outside of Mass. When they began to talk about making the sign of the cross, the conversation grew animated. "We cross ourselves after grace or when we pray to a particular saint." "We make the sign of the cross whenever we leave the house to go on a trip." "My grandmother makes us all sign ourselves when we pass a cemetery." "Same thing if we pass the scene of an accident." "If we have a relative in the hospital, and someone mentions their name, we all cross ourselves."

I experienced an eerie feeling of déjà vu during this conversation. The words of ancient Christians sounded in my head as I listened: Lactantius's claim that signing controls demons; Tertullian's admonition to sign "in all the ordinary actions of daily life"; Chrysostom's suggestion that mothers use the cross instead of mud to protect children.[1] Here were my students describing the same ritual, practiced in their own lives in ways very much like those suggested by the ancient evidence. They sign their bodies with the cross at moments of transition and vulnerability, marking themselves as belonging to Christ.

When I asked why they do it or what the signing does, they found it difficult to articulate specific answers. They know what to do and when to do it, and they know that it is important, but they lack the vocabulary to explain it theologically. This is a practice they first learned not in Mass or catechism class but in the context of family life.

This was an eye-opening experience for me. After hours trawling through scraps of evidence for daily-life practices among early believers, and after developing an understanding of the pervasive and early use of this gesture among Christ followers, I discovered the very same practice alive and well among my own students. Contrary to my usual caution in the classroom that Roman-period Christianity is markedly different from what we know today, I found myself exclaiming over the opposite phenomenon. Adaptive, powerful, and portable, this gesture forms a common thread reaching across the centuries.

In this book I have tried to bring to life this kind of ritual in its ancient context. I have argued that it, along with many other practices, belongs to a tradition of household cult practices developed by followers of Christ in the first through early fourth centuries. My hope is that this research helps us understand, in more complex ways, how early Christianity developed. The book belongs to a larger trend of rethinking this history, calling attention to the ways later definitions of Christianity have shaped what we see as well to the ways our own biases influence our interpretations. My research builds on and contributes to insights and themes from earlier generations as well as the many scholars whose work is reflected in my notes. Wayne Meeks, for example, famously called attention to the importance of studying ordinary Christians.[2] The work of scholars involved in the Redescribing Christian Origins group of the Society of Biblical Literature—including Burton Mack and J. Z. Smith, but also generations of scholars after them—have fruitfully challenged us to integrate Christian material more fully into its context rather than treating it as though it were unique. In part through contributions to this group, Stanley Stowers developed a theoretical framework—religion as a social kind—that opened up new ways of thinking about everyday religious practices.[3] And perhaps most fundamentally, the work of feminist historians has fueled my curiosity about the lives of those who were subordinate in the Roman world. From them I learned to read "against the grain," ask new questions, seek new approaches, and harness my historically informed imagination to help interpret evidence.[4] This book is a product of my bringing together these various threads to seek out the daily lives of early followers of Christ.

As discussed in the introduction, one of the challenges of this project has been the seeming lack of evidence. Fleeting rituals practiced by ordinary people do not tend to make a mark on the historical record. Addressing a similar issue, Michel-Rolph Trouillot argues that all historical evidence implicitly carries with it "silences." In order for an artifact or piece of writing to have survived, someone along the way (whether in its original time period or later) had to choose to preserve it rather than something else. The very act of focusing on one thing necessarily means that other things are ignored or not seen. When evidence is scarce, Trouillot notes, one option for the historian is to "reposition that evidence to generate a new narrative."[5]

This strikes me as an apt description of what I do in this book. Using the modes of religion framework—which reorganizes the categories we typically use for religious practices and identities—I have "repositioned the evidence" to illuminate a component of early Christian history that is rarely examined. I show that ordinary Christ followers participated in everyday exchanges with the divine, incorporating and adapting their god into daily-life practices. The modes of religion theoretical model has allowed me to bring new questions to the material, prompting me to "re-see" evidence in new ways.[6]

This research has taken me through a variety of types of evidence in a variety of places around the Mediterranean world. I have not argued for a one-size-fits-all model but have built the case that Christians, like their neighbors and family members, used available and trusted methods for interacting with the divine and other powerful beings in this world. Thus the Christian household cult, like household cult practices across the empire, was flexible, woven into daily life, practiced in various unsupervised spaces, and perceived as potent.

Several important implications for understanding Christian history emerge from this proposal. First, it challenges us to continue to rethink what "Christianity" was in its early centuries. Contrary to what most evidence proclaims (written by literate producers attempting to shore up and define the tradition), Christianity was not a well-bounded, well-defined entity but "an ongoing process of negotiation," a series of experiments.[7] We therefore need to be aware of our assumptions about what Christianity is in this early phase, even to the point of questioning the notion that Christianity is something that people recognized as a distinct cult, community, or organization. As Nicola Denzey Lewis puts it, "The identity 'Christian' was not totalizing but could be activated or invoked within a particular spatial context: in the home, within a titular church, at a cemetery."[8] It is possible that interacting with the cult of Christ did not necessarily imply any kind of radical change for many people. Instead, it might mean including its symbols and representations of the divine in daily prayers or offerings along with those of other relevant cults. When we open ourselves to this perspective, we see new and sometimes surprising ways of being Christian in this period (see chapter 3).

A second implication of this study is that those without power had a hand in expanding and shaping this new cult through their everyday religious practices. This is not a new idea in the study of early Christianity. We know from early sources (such as Paul's letters) that enslaved people and women were active in the movement.[9] This study offers a different angle, however, suggesting that subordinate members of households might have been able to bring the cult of Christ into their daily lives, incorporating their new god into the traditional cast of deities of the household. The power dynamics in this scenario are complex, involving not only divine/human hierarchies but also social hierarchies among people of different status positions. Most of our reconstructions of the early Christ cult have focused on communities and on leaders; with this research I illuminate other possible agents, including people who hold subordinate positions, such as women and slaves (see chapter 4). With this focus I join others who have attempted to recover, or at least imagine, the contributions of women and enslaved people to history in general and to the development of Christianity in particular.

A third implication is that daily-life practices, specifically mortuary rituals, shaped what would become an institutionalized church in the fourth century and beyond. The cult of the dead, which extends household religion to the graveside and to the larger community, is both powerful and ubiquitous, drawing the attention of those seeking to strengthen or expand their own social or political power. Archaeological evidence of Christian structures built on graves helps us trace this phenomenon in the third and early fourth centuries (see chapter 5). This evidence highlights an important feature of the modes of religion theoretical framework: the boundaries of the different modes are themselves fluid and often interact with one another. Indeed, the practices of daily-life religion inform Christian practices from the beginning. The earliest communal rituals (meals, prayer, washing/baptizing, offerings) are simply iterations of daily-life practices.[10] And, as I have discussed in earlier chapters, followers of Christ incorporate parts of communal rituals into their own observances (bringing home the communion bread, for instance). Thus there is a regular flow, back and forth, between the daily-life mode and the institutional mode.

Taken together, these implications contribute to our thinking about a larger question in early Christian history: How did it ever succeed? One popular narrative about Christianity's surprising success in these early centuries is that it offered something new, satisfying some kind of spiritual longing that other cults could not. Another popular theory is that it drew people because of the opposition it faced; persecution created martyr-heroes that were admired by many. My research suggests a different theory. The success of this new cult is owed, at least in part, to its familiarity and ability to integrate.[11] That is to say, Christianity took hold because it became part of everyday life. Perceived as powerful, its symbols and gestures were integrated into a kind of organic flow of daily activity, mixed with those of other gods and propelled by the hands, feet, and mouths of ordinary people who needed protection and healing. In contrast to the very intentional work of literate producers and institutional experts, who labor at defining this new cult as unique by articulating theologies and liturgies, the dynamic of everyday religion is habitual, unstudied, and instinctual.

One of those literate producers, a favorite companion of mine throughout this project, is Tertullian, who inadvertently offers a humorous glimpse of how easily Christianity might seep into the household. In his essay railing against Christian women marrying "heathen" men, after listing in detail the myriad ways such spouses would be incompatible (most of which relate to household religious practices), the jurist names the most infuriating problem of all: the tolerant husband! He bemoans the non-Christian husband who tolerates his Christian wife's practices (*Ux.* 2.51). Tertullian thus raises the specter that Christ followers may have lived quite peacefully with their non-Christian families. This indignant comment, almost an aside in this lengthy treatise advising wives, invites us to imagine just such a scene: Christ followers integrating their new cult into the traditional practices of the household without secrecy or censure. Without fanfare, without boundary-making, conflict, or theologizing, in the quotidian actions of daily life, and perhaps even without notice, the cult of Christ thus joins the traditional cults of the household.

I find it compelling to imagine that Christianity, in its various iterations, spread this way. The very nature of the everyday mode of religious practice is to be adaptable and inclusive, characteristics that facilitate the integration of new cults. I would suggest that this development, which I have documented for the second, third, and early fourth centuries, lays the foundation for the spectacular growth Christianity experiences once it gains imperial recognition and support in the fourth century. By the time it gains public sanction and begins to enjoy the patronage of Constantine, it has already found a place in houses and shops around the empire.

In chapter 3 I referred to Douglas Boin's discussion of how new cults take hold in the Roman world, and I return to his argument here. He observes that successful new cults "found ways to hybridize with Roman tradition. These creative efforts at outreach . . . are the very characteristics that ensured the growth of their movements—without having to convert the entire population to their practices and beliefs."[12] These strategies worked because the "Roman religious landscape proved to be a highly flexible, accommodating one for those who wanted to work within the system."[13] This study has shown the same to be true for the new cult of Christ in the first through early fourth centuries. Particularly through everyday religious practices, followers of Christ found ways to "work within the system." Their cult took its place among many others, fitting into the same logic of exchange with the gods deployed by most people in the ancient Mediterranean world. In the hands of laborers, mothers, householders, shopkeepers, enslaved people, and the like, the cult of Christ offered protection, healing, and blessing through familiar forms of petition and offering.

NOTES

Introduction

1. Acts of Thecla 42. Greek: Lipsius and Bonnet, *Acta apostolorum apocrypha*, 1:268. Translation: Hennecke, *New Testament Apocrypha*, 246.
2. Frankfurter, "Spaces of Domestic Religion," 7.
3. Frankfurter, *Christianizing Egypt*, 48–54. See also Frankfurter, "Spaces of Domestic Religion."
4. "Extra-domestic" is Frankfurter's phrase ("Spaces of Domestic Religion," 7).
5. Some have suggested, however, that we have overlooked other possible meeting places for early Christians, including shops, barns, and gardens. See Adams, *Earliest Christian Meeting Places*. See also Bremmer's refutation of Adams's theory: "Urban Religion."
6. At the time, the Greek word *ekklesia* meant assembly, gathering, or congregation and is translated in the NRSV as "church." For a short discussion of this choice, see Runesson, "Ekklesia."
7. Examples of studies include White, *Building God's House* (architecture); Bradshaw, *Search for the Origins* (liturgy); Peppard, *World's Oldest Church* (art).
8. Bowes, *Private Worship*; Frankfurter, *Christianizing Egypt*; Sessa, *Daily Life*; Fugger, "Shedding Light." Of course, Peter Brown's work has been foundational for many of these studies, as it has been for my own. See especially *Cult of the Saints*.
9. See Denzey Lewis, *Early Modern Invention*.
10. I am grateful for conversations with Stanley Stowers for these ideas.
11. This is a different approach from region-specific studies, which I have benefited from enormously. Some examples are Burns and Jensen, *Christianity in Roman Africa*; Frankfurter, *Christianizing Egypt*; Denzey Lewis, *Early Modern Invention*. For a discussion of Mediterranean-wide approaches, see Yasin, *Saints and Church Spaces*, 6–7, and the notes cited there.
12. Stowers, "Why Expert," 140–41. See also Frankfurter's discussion of "pagan survivals" (*Christianizing Egypt*, 10–12). For other discussions of this issue, see the collection of "Viewpoint Essays" by Denzey Lewis, Frank, Frankfurter, Grig, and Klingshern in *Studies in Late Antiquity* 5, no. 1 (2021); Gasparini et al., *Lived Religion*; Frank, *Unfinished Christians*; and Peter Brown's earlier call to scholars to widen their notions of what Christian practices might entail rather than buying into labels such as "superstitious," "popular," or "vulgar" (P. Brown, *Cult of the Saints*, 30, and his chapter 2 generally).
13. For recent discussions of this, see Nongbri, *Before Religion*; Barton and Boyarin, *Imagine No Religion*. Heidi Wendt offers a helpful response to the notion that we should abandon the term "religion" (*At the Temple Gates*, 30–36), and see Stowers, *History and the Study*.
14. This work has unfolded over the last few decades in a variety of publications, many of which are collected in Stowers, *Christian Beginnings*. For a detailed elaboration of the argument for religion as a social kind, see Stowers, *History and the Study*, especially chapter 4.
15. I am not arguing for the removal of the terms "Christian" or "Roman" from scholarly discourse, especially to the extent that ancient people described themselves or others that way. But it is useful to question whether they necessarily represent a stable set of religious practices that everyone recognized and to see what we learn from a new way of theorizing

these practices. For another study that challenges these categories, see Marx-Wolf, *Spiritual Taxonomies*.

16. In this paragraph I am summarizing Stowers, "Religion of Plant and Animal Offerings," 36–41 (and his *Christian Beginnings*, 33–56). See also *Christian Beginnings*, 12–13, and *History and the Study*, 1–26.

17. De Bruyn, *Making Amulets Christian*, 204.

18. Stowers, "Religion of Plant and Animal Offerings," 38.

19. Neighborhoods and grave sites are examples of others. See Stowers, "Religion of Plant and Animal Offerings," 8.

20. Larson, *Understanding Greek Religion*, 3. For an introduction to cognitive science as it applies to religion, see Larson's bibliographical essay at the end of the book, "Cognitive Science of Religion," 378–84.

21. Larson, *Understanding Greek Religion*, 3 (and sources cited there). See also Stowers, *History and the Study*, 116–24.

22. Stowers, *History and the Study*, 16–18. I am grateful to Stowers for sharing this work in progress before publication.

23. See Stowers, "Theorizing the Religion," 10.

24. Stowers, "Religion of Plant and Animal Offerings," 41, and *History and the Study*, 113–16, 227–83 (and throughout).

25. Stowers, "Religion of Plant and Animal Offerings," 41.

26. For the sake of efficiency, I am oversimplifying this mode. Stowers explains that in the ancient Mediterranean world, there were many subfields of this mode, and there tended to be two poles within it that were often in tension. One of these was less radical and depended upon the patronage of the elite. The other was more independent and more radical, often criticizing the status quo. See "Religion of Plant and Animal Offerings," 42.

27. Larson, *Understanding Greek Religion*, 11.

28. Stowers, "Religion of Plant and Animal Offerings," 45, and "Kinds of Myth," 112.

29. Stowers, "Religion of Plant and Animal Offerings," 49; *History and the Study*, 116; and *Christian Beginnings*, 13.

30. Stowers, "Religion of Plant and Animal Offerings," 50, and *History and the Study*, chapter 8.

31. Many of these same dynamics could be traced in a study focusing on Jewish practices of this period. Most of the chapters of this book address Jewish practices as they influence, overlap, and sometimes cannot be distinguished from Christian ones. See Hezser, *Oxford Handbook*; Meyers, "Aspects of Everyday Life"; Stowers, "Why 'Common Judaism.'"

32. Stowers makes this point in "Religion of Plant and Animal Offerings," 46.

33. This point recalls earlier challenges to the uniqueness of Christianity made by Mack in *Myth of Innocence* and J. Z. Smith in *Drudgery Divine*, especially chapter 2.

34. Frankfurter, *Christianizing Egypt*, 15–25. Some scholars have called for a rethinking of the concept of "Christianization" because it assumes the triumph of the Christ cult at a time when it was by no means guaranteed. See Boin, *Ostia in Late Antiquity*, 31–33.

35. Frankfurter, "Restoring 'Syncretism,'" 130. See also Sanzo's caution about the limitations of this concept (*Ritual Boundaries*, 17–19).

36. Frankfurter, *Christianizing Egypt*, 4.

37. Concannon, *Assembling Early Christianity*, 66. See also 46–47, where Concannon describes Latour's call to "multiply the agents at work in our historical reconstructions" because "there will always be more agents in any given situation than we can count, each making some difference and pursuing some set of ends" (47). Latour makes these arguments in *Pasteurization of France*.

38. Concannon makes a similar comment: *Assembling Early Christianity*, 64–65.

39. Both quotations from MacMullen, *Second Church*, 50.

Chapter 1

1. For caution against interpreting daily-life objects as religious, see Allison, *Pompeian Households*, 51, 102. Bowes comments that many utilitarian spaces in the home (hearths, kitchens) are also spaces of ritual ("At Home," 211). See also Cianca, *Sacred Ritual*, 34–79.

2. See the work of scholars such as Caitlín Barrett, Kim Bowes, Nicola Denzey Lewis, and David Frankfurter, among others.

3. Bodel, "Cicero's Minerva," 258–62.

4. Bodel, "Cicero's Minerva," 261 (with references in note 41).

5. Foss, "Watchful *Lares*," 218; George, "Servus and Domus"; George, "Lives of Slaves," 540; Bodel, "Cicero's Minerva," 265.

6. Frankfurter, *Religion in Roman Egypt*, 132.

7. Toynbee, *Death and Burial*, 43–50.

NOTES TO PAGES 16–24

8. Johnson Hodge, "'Holy Wives,'" 7.
9. Latin: "On His House" (Clark). Translation: Treggiari, *Roman Social History*, 80–81.
10. Latin: *De legibus* (de Plinval). Translation: Bodel, "Cicero's Minerva," 250.
11. Greek: Burnet, *Platonis Opera*. Translation: Plato, *Laws* (Bury, LCL 192), 2:385.
12. Frankfurter, "Beyond Magic and Superstition," 265–66; Bowes, *Private Worship*, 44–48.
13. Gazda, *Guardians of the Nile*, 9.
14. Boak and Peterson, *Karanis*; Husselman, *Karanis Excavations*.
15. Gazda, *Guardians of the Nile*, 13–14, 35; Yandek, "Pagan Roman Religious Acculturation?," 86.
16. M. Allen, "Terracotta Figurines from Karanis," 137, 414–57.
17. Gazda, *Guardians of the Nile*, 13, 42; Yandek, "Pagan Roman Religious Acculturation?," 71.
18. Gazda, *Guardians of the Nile*, 14, 54, 64.
19. Gazda, *Guardians of the Nile*, 60.
20. Husselman, *Karanis Excavations*, 47, 73.
21. Yandek, "Pagan Roman Religious Acculturation?," 56, 60, 80–81.
22. Greek accessed at Papyri.info (https://papyri.info/ddbdp/p.athen;;60). Translation: Frankfurter, "Religious Practice and Piety," 322.
23. Gazda, *Guardians of the Nile*, 14, 53.
24. Zimmermann et al., *Wall Painting in Ephesos*, 41, 53.
25. Zimmermann et al., *Wall Painting in Ephesos*, 43; Zimmermann, "Archaeological Evidence"; Rathmayr, "Meaning and Use."
26. Zimmermann et al., *Wall Painting in Ephesos*, 53–54.
27. Rathmayr, "Götter- und Kaiserkult," 108–9.
28. Residential Unit 4. Fugger, "Shedding Light," 206–8; Rathmayr, "Götter- und Kaiserkult," 112; Zimmermann et al., *Wall Painting in Ephesos*, 126.
29. Fugger, "Shedding Light," 207.
30. Zimmermann et al., *Wall Painting in Ephesos*, 126.
31. These were located in a niche of Residential Unit 7 and were in place at the time of the earthquake in 230 CE. For discussions of why these first-century imperial figures were honored in the third century, see Rathmayr, *Hanghaus 2 in Ephesos*, 545–46, 562–63, 654–59; Rathmayr, "Götter- und Kaiserkult," 124–28; Zimmerman et al., *Wall Painting in Ephesos*, 127, 75 fig. 107.
32. Archaeologists have also found paintings of Nike, Asclepius, and a woman making offerings at an altar in this apartment (Zimmerman et al., *Wall Painting in Ephesos*, 127).
33. Residential Unit 2. The connection between this apartment and this particular man is based on a rather unflattering inscription near the latrine of Residential Unit 2 (Rathmayr, "Götter- und Kaiserkult," 123–24; Zimmerman et al., *Wall Painting in Ephesos*, 54).
34. For a study of the procession and the inscription that describes it, see Rogers, *Sacred Identity*. Rogers includes the Greek and English translation of the Salutaris inscription (152–85).
35. Whether these two statuettes were carried in the processions is understood differently by different scholars. Rogers treats them as though they were part of the processions (*Sacred Identity*, 91, 94–95). Shaner assumes the same and imagines the participation of enslaved members of Salutaris's household in this ritual: *Enslaved Leadership*, 20. Kokkinia argues that the statues would stay in Salutaris's home. See her careful discussion of the relevant lines (152–58) in "Roman Financier's Version," 221, 233–35.
36. Flower, *Dancing Lares*, 1–2; Orr, "Roman Domestic Religion"; Bodel, "Cicero's Minerva."
37. Boyce, *Corpus of the Lararia*, 77, plate 31; Van Andringa, *Quotidien des dieux*, 258–59; Flower, *Dancing Lares*, 50–52.
38. Boyce, *Corpus of the Lararia*, 77.
39. Van Andringa, *Quotidien des dieux*, 253–56; Flower, *Dancing Lares*, 58; Giacobello, *Larari pompeiani*, 100n28.
40. Flower, *Dancing Lares*, 154, plate 18; Fröhlich, *Lararien- und Fassadenbilder*, 308.
41. Translation from Flower, *Dancing Lares*, 154.
42. Flower, *Dancing Lares*, 149.
43. E. M. Meyers finds the faunal evidence convincing that this was primarily a Jewish city during the Roman period: There were no pig bones found during these centuries. They begin to appear when Christians move in after 363 CE (the year of a large earthquake). See Meyers, "Aspects of Everyday Life," 205.

Meyers cites the work of Grantham, whose findings are reported in "Faunal Remains," 871–88.

44. Galor, "Stepped Water Installations," 201.

45. Many of these prescriptions can be found in the Mishnaic text Miqva'ot. For the debate on these stepped pools, see Eshel, "They're Not Ritual Baths"; Meyers's response, "Yes, They Are"; and Eshel's additional response, "We Need More Data." See also Meyers, "Aspects of Everyday Life," 211–13. Galor offers a helpful discussion of the issues involved with interpretation in "Stepped Water Installations"; note 2 offers further bibliography on the nomenclature.

46. Galor, "Stepped Water Installations," 205–9; Meyers, "Aspects of Everyday Life," 211–20.

47. Galor, "Stepped Water Installations," 202–3.

48. For reviews of biblical and rabbinic treatments, see Sanders, *Jewish Law*, 214–27; Meyers, "Aspects of Everyday Life," 211–12; and Zissu and Amit, "Common Judaism," 47–48. Galor offers a helpful caution against the assumption that the literary tradition represents widespread practice and can therefore determine interpretation of archaeological finds ("Stepped Water Installations," 204).

49. Galor, "Stepped Water Installations," 209–10; Zissu and Amit, "Common Judaism," 51–61.

50. Zissu and Amit make this point and include ritual bathing in the category "common Judaism" (using E. P. Sanders's phrase). See "Common Judaism," 47–48. Sanders uses "common Judaism" in *Judaism*. Note the critique of Stowers, however, who challenges the notion of widespread uniformity of practice among Jews: Stowers, "Why 'Common Judaism,'" and *Christian Beginnings*, 80–98.

51. Rutgers, "Incense Shovels"; Meyers, "Ceramic Incense Shovels."

52. Rutgers, "Incense Shovels," 192–196.

53. Meyers, "Ceramic Incense Shovels," 876–77.

54. E. M. Meyers conjures the image of the full house in "Ceramic Incense Shovels," 876.

55. Rutgers, "Incense Shovels," 179–81. The theory is that the ritual objects represented in synagogue mosaics, for example, refer to temple worship (menorah, *lulav, shofar,*

incense shovel) on different holy days. The incense shovel was carried into the Holy of Holies on Yom Kippur (Rutgers, "Incense Shovels," 181).

56. Lapp, "Lamps"; Lapp, *Sepphoris II*; Meyers, "Aspects of Everyday Life," 203–4. These range in date from the first century CE to the fourth century CE, with the menorahs and Torah shrines tending to belong to the fourth through sixth centuries.

57. Lapp, "Lamps," 222n118; Lapp, *Sepphoris II*, 96–97, 99, 103. Lapp calls this a "graffito" style of artisanship in contrast to the professionally cut menorahs of larger workshops (*Sepphoris II*, 113). For a discussion of menorahs on lamps and other materials in Sepphoris, see Meyers and Meyers, "Image and Identity."

58. Lapp, *Sepphoris II*, 97; Meyers and Meyers, "Image and Identity," 388.

59. McKay, *Sabbath and Synagogue*, 203; Archer, "Role of Jewish Women," 283; Lapp, *Sepphoris II*, 199.

60. Sanders, *Judaism*, 190–212; McKay, *Sabbath and Synagogue*; Goldenberg, "Jewish Sabbath."

61. Chancey and Meyers, "How Jewish Was Sepphoris?," 28–29.

62. Kraemer, "On the Meaning," 46. The inscriptions are from the mid-second to late first century BCE.

63. Stern, "Vandals or Pilgrims?," 188. Lieu makes a similar point, arguing that if you look for "'Jewish' particularity" you will miss the Jews, who were integrated into daily life and who, like others, occupied multiple identities, especially in the context of family and home: "Household and Family," 76.

64. See Stowers, "Why 'Common Judaism,'" and *Christian Beginnings*, 80–98, for discussions of everyday practices associated with Judaism.

Chapter 2

1. Minucius Felix, *Octavius* 10.2. Latin and English translation: Tertullian, Minucius Felix (Rendall, LCL 250), 338 and 340 (Latin), 341 (English).

2. The Christian building at Dura Europos, dating to the middle of the third century, is an early example of a structure dedicated to communal meetings. Large churches were supported by Constantine's building campaign in the first half of the fourth

NOTES TO PAGES 26–30

century. See White, *Building God's House*; Peppard, *World's Oldest Church*.

3. An early exception to this lack of attention is Deissman, who promotes the study of daily-life Christianity in *Light from the East*. Recent decades have witnessed new interest in daily-life history, especially in the fourth through seventh centuries. Examples of studies include Bowes, *Private Worship*; Frankfurter, *Christianizing Egypt*; Sanzo, *Ritual Boundaries*; Öhler, "Das ganze Haus"; Sessa, *Daily Life*; Frankfurter and Varhelyi, *Sacra Privata*; and Gasparini et al., *Lived Religion*.

4. Sanzo argues, however, that quotidian practices, too, were interested in establishing boundaries among different groups (*Ritual Boundaries*).

5. Frankfurter, *Christianizing Egypt*, 4.

6. Acts of Thecla 42. Greek: Lipsius and Bonnet, *Acta apostolorum apocrypha*, 1:268. Translation: Ehrman, *After the New Testament*, 284.

7. Stowers, "Religion of Plant and Animal Offerings," 38; Stowers, "Locating the Religion of Associations," 317; Pulleyn, *Prayer in Greek Religion*, 4, and throughout. A central thesis of Pulleyn's study is that Greek religious practice is based on reciprocity and exchange between humans and gods. For the larger theoretical framework I draw upon here, see Stowers, *History and the Study* (discussed in the introduction).

8. See Stern's *Writing on the Wall*, 35–79, for an argument that writing graffiti is a form of prayer. See also chapter 5 for my discussion of this phenomenon at the Memoria Apostolorum.

9. As I discuss in chapter 3, this practice-based way of thinking about the varieties of early Christian prayer offers a way to move beyond binaries that may not be as helpful, such as magic vs. religion. See Frankfurter, *Guide to the Study*, especially Frankfurter's introductory essay, "Ancient Magic in a New Key."

10. For text, translation, and commentary, see Kotansky, *Greek Magical Amulets*, 301–5. The date of this amulet is uncertain, but Kotansky decides that the late third century is most likely (301).

11. See Kotansky, *Greek Magical Amulets*, 303–4, for a discussion of "*Raba Skanomka loula amriktorathena thabytharorak*." Scholars are unsure what these names refer to or even how to divide the letters to arrive at distinct names. "Iaô" represents YHWH in Greek (Meyer and Smith, *Ancient Christian Magic*, 393). Unintelligible words are part of the typical repertoire of spell prayers in the ancient world, especially those related to healing or exorcism. One theory is that these are appropriate for communicating with a variety of powerful beings, some of whom might be "foreign" and therefore would understand these words better than Greek (Gager, *Curse Tablets*, 7–10). See further discussion in chapter 3.

12. Greek: P 21 in *PGM* II.229–30. Translation from Meyer and Smith, *Ancient Christian Magic*, 55–56n36. Preisendanz (in *PGM*) and Meyer and Smith give a date of 300 CE for this prayer (55), although other dates are offered by other sources. See de Bruyn and Dijkstra, "Greek Amulets," 190 (#39) and 190n136.

13. Meyer and Smith also make this point in *Ancient Christian Magic*, 5.

14. Stowers, "Locating the Religion of Associations," 315.

15. For Christian adaptation of "magical texts," see Meyer and Smith, *Ancient Christian Magic*; de Bruyn, *Making Amulets Christian*. See also chapter 3, where this issue is discussed more fully.

16. Sources on spell experts are Nagy, "Engineering Ancient Amulets"; Frankfurter, "Dynamics of Ritual Expertise"; de Bruyn, *Making Amulets Christian*, 6–9, 89–183; Luijendijk, "Gospel Amulet"; Sanzo, *Scriptural Incipits*; and Sanzo, *Ritual Boundaries*, chapter 3.

17. Luijendijk, "Gospel Amulet," 427, building on the work of de Bruyn. See also Johnson Hodge, "Ritual Epiclesis." See the discussion of amulets below and also chapter 3.

18. Greek and translation in Maravela, "Christians Praying," 300. Greek for P.Oxy. III 407: Grenfell and Hunt, *Oxyrhynchus Papyri*, 12–13.

19. De Bruyn and Dijkstra, "Greek Amulets," 212–13 (#173).

20. Maravela, "Christians Praying," 300.

21. E. P. Sanders comments that daily prayer (the Shema among others) was common: *Judaism*, 196. Reif points out that Second Temple Judaism had a wide variety of practices and no central authority to determine a unified format for prayer; see Reif, "Prayer and Liturgy." See Stern, *Writing on the*

Wall, 35–79, for a discussion of writing graffiti as a form of Jewish prayer. For discussions of Jewish prayers and their influence on Christianity, see McGowan, *Ancient Christian Worship*, 184–90; Bradshaw, *Daily Prayer*, 1–22; Bowes, *Private Worship*, 52–53.

22. See Bradshaw, *Daily Prayer*, 62; Burns and Jensen, *Christianity in Roman Africa*, 554–55. Nearly a third of Tertullian's treatise on prayer (*Or.* 2–9) deals directly with the Lord's Prayer. Origen expands upon this prescription and develops a five-part schema for each prayer session (*Or.* 33). Bradshaw offers a review of the evidence from Christian writers in the second and third centuries (*Daily Prayer*, 47–71).

23. Clement (second century) explains that the "gnostic" (his word for the ideal Christian) lives his or her life in constant prayer (*Stromateis* 7.7); see also Origen, *Or.* 12.2. For a discussion of these and other texts, see Bradshaw, *Daily Prayer*, 47–71; McGowan, *Ancient Christian Worship*, 183–215. On the timing of prayer, see Hvalvik, "Praying with Outstretched Hands," 72–76.

24. Tertullian associates the third, sixth, and ninth hours with biblical events (*Or.* 25; see also Cyprian, *De dominica oratione* 34–36. Clement (*Stromateis* 7.7) and Origen (*Or.* 12.2) also discuss praying three times a day. Tertullian (*Or.* 25) and Cyprian (*De dominica oratione* 35) include morning and evening as appropriate prayer times as well. The *Apostolic Tradition* advises similar times for prayer (41). See McGowan, *Ancient Christian Worship*, 199–200, for an attempt to sort out the different layers of tradition represented in *Apostolic Tradition* 41 and how the two patterns of daily prayer (three times at the third, sixth, and ninth hours vs. two times at morning and evening) might interact.

25. Mealtimes: Clement, *Stromateis* 7.7; Tertullian, *Or.* 25. Departure of a fellow believer: Tertullian, *Or.* 26. Nocturnal: Tertullian, *Ux.* 2.5.3; Origen, *Or.* 12.2.

26. See also McGowan, *Ancient Christian Worship*, 198.

27. Translations from Bradshaw, Johnson, and Phillips, *Apostolic Tradition*, 194 (41.3) and 196 (41.5). These translations both come from the Sahidic version; see Bradshaw's discussion of this specific version (8) and the process of reconstructing the text from multiple sources (11–17).

28. Latin and English translation amended from *Catullus, Tibullus, Pervigilium Veneris* (Postgate, LCL 6), 331. Circulated in a collection authored by Tibullus, this poem is attributed by some scholars to a woman named Sulpicia. See Hallett, "Eleven Elegies"; Argetsinger, "Birthday Rituals."

29. A sampling of studies is listed here: Fröhlich, *Lararien- und Fassadenbilder*; Boyce, *Corpus of the Lararia*; Harmon, "Family Festivals"; Orr, "Roman Domestic Religion"; Bakker, *Living and Working*; Williams, "Roman Corinth"; Bodel, "Cicero's Minerva"; Flower, *Dancing Lares*; Rathmayr, "Götter- und Kaiserkult"; Frankfurter, *Religion in Roman Egypt*.

30. Fugger, "Shedding Light."

31. Fugger makes this point as well ("Shedding Light," 203). On places of Christian prayer, see Hvalvik, "Praying with Outstretched Hands," 58–63.

32. Latin: Evans, *Tertullian's Tract on the Prayer*.

33. Greek: Koetschau, *Origenes Werke*, 2:397–8.

34. Latin: PL 4:521. Translation: Schaff, *ANF* 5. For a discussion of Cyprian's comments on prayer, see Burns and Jensen, *Christianity in Africa*, 556–57.

35. Sessa, "Christianity and the *Cubiculum*"; Riggsby, "'Public and Private.'" See also Allison, "Roman Households"; Berry, "Household Artefacts."

36. See chapter 4 for an extended discussion of this passage.

37. Latin: Tidner, *Didascaliae apostolorum*, 146–47. Translation: Bradshaw, Johnson, and Phillips, *Apostolic Tradition*, 198.

38. Sessa, "Christianity and the *Cubiculum*," 179–80.

39. For a discussion of these, see Hvalvik, "Praying with Outstretched Hands," 76–85.

40. Corbeill, *Nature Embodied*, 29. Van Straten describes gestures in Greek prayer and offers some images of what he calls the most common prayer position in iconography (one hand up, sometimes two) in "Gifts for the Gods." See also Pulleyn, *Prayer in Greek Religion*, 188–95.

41. Latin: Evans, *Tertullian's Tract on the Prayer*. Translation: *ANF* 3 (Thelwall).

42. See Hvalvik, "Praying with Outstretched Hands," 77–82, on references to kneeling in Jewish and Christian texts. Tertullian instructs catechumens who are about to be baptized

to "pray, with frequent prayers, fastings, bendings of the knee, and all-night vigils" (*Bapt.* 20). Latin and English translation: Evans, *Tertullian's Homily on Baptism*, 40 (Latin), 41 (English).

43. On the difficulties in dating these paintings, see Denzey, *Bone Gatherers*, 101; Grabar, *Beginnings of Christian Art*, 59–143 (for pre-Constantinian art), 98–99 (for the difficulties of dating the frescoes in the catacombs in Rome), 123–43 (for sarcophagi reliefs).

44. Jensen, *Understanding Early Christian Art*, 35–37. See also Milburn, *Early Christian Art*, 27–36. On the orant in Jewish contexts, see Fine, "Jewish Art," 43–44. See also Hvalvik, "Praying with Outstretched Hands," 82–85.

45. Jensen, *Understanding Early Christian Art*, 35; Hvalvik, "Praying with Outstretched Hands," 82–85. See Denzey's fascinating reinterpretation of several of the catacomb paintings in *Bone Gatherers*, 58–88, 109–13.

46. For authors who connect this stance to the shape of the cross, see Minucius Felix, *Octavius* 29, and Tertullian, *Apol.* 30.7.

47. Greek: Lipsius and Bonnet, *Acta apostolorum apocrypha*, 1:115. Translation: Hennecke, *New Testament Apocrypha*, 262. See Hvalvik, "Praying with Outstretched Hands," 64–72, for a review of the evidence for facing east during prayer; McGowan, *Ancient Christian Worship*, 194.

48. Likewise, in the *Apostolic Tradition*, ritual blowing of moist breath is included in the section on prayer (*Apostolic Tradition* 41; Bradshaw, Johnson, and Phillips, *Apostolic Tradition*, 198). For more discussion of these practices, see below and chapter 4.

49. Another example of such a gesture is ritual kissing, practiced by Christians especially in liturgical settings but also in less scripted contexts (such as greeting other believers or martyrs; see *Ux.* 2.4.2). See Penn, *Kissing Christians*. For a helpful discussion of gestures, see Frankfurter, *Christianizing Egypt*, 111–14.

50. Latin and English translation: Pliny, *Natural History* (Jones, LCL 418), 18–19.

51. Latin and English translation: Pliny, *Natural History* (Jones, LCL 418), 18 (Latin), 19 (English).

52. As noted by Corbeill, ritual spinning has been variously explained both by ancient literate specialists and modern scholars. One theory is that turning in circles creates a protective sphere. See Corbeill, *Nature Embodied*, 28–29n76, and sources cited there.

53. Latin and English translation: Apuleius, *Golden Ass* (Adlington, LCL 44), 186–87. For a similar gesture, see Lucian, *Demosthenis encomium* 49. Christian apologist Minucius Felix depicts a non-Christian character greeting a statue of a god with this same motion: "Caecilius noticed an image of Serapis and—as is the superstitious habit of the vulgar—put his hand to his mouth and blew it a kiss" (*Octavius* 2). Latin and English translation: Tertullian, Minucius Felix (Rendall, LCL 250), 316–17.

54. I have relied on several studies of the cross in early Christian tradition: Jensen, *Cross*; Longenecker, *Cross Before Constantine*; Longenecker, *Crosses of Pompeii*; Viladesau, *Beauty of the Cross*.

55. Latin: *De corona* (Fontaine). Translation amended from *ANF* 3 (Thelwall). Cyril of Jerusalem (fourth century CE) also recommends daily signing (*Catechetical Lectures* 4.14).

56. Latin and English translation (amended) from *Adversus Marcionem* (Evans). The Ezekiel passage referred to here is 9:4–6.

57. *Selecta Ezehielem* 9 (PG 13:800–801). This passage is also discussed by Jensen, *Cross*, 36, and Longenecker, *Cross Before Constantine*, 59.

58. Both quotes from *To Demetrianus* 22. Latin: CSEL 3.1. Translation: *ANF* 5 (Wallis). See also Cyprian, *Testimonies* 22.

59. Jensen, *Cross*, 38.

60. Cyprian, *Letter to Jubaianus* 73.9. Translation: Donna, *Saint Cyprian*, 274.

61. Acts of Peter 5. Latin: *Actus Petri cum Simone* 5 in Lipsius and Bonnet, *Acta apostolorum apocrypha*, 1:50, 51. Translation: Hennecke, *New Testament Apocrypha*, 291–92.

62. *Appendix to the Works of Hippolytus* (or Elucidations) 48. Greek: PG 10:949. Translation: *ANF* 5.

63. *Contra Judaeos et gentiles quod Christus sit deus* 9. Greek: PG 48:826. Translation: Jensen, *Cross*, 34.

64. *Homily 12 on 1 Corinthians* 13–14 (PG 61:106). More on this passage in chapter 3.

65. See Frankfurter, *Christianizing Egypt*, 156–61, 171–73, and 180–82 for a discussion of how widespread the symbol of the cross was in the ancient Mediterranean world in late antiquity, especially in stone and textile workshops. It was deployed for protective and

apotropaic purposes. See also Sanzo, *Ritual Boundaries*, 81–87.

66. Translation from Bradshaw, Johnson, and Phillips, *Apostolic Tradition*, 198, 200. See 204–5 for the difficulties of translating this passage (e.g., *spm* could be *spitum* or *spiritum*), and see Tidner, *Didascaliae apostolorum*, 146–47, with notes. See also *Apostolic Tradition* 42.2 for a comment that seems to undermine the gesture mentioned in 41.14: "the adversary . . . will be routed by the not spitting but breathing mouth" (Bradshaw, Johnson, and Phillips, *Apostolic Tradition*, 216; see also Tidner, *Didascaliae apostolorum*, 149).

67. The Latin phrase in Tertullian is "cum aliquid immundum flatu explodis" (when you blow away some unclean thing). Latin: *À son épouse* (Munier). Translation from Le Saint, *Tertullian*, 30. See Le Saint for a connection between the gestures mentioned in *Ad uxorem* and in the *Apostolic Tradition* (129n117). Bradshaw thinks the two texts are referring to the same ritual (Bradshaw, Johnson, and Phillips, *Apostolic Tradition*, 211). I discuss this passage further in chapter 4.

68. See Chowdharay-Best, "Notes on the Healing Properties."

69. Latin and English translation: Celsus, *De medicina* (Spencer, LCL 304), 2:170 (Latin), 2:171 (English).

70. As a rather unappetizing example, Galen asks the reader to recall how food that is stuck between your teeth changes in your mouth: Bread is no longer quite bread, nor is meat meat. A further sign of this is the stench that develops in your mouth as a result (3.7). Greek and English translation: Galen, *On the Natural Faculties* (Brock, LCL 71), 252 (Greek), 253 (English).

71. For a quick and helpful discussion of Mark 7:33 in the context of Roman-period healing using saliva, including among Jews, see Marcus, *Mark 1–8*, 473–74.

72. A similar story is famously told about Vespasian, as recorded by several Roman historians: Tacitus, *Histories* 4.81; Suetonius, *Divine Vespasian, Lives of the Caesars* 7.2; Dio Cassius, *Roman History* 65.8. For these passages presented together in translation, see Cotter, *Miracles in Greco-Roman Antiquity*, 40–42.

73. See Eitrem, *Some Notes on the Demonology*, 47–49.

74. Latin: Tertullian, Minucius Felix (Rendall, LCL 250), 128. Translation: *ANF* 3:38 (Thelwall). See also *Idol.* 11 for a reference to believers spitting and blowing on altars with burning incense (I discuss this passage further in chapter 3).

75. Greek: Koetschau, *Origenes Werke*, 122. Translation: *Contra Celsum* (Chadwick), 63. Celsus is likely thinking here of stories like those mentioned above, where Jesus heals using his hands, mud, and saliva.

76. Original language (Coptic and Greek) edition: *PGM* I.170–72. Translations: Betz, *Greek Magical Papyri*, 97. For an extensive treatment of *PGM* IV, see Love, *Code-Switching with the Gods*. See also Twelftree, "Jesus the Exorcist," 72n70. For a discussion of the relationship between "magic" and early Christian practices, see chapter 3.

77. For studies of this complex phenomenon, see D. Smith, *From Symposium to Eucharist*; McGowan, *Ascetic Eucharists*; Smith and Taussig, *Meals*; Taussig, *In the Beginning*.

78. McGowan, *Ancient Christian Worship*, 43–55.

79. Dix, *Detection of Aumbries*, 7–8. For another study of this phenomenon, see Freestone, *Sacrament Reserved*.

80. Latin: PL 4:231. Freestone cites this passage as *Epistle* 5; see *Sacrament Reserved* 24. Translation here by the author.

81. Latin and English translation (amended): Evans, *Tertullian's Tract on the Prayer*.

82. Latin: *Exhortation à la chasteté* (Moreschini). Translation amended from *ANF* 4:54 (Thelwall).

83. For the householder as an important ritual agent in the Roman world, see Ullucci, "Toward a Typology," 96–97.

84. Bowes, *Private Worship*, 58.

85. Latin: Tidner, *Didascaliae apostolorum*, 143. Translation: Bradshaw, Johnson, and Phillips, *Apostolic Tradition*, 180, 182.

86. Latin: Tidner, *Didascaliae apostolorum*, 143. Translation: Bradshaw, Johnson, and Phillips, *Apostolic Tradition*, 184.

87. And in that passage Tertullian, too, cautions against the cup or the bread, "even though our own (*etiam nostri*)," being thrown to the ground (*Cor.* 3). The reference to "our own" cup and bread could imply a domestic context. Freestone thinks either domestic or communal worship is possible (*Sacrament Reserved*, 37). Latin: *De corona* (Fontaine).

88. Latin: *À son épouse* (Munier).

NOTES TO PAGES 42–44

89. Latin: CSEL 3.1, 8. See also CCSL 4:173–4. Translation amended from *ANF* 5:577.

90. Latin: PL 4:480. Translation: *ANF* 5:444. The "box" referred to here is likely a pyxis, made for the purpose of transporting the bread. See Bowes, *Private Worship*, 77; Bradshaw, Johnson, and Phillips, *Apostolic Tradition*, 181.

91. Shipwrecks (Ambrose, *De excessu fratris sui Satyri* 1.43); evil spirits (Augustine, *De civitate Dei* xxii.8).

92. Jerome: Epistles 71.6 (Lucinius) and 49 (48).15 (Pammachius). Basil of Caesarea: *Epistle (xciii) ad Caesariam patriciam* 53–58. On the common practice of the reserved eucharist, especially in Rome, see Bowes, *Private Worship*, 76. On the fourth-century councils that address this issue, see Freestone, *Sacrament Reserved*, 29.

93. Bowes's excellent study of this phenomenon (*Private Worship*) traces these tensions into the sixth century.

94. Faraone discusses the media of amulets as found in the archaeological record (*Transformation of Greek Amulets*, 79–101).

95. Note the similar Jewish practice of wearing tefillin, which attach scripture to the arms and forehead (Sanders, *Judaism*, 196).

96. For a helpful study of this phenomenon, see de Bruyn, *Making Amulets Christian*; de Bruyn and Dijkstra, "Greek Amulets." See also Faraone, *Transformation of Greek Amulets*.

97. The Fayum mummy portraits offer iconographic evidence for this practice in Egypt. See Kotansky, "Incantations and Prayers," 114 and 130n47; Luijendijk, "Gospel Amulet," 431n1, 433n10.

98. *Hom. Matt* 72 (PG 58:669). Cited in Luijendijk, "Gospel Amulet," 418 and 431n2 (note also gives the Greek).

99. P.Oxy. LIIIVI 5073 (Trismegistos 140277). Original edition with Greek, translation, and notes: Smith and Bernhard, "5073. Mark I 1–2: Amulet," 19–23. Greek and translation also found in Blumell and Wayment, *Christian Oxyrhynchus*, 336 (the amulet is discussed on 335–37). Regarding the date, note that while Smith and Bernhard have placed this gospel in the late third or fourth century (21), Sanzo cautions that this would make this text the earliest of the extant gospel incipits and perhaps warrants further study: *Scriptural Incipits*, 98n91. B. Jones, however, situates the writing style in the third century, citing several close parallels (while also admitting that paleographical dating of papyri is necessarily tentative): *New Testament Texts*, 131. De Bruyn agrees with a possible third-century date and adds more evidence to Jones's assessment (*Making Amulets Christian*, 147–48).

100. Blumell and Wayment, *Christian Oxyrhynchus*, 335.

101. Luijendijk, "Gospel Amulet," 424–25, 440n63.

102. Sanzo, *Scriptural Incipits*, 141.

103. Blumell and Wayment, *Christian Oxyrhynchus*, 335, referring to the editors of this manuscript, Smith and Bernhard, "5073. Mark I 1–2: Amulet," 19–23. See B. Jones, *New Testament Texts*, 132n218 for third-century parallels mentioning angels. Another possible third-century amulet text contains the Letter of Jude and is also thought to protect against evil spirits. Wasserman argues that the original papyrus contained more of the letter than the fragment we have and included portions that support an apotropaic function: see Wasserman, "P78 (Oxy. XXXIV 2684)." Others have cautioned that this manuscript might date to later centuries: B. Jones, *New Testament Texts*, 175–80 (fifth or fourth century); Orsini and Clarysse, "Early New Testament," 459 (fifth century).

104. P.Ant. 2.54. Greek: Barns, Zilliacus, and Roberts, *Antinoopolis Papyri, Part 2*, 6–7. Translation from B. Jones, *New Testament Texts*, 117 (Greek is also cited; p. 118 has a photo of the papyrus). For the full discussion of the amulet, see 117–22. De Bruyn and Dijkstra list this amulet as belonging to the third century ("Greek Amulets," 208, #156).

105. B. Jones, *New Testament Texts*, 119.

106. *Making Amulets Christian*, 181–83. P.Ant. 2.54 is discussed on pp. 162–64 (and a discussion of the Lord's Prayer on amulets begins on p. 157).

107. De Bruyn, *Making Amulets Christian*, 157–72.

108. De Bruyn, *Making Amulets Christian*, chapter 5 in general (pp. 139–83), esp. 171, 181–83 (182 for "habits of prayer"). See also de Bruyn's chapter 6 for more on liturgical settings.

109. Frankfurter, "Healing Spells," 81.

110. The following scholars address the rituals that accompanied these texts: Luijendijk, "Gospel Amulet," 421; Kotansky, "Incantations and Prayers"; Frankfurter, "Narrating Power," 462–63.

111. De Bruyn, "Appeals to Jesus," 79. Arguing along the same lines, Buell writes, "Amulets thus are part of [a] larger set of ancient practices 'constantly entangled with things' and 'fundamentally grounded in both incantations and physical actions'": "Embodied Temporalities," 465. Buell quotes Wilburn, *Materia Magica*, 8.

112. See Buell, "Embodied Temporalities," for a discussion of how amulets are used by ancient Mediterranean people to manage the vulnerability of bodies to illness, disease, and other unfriendly invaders.

113. See Marshall, *Catalogue of the Finger Rings*, xv–xxx, for an overview of the use of Roman finger rings. See also Hawley, "Lords of the Rings."

114. Hawley, "Lords of the Rings," 106–7.

115. Marshall, *Catalogue of the Finger Rings*, xxi–xxii.

116. Marshall, *Catalogue of the Finger Rings*, xxii–xxiii, xxix–xxx.

117. For a discussion of this spell and the argument that the engraving of a deity on a gemstone could be understood as itself a miniature version of a cult statue, see Moyer and Dieleman, "Miniaturization." For a translation of the text, see Betz, *Greek Magical Papyri*, 163–65 (see also the preceding ring spell, *PGM* XII.201–69, in Betz, *Greek Magical Papyri*, 161–63).

118. Marshall, *Catalogue of the Finger Rings*, xxix–xxx.

119. Boin cautions against using symbols typically associated with the Christ cult to identify the wearers as Christians (*Ostia in Late Antiquity*, 39–43). This is an important caution, even if I am less persuaded by his argument about people trying to "pass" as something they are not.

120. Spier, *Late Antique*, 18, and catalogue nos. 1–3. The Greek is simply the genitive case of Jesus Christ; Spier suggests "servant of Christ" as a translation.

121. Spier sees the fish as further support that this is a Christian ring (*Late Antique*, 18, no. 3).

122. Spier, *Late Antique*, 18.

123. See Spier, *Late Antique*, 474–76.

124. Spier, *Late Antique*, 29–30.

125. Spier, *Late Antique*, 30–34.

126. Spier, *Late Antique*, 34–35, including the notes on 35. See also Harley-McGowan, "Constanza Carnelian," 214.

127. Spier, *Late Antique*, 36.

128. Spier, *Late Antique*, 36. Spier notes that the verb *tēreō* is rare on amulets, and it might be a reference to John 17:15: "I am not asking you to take them out of the world, but I ask you to protect (*tērēsēs*) them from the evil one."

129. Spier, *Late Antique*, 41. See pp. 41–52 for a discussion of different images on rings thought to be Christian.

130. Spier, *Late Antique*, 53–62. One example belongs to the MFA in Boston, acc. no. 03.1010: https://collections.mfa.org/objects/181439. See also the exhibition catalogue edited by Miner, *Early Christian and Byzantine Art*, 115, no. 562 and plate 78. Biblical narratives also appear on rings in this period, with the story of Jonah being popular (as it was in other art forms). See Spier, *Late Antique*, 63–79 and 67–68, on the popularity of Jonah.

131. The full passage is 3.57.1–3.60.1. See Finney, "Images on Finger Rings," 181–86.

132. See Harley-McGowan, "Constanza Carnelian," 215.

133. Aune, "Magic in Early Christianity," 407–11.

134. Harley-McGowan, "Constanza Carnelian," 215–16.

135. S. Mitchell documents the importance of lamp-lighting among devotees of *theos hypsistos*: "Cult of Theos Hypsistos," 81–148.

136. The sources on this are many. A few that have been useful to me are Brussière and Wohl, *Ancient Lamps*; Lapp, *Sepphoris II*; and G. Gardner, "City of Lights" (see also sources cited in his bibliography).

137. Nilsson, "Divine Service," 64–65; Dix, *Shape of the Liturgy*, 85–87; Dölger, *Lumen Christi*, 13–24; Bowes, *Private Worship*, 154.

138. Heliodorus offers an example of this practice in his novel, *Aethiopica*, in which the characters bring in a lighted lamp, pour libations, and call upon the gods before retiring for the night (*Aethiopica* III.4.11–5.1).

139. G. Gardner, "City of Lights," 284; Bradshaw, *Daily Prayer*, 22; Dix, *Shape of the Liturgy*, 87. See Berakhot viii.5–6 for a discussion by the rabbis of saying prayers over lamps.

140. Hadley points out that the ritual use of household lamps is a good example of the "adaptation of religious precedent" argued for by Murray (Hadley, "Early Christian Perceptions," 93). See Murray, "Art and the Early Church," and her *Rebirth and Afterlife*.

141. See Brussière and Wohl, *Ancient Lamps*, 353–58 for possible Christian iconography.
142. Spier, *Picturing the Bible*, 171–72. Spier also mentions this lamp and workshop in *Late Antique*, 63, 54n14. See also Hadley, "Early Christian Perceptions," 94.
143. Spier, *Picturing the Bible*, 171.
144. Bowes, *Private Worship*, 54. Lamps were also used in burial rituals. See M. Johnson, "Christian Burial Practices," and MacMullen, *Second Church*, 29.
145. Latin: CSEL 20, 30–58. Translation amended from *ANF* 3 (Thelwall).
146. *Apostolic Tradition* 29C (Bradshaw, Johnson, and Phillips, *Apostolic Tradition*, 156); Tertullian, *Apol.* 39.18.
147. Frankfurter, "Spaces of Domestic Religion," 12.
148. Maxwell, "Lay Piety," 38.

Chapter 3

1. For a brief discussion of this scene, and a larger discussion of household religion in the Apocryphal Acts of the Apostles, see Frenschkowski, "Domestic Religion," 146–47.
2. Acts of John 27. Greek: Lipsius and Bonnet, *Acta apostolorum apocrypha*, 2.1, 165–66. Translation (amended): Hennecke, *New Testament Apocrypha*, 176.
3. Sanzo talks about the "prototype" problem in the context of late antique amulets: when scholars have a well-defined understanding of what true Christianity is and bring that to their work, they tend to privilege certain symbols as more authentically Christian than others. See *Scriptural Incipits*, 12 and references in note 34.
4. I build here on the work of others who have explored this same idea, including MacMullen, *Second Church*; MacMullen, *Christianizing the Roman Empire*; Frankfurter, *Religion in Roman Egypt*; Frankfurter, *Christianizing Egypt*; Rebillard, *Christians and Their Many Identities*; Boin, *Coming Out Christian*; Sanzo, *Scriptural Incipits*; and Sanzo, "Magic and Communal Boundaries."
5. The bibliography on "magic" and the usefulness of this term is enormous. For a recent discussion, see Frankfurter, *Guide to the Study*, especially his opening essay, "Ancient Magic in a New Key." The notes in this chapter cite many other important contributions.
6. J. Z. Smith, "Trading Places," 21. Smith also adds that there are other collections of similar types of texts as well (21n15). For information on the Greek Magical Papyri, see Brashear, "Greek Magical Papyri." For a translation of *PGM* texts, see Betz, *Greek Magical Papyri*. For a helpful description of these texts as well as a recounting of the history of scholarship, see Dieleman, "Greco-Egyptian Magical Papyri."
7. Frankfurter, *Religion in Roman Egypt*, 224–37; Frankfurter, "Dynamics of Ritual Expertise"; Luijendijk, "Gospel Amulet."
8. J. Z. Smith, "Trading Places," 23–25.
9. Sanzo makes a similar point with respect to amulets (*Scriptural Incipits*, 13; *Ritual Boundaries*).
10. De Bruyn, *Making Amulets Christian*, 41. This is also the argument of Boyarin's *Border Lines*, which focuses primarily on the boundary-making between Christians and Jews. Joseph Sanzo's work argues against what he identifies as a widespread scholarly assumption that while Christian writers asserted boundaries, those practicing everyday religion blurred them. This assumption keeps us from seeing not only the importance of boundary construction in amulets and spells but also the different conceptualizations of Christianity that these suggest. See *Ritual Boundaries*, chapter 2, and further discussion of Sanzo's ideas below.
11. These treatises include, but are not limited to, *De idolatria*, *De spectaculis*, *De corona*, *De cultu feminarum*, *Ad nationes*, and *De anima*. See Rébillard, *Christians and Their Many Identities*, 20–21. I have chosen Tertullian here because the evidence is rich in his corpus, but his sentiments are echoed among other writers as well. Church canons, too, address boundary crossings with similar disapprobation. See Benga, "'Defining Sacred Boundaries,'" and de Bruyn, *Making Amulets Christian*, 34–41.
12. Latin: CSEL 20. Translation amended from *ANF 3* (Thelwall).
13. For a discussion of this practice, see Hvalvik, "Praying with Outstretched Hands," 64–72.
14. Latin: *De anima* (Waszink). Translation: *ANF* 3:219 (Holmes).
15. Tertullian does not comment here on how difficult it might be for subordinates to walk this fine line, unlike in *Ad uxorem*, where he is attentive to this tension for Christian wives married to unbelieving husbands (see *Ux.* 2.4 for an example).

16. This language is similar to the discourses that develop about Christians married to non-Christians by these same authors. See Johnson Hodge, "Mixed Marriage," and Cohen, "From Permission to Prohibition."

17. Latin: CSEL 20. Translation: *ANF* 3:64 (Thelwall).

18. Latin: CSEL 3.2, 248. Translation: *ANF* 5 (Wallis).

19. For discussions of the evidence from early Christian writers, see Thee, *Julius Africanus*, 316–448; Stander, "Amulets and the Church Fathers"; de Bruyn, *Making Amulets Christian*, 17–42; Sanzo, "Early Christianity," 226–37. For discussions of non-Christian views of magic, see the essays in part 2 of Frankfurter, *Guide to the Study*; Beard, North, and Price, *Religions of Rome*, 211–44; Aune, "Magic in Early Christianity," 377–84.

20. Justin: *First Apology* 14:1–3; 26:2, 4; 56:1; *Second Apology* 5.

21. *Against Heresies* 1.13.1; 1.23.1; 1.23.4; 1.23.5; 1.24.5; 1.25.3 (as just a sampling). See Thee, *Julius Africanus*, 367–86, and de Bruyn, *Making Amulets Christian*, 22, for more examples.

22. *Cels.* 1.6; 1:28. See Thee, *Julius Africanus*, 367–86.

23. Sanzo, "Early Christianity," 230.

24. *De amuletis* (PG 26:1320, section a). Cited by Stander, "Amulets and the Church Fathers," 63.

25. Latin: Tertullian, Minucius Felix (Rendall, LCL 250), 128. Translation: *ANF* 3:38 (Thelwall).

26. Note that Celsus accuses Jesus of being a magician, who, like others in the trade, "blow[s] away diseases (νόσους ἀποφυσώντων)" (Origen, *Cels.* 1.68). Greek: Koetschau, *Origenes Werke*, 122. Translation: *Contra Celsum* (Chadwick), 63. For more on this text, see chapter 2.

27. Greek: Koetschau, *Origenes Werke*, 59. Translation: *Contra Celsum* (Chadwick), 10.

28. For a similar comment, see Lactantius, *Manner in Which Persecutors Died*, 10. See also chapter 2 for a discussion of signing among believers.

29. John Chrysostom, *Homily 12 on 1 Corinthians* (on 1 Cor 4:6–10), section 13.

30. John Chrysostom, *Homily 12 on 1 Corinthians* (on 1 Cor 4:6–10), section 14. Greek: PG 61:106. Translation: *NPNF* 1/12 (Chambers).

31. John Chrysostom, *Homily 54 on Matthew*, section 7 (PG 58). Translation: *NPNF* 1/10 (Prevost and Riddle).

32. Antony instructs his ascetic followers to sign themselves and their dwellings to repel the ever-attacking demons (*Life of Antony* 13, 35, and 80). Jensen discusses this text in *Cross*, 36–37. For later examples of Christian symbols used for protection, see Maguire, Maguire, and Duncan-Flowers, *Art and Holy Powers*.

33. *Homily 12 on 1 Corinthians* (on 1 Cor 4:6–10), section 13.

34. MacMullen, *Christianizing the Roman Empire*, 77, and the general discussion on 74–85.

35. *Sermones* 286.7 (PL 38:1300–1301). Discussed and cited by de Bruyn, *Making Amulets Christian*, 27.

36. Severus of Antioch, *Homily* 79.S.

37. For an introduction to this figure, see Wallraff, *Iulius Africanus*, XII–XVII, and Thee, *Julius Africanus*, 1–3. Wallraff's volume also contains the Greek and English of *Chronographiae* (trans. Adler).

38. Adler notes that these are typical of his time period: "Cesti and Sophistic Culture," 11. Thee offers a translation of *Cesti*: see *Julius Africanus*, 102–92.

39. Adler, "Cesti and Sophistic Culture," 1.

40. See Thee, *Julius Africanus*, 11–101 (a survey of scholarship on Julius Africanus) and 449–67 (Thee's views of how Africanus fits into Christian thinking at the time).

41. Sanzo, "Early Christianity," 238.

42. Kotansky, "Early Christian Gold *Lamella*," 37.

43. Kotansky, "Early Christian Gold *Lamella*," 37–39.

44. For a discussion of different possible reconstructions of the text, alternative translations, and the identity of the demon, see Kotansky, "Early Christian Gold *Lamella*," 40–42.

45. Kotansky, "Early Christian Gold *Lamella*," 43. Kotansky views this as an independent counterpart to Paul's use of *doulos/doule* for believers.

46. For a study of Jewish tradition and "magic," see Bohak, *Ancient Jewish Magic*.

47. Kotansky raises the question of whether Jesus is being conflated with god here ("Early Christian Gold *Lamella*," 45).

48. Kotansky, "Two Amulets," 181.
49. Kotansky, "Two Amulets," 181.
50. Kotansky, "Two Amulets," 183.
51. Kotansky, "Two Amulets," 182.
52. Kotansky, "Two Amulets," 182–84.

53. Kotansky, *Greek Magical Amulets*, 169. Kotansky discusses his rendering of the inscription (which differs from Robinson's first edition) on 170. For the name of the demon here, Phoathphro, and for a discussion of "her [*sic*] angels," see 171–73.
54. Kotansky, *Greek Magical Amulets*, 172 and excursus on 174–80.
55. Chepel, "Invocations," 69–70.
56. Chepel, "Invocations," 70.
57. Evil spirits: Cyril of Jerusalem, *Mystagogica* 1.3. Demons: Chrysostom, *Homiliae in Joannem* 46.3. Both are cited in Chepel, "Invocations," 65–66.
58. Trnka-Amrhein, "Seal of the Living God," 87 (measurements), 88–89 (photos).
59. Trnka-Amrhein, "Seal of the Living God," 91. Although one similar hand dates to 372, others belong to earlier in the century.
60. Trnka-Amrhein, "Seal of the Living God," 96.
61. Trnka-Amrhein, "Seal of the Living God," 92–93. See Trnka-Amrhein's article for a thorough discussion of the symbolism of these markings and their parallels.
62. Trnka-Amrhein, "Seal of the Living God," 98. For a discussion of the use of multiple modes of communication on amulets, see Sanzo, *Ritual Boundaries*, 65–88.
63. Trnka-Amrhein, "Seal of the Living God," 104.
64. *Apostolic Tradition* 41.14.
65. Trnka-Amrhein also makes this point: "The amulet appears to have been designed to continue the cleansing and protection received at baptism into everyday life and assert a saving Christian identity" ("Seal of the Living God," 104).
66. M. Smith, "Jewish Elements," 245.
67. Boustan and Sanzo, "Christian Magicians," 239. See also Sanzo's development of these ideas in *Ritual Boundaries*.
68. Frankfurter, *Christianizing Egypt*, 15–25 (and see the introduction for a discussion of Frankfurter's use of this term).
69. Boustan and Sanzo, "Christian Magicians," 239. This article and Sanzo's later work, *Ritual Boundaries*, have been helpful to me in thinking about these issues. Sanzo has offered an important corrective to the tendency of scholars to assert that those practicing everyday religion were not concerned with boundaries (*Ritual Boundaries*, chap. 2). His work has shown that this is not necessarily true, at least in some examples. There is value to recognizing that boundary-making takes place in multiple modes of religious practice; it helps us see different configurations of what Christianity is (as they argue and as I am arguing in this chapter). I am still open to the possibility, however, that many people who followed Christ did not perceive this as something that was particularly bounded. I would like to hold that as a possibility as we rethink our categories.
70. See the British Museum website for catalogue entry BM 1986,0501.1: https://www.britishmuseum.org/collection/object/H_1986-0501-1. Originally in the private collection of Roger Pereire, the British Museum acquired the gem in 1986. It was first published by Philippe Derchain in 1964 in "Die älteste Darstellung." See also Delatte and Derchain, *Les intailles magiques gréco-égyptiennes*.
71. For more examples of possibly Christian symbols on gems, see Spier, *Late Antique*, 81–86, and the corresponding catalogue numbers for images. Spier does not give dates for most items, although he makes a blanket statement at the beginning of the chapter about "magical amulets engraved on gemstones, most of which belong to the second and third centuries" (81). A handful seem to belong to the third and fourth centuries (82–83), and another group to the fifth century (84). Only two gems with dates explicitly noted land in our period: #477 (p. 84) and #443 (our bloodstone gem, p. 81 and also p. 73).
72. Harley-McGowan and Spier, "Magical Amulet with Crucifixion," including bibliography. Harley-McGowan, "Images," 131n520 for sources. In the fall of 2020, through personal communication, Felicity Harley-McGowan commented that she remains convinced of this early date.
73. Harley-McGowan, "Images," 131–32; Harley-McGowan and Spier, "Magical Amulet with Crucifixion."
74. Harley-McGowan, "Constanza Carnelian," 217.
75. Harley-McGowan, "Constanza Carnelian," 217. See also Derchain, "Die älteste Darstellung."
76. Kotansky, "Magic 'Crucifixion Gem,'" 644–45. Kotansky argues that this form of the word cannot refer to the act of hanging (Derchain's "hung up") because "feminine nouns in -ανη are always instrumental nouns"

(644 and note 21). Instead, it likely refers to a suspension device, which on this gem means the crossbeam (644–45). Sanzo makes this point in *Ritual Boundaries*, 101 and 139n65.

77. Sources for text and translation of both the obverse and reverse: Kotansky, "Magic Crucifixion Gem," 636; Harley-McGowan and Spier, "Magical Amulet with Crucifixion," 228.

78. Kotansky, "Magic 'Crucifixion Gem,'" 648 and note 27. Kotansky hypothesizes that a different drilling instrument was used and also notes that the letters have different forms, indicating a different artisan.

79. Iadêtophô/th, which likely means Badetopthoth: Kotansky, "Magic 'Crucifixion Gem,'" 650; Kotansky identifies this as the god of the second hour in *Greek Magical Amulets*, 335. The second name is A/straperkmê/th, which refers to Satraperkmeph (Kotansky, "Magic 'Crucifixion Gem,'" 651; Sanzo, *Ritual Boundaries*, 101). According to Brashear, Satraperkmeph refers to the Egyptian "Great Satrap Kmeph" (Brashear, "Greek Magical Papyri," 3598). See also Harley-McGowan and Spier, "Magical Amulet with Crucifixion."

80. Kotansky, "Magic 'Crucifixion Gem,'" 651 (sources cited here document other gems with this name). Biblical references to Emmanuel are Isaiah 7:14 and Matthew 1:23. Kotansky remarks that the name is here written as an "angel-name" and that its poor spelling is evidence of a non-Christian writer (651, notes to lines 5–6).

81. Sanzo explains that crucifixion does not necessarily involve piercing but could also be done by tying the victim to the cross (*Ritual Boundaries*, 101 and 140n69).

82. Jensen, *Cross*, 10.

83. Harley-McGowan suggests a pendant rather than a ring because of its size ("Images," 132). Kotansky maintains that the chipped portions suggest its original setting in a ring ("Magic 'Crucifixion Gem,'" 635). See Bonner, *Studies in Magical Amulets*, 8–10, for a discussion of stones, sizes, and settings.

84. In "Engineering Ancient Amulets," Nagy describes this scenario not specifically for this gem but for "magical gems" in general.

85. Harley-McGowan, "Constanza Carnelian," 216.

86. Harley-McGowan, "Constanza Carnelian," 218, and Yarbrough, "Alexamenos Graffito." Harley-McGowan offers the imperative translation "Alexamenos, worship god" (218), while Yarbrough favors the third person ("Alexamenos worships god," 233).

87. We might also note a graffito from Pozzuoli, which depicts a woman being crucified with the same splayed-leg position. This image, which was found on a shop wall among beast-fighting scenes, might have been an advertisement for the games. See Jensen, *Cross*, 11; Cook, "Crucifixion as Spectacle"; and Chapman, *Ancient Jewish and Christian Perceptions*, 92–98. Harley-McGowan mentions two additional possible companion pieces. The first is a hematite gem in the Metropolitan Museum of Art showing a man with wrists bound in front of him, second–fourth century (Harley-McGowan, "Images," 140, 263–65, and plate 17c); Bonner discusses the possibility that the figure is Christ (*Studies in Magical Amulets*, 112, 224, 278 [#154]). The second is the Köln gem from the second century, with the same symbols as the Metropolitan gem (Harley-McGowan, "Images," 140). If Bonner is right that the Metropolitan gem is an image of Christ, then we see a trend of the sufferings of Christ on magical gems for prophylactic purposes in the second and third centuries (Harley-McGowan, "Images," 140).

88. Depictions of Christ's death are rare before the sixth century; those we do have appear on other intaglios or on sarcophagi and often show the procession of apostles, a halo over Christ's head, or a fairly lively looking body on a cross. They do not portray the same kind of humiliation we see on the bloodstone gem (Jensen, *Cross*, 74–82). See also Jensen, *Understanding Early Christian Art*, 130–37; Harley-McGowan, "Constanza Carnelian," 214–18.

89. Sheckler and Leith make this suggestion in "Crucifixion Conundrum," 74–75. For a discussion of these two interpretations of the crucifixion, triumphant and shameful, see Sanzo, *Ritual Boundaries*, 89–108.

90. Harley-McGowan, "Images," 132.

91. Harley-McGowan, "Images," 133.

92. Harley-McGowan, "Images," 121.

93. Harley-McGowan and Spier, "Magical Amulet with Crucifixion."

94. Harley-McGowan, "Images," 131: "Whilst it cannot be classified as a specifically Christian devotional representation, the image and the text within which it operates does illustrate a perception of the crucified Jesus' power that extends beyond the parameters of

Christianity in Late Antiquity . . . this tension between magical and Christian expressions of Jesus' power" is characteristic of the cohort of gems to which this one belongs.

95. Longenecker, *Cross Before Constantine*, 104. Longenecker's mention of "those whose religious allegiance was not restricted to a monotheistic form of Christianity" anticipates my argument below.

96. Harley-McGowan and Spier, "Magical Amulet with Crucifixion." See also Harley-McGowan, "Images," 137, and "Constanza Carnelian," 218.

97. Harley-McGowan and Spier note that the idea that Christ overcame the brutality of the cross and defeated evil draws from biblical references. They cite Mk 9:38–41, Lk 9:49–50, and Acts 19:13–17 for examples of Jesus's name being used "for magical purposes" ("Magical Amulet with Crucifixion," 229); in Acts 4:10, too, Peter heals a cripple in name of Christ "whom you crucified," whom God raised from the dead (229). It is important to be cautious about the complex relationship between different kinds of evidence and how we make assumptions that our textual evidence can help us interpret material evidence. Scholars of Christianity in particular tend to treat textual evidence, especially canonical texts, as a reliable representation of "true" Christianity and then use that to interpret other types of evidence. See the discussion in Hijmans, "Language, Metaphor." Such a practice is especially problematic because not all texts agree on how to interpret the crucifixion. The Coptic Apocalypse of Peter, for example, mocks those who believe in the one being put to death on the cross, the "substitute" for the Savior (CAP 81; translation from Ehrman, *After the New Testament*, 229). See also Sanzo, *Ritual Boundaries*, 106.

98. Kotansky, "Magic 'Crucifixion Gem,'" 636, 647–48. Kotansky, who states in his article that he examined photos of the gem (634), reconstructs lines 8–9 of the obverse as "*lusiou huiou*" (redeeming son). His overall reading is that "some Christian group is representing on a gem a genuinely early Crucifixion image along with the invocation of an unorthodox Trinitarian formula, a 'secret' anagrammatic soteriological slogan, mystical and vocalic names of God, and a non-biblical acclamation of the very cross upon which the redemptive figure of Jesus is shown to be hanging" (655).

99. Sanzo questions Kotansky's reconstruction of line 8 based on his own in-person examination of the gem. Sanzo saw no sign of a mark that would indicate a lambda as the first letter (*Ritual Boundaries*, 140–41n79; discussion of Kotansky's theory on 102).

100. Harley-McGowan, "Picturing the Passion," 291.

101. Longenecker, *Cross Before Constantine*, 104.

102. Harley-McGowan, "Images," 133, citing Kotansky, who writes: "It is simply wrongheaded to suspect the piety of the person using an abbreviated prayer formula simply because it is found in the context of an otherwise entirely 'magical' ritual" ("Incantations and Prayers," 122). Kotansky also talks about the difficulties of distinguishing among the categories we have set up (such as magic and religion), and he remarks that this should cause us to rethink our categories (122).

103. Harley-McGowan and Spier, "Magical Amulet with Crucifixion."

104. Harley-McGowan writes that not all believers would have had "qualms about seeing the tormented body of Jesus that certain of his followers no doubt had" ("Images," 141).

105. See the introduction for an initial discussion of Frankfurter, and below for further comments.

106. Harley-McGowan, "Images," 134.

107. Sheckler and Leith, "Crucifixion Conundrum," 72n19; see also Maguire, "Magic and the Christian Image," 64.

108. Boustan and Sanzo, "Christian Magicians," 234. See Sanzo's development of this argument in *Ritual Boundaries*, chapter 2, where he argues that those practicing lived religion, as illustrated by amulets and spells, were not necessarily blending traditions but creating different kinds of boundaries than other Christ followers.

109. See Nagy, "Engineering Ancient Amulets," for a description of the different types of labor that would have gone into creating an amulet like this.

110. "Magic and Communal Boundaries," 246.

111. Sheckler and Leith, "Crucifixion Conundrum," 72n19. Crucifixion was sexually humiliating, rendering the crucified body as vulnerable, naked, and feminized: Moore, "'Oh Man, Who Art Thou?,'" 11. Other studies

that make this point are Tombs, "Lived Religion"; Tombs, "Crucifixion, State Terror." Harley-McGowan points out that the brutality of the image "should be seen as integral to the magical nature of the gem" ("Images," 140).

112. Sheckler and Leith argue that the shame associated with crucifixion accounts for its absence in art ("Crucifixion Conundrum," 74). Harley-McGowan disagrees with this point in "Jesus the Magician," 106. Jensen, *Understanding Early Christian Art*, 133–36, discusses theories for the absence of crucifixion. Conway charts how the Deutero and Pastoral Epistles turn Paul's crucified Christ into a reigning emperor figure: *Behold the Man*, 67–88. For helpful studies of Roman-period crucifixion, see Cook, *Crucifixion in the Mediterranean World*, and Chapman, *Ancient Jewish and Christian Perceptions*.

113. Sanzo, *Ritual Boundaries*, 102.

114. Sanzo, *Ritual Boundaries*, 99–108. The following discussion of evidence for the "restless dead" relies in large part on Sanzo's research.

115. Johnston, *Restless Dead*.

116. See *PGM* II.166; *PGM* IV.1928–2005, at l. 1950; *PGM* IV.2145–2240; *PGM* V.73–74 (cited by Sanzo, *Ritual Boundaries*, 104).

117. Pliny, *Natural History* 28.11.46; Lucan, *Pharsalia / De bello civili* 6.547; Apuleius, *Metamorphoses* 3.17; Lucian, *Philopsuedes sive incredulus* ["The Liar" or "The Lover of Lies"] 17.

118. *Natural History* 28.11.46. Latin and English translation: Pliny, *Natural History* (Jones, LCL 18), 34–35.

119. See *m.Šabb.* 6:10. Translation and Hebrew in Chapman, *Ancient Jewish and Christian Perceptions*, 182. Sanzo, citing Chapman (182–84), comments that "this passage betrays a knowledge of the magical use of crucifixion nails and probably reflects a practice among certain Jews" (*Ritual Boundaries*, 144n108). See Sanzo's note 108 and other sources cited there for a discussion of the role of crosses in Jewish practices and the possible connection to the power of crucifixion (note that how these crosses are used is debated). For a study of the ritual power of nails on *defixiones* (curse tablets), see Nasrallah, "Work of Nails."

120. See Stowers, *History and the Study* and *Christian Beginnings*, as well as my discussion in the introduction.

121. Frankfurter, *Christianizing Egypt*, 2. Frankfurter argues for a redefinition and resuscitation of the term "syncretism" so that it signals this process, or multiple processes, of integrating traditional symbols with Christian ones (15). I would argue that one important characteristic of this process is the lack of intentionality or central organization. The impulse to combine symbols in new ways is rooted in local tradition and wisdom.

122. Frankfurter, *Christianizing Egypt*, 6.

123. Frankfurter, *Christianizing Egypt*, 17.

124. Luijendijk, "Gospel Amulet," 419.

125. Boin, *Ostia in Late Antiquity*, 36–37.

126. Boin, *Ostia in Late Antiquity*, 37.

127. Sanzo, *Scriptural Incipits*, 12–14.

128. Frankfurter discusses a similar point in *Religion in Roman Egypt*, 267–72.

129. This is one of Frankfurter's arguments in *Christianizing Egypt*, 38 and passim.

130. Canon 36 (traditionally this has been identified as part of the Synod of Laodicea; see de Bruyn, *Making Amulets Christian*, 39, and Sanzo, "Early Christianity," 222). Greek: Mansi, *Sacrorum Conciliorum Nova*. Translation: *NPNF* 2/14, 216. This canon and others after it are discussed by Graf, "Christian Transformation of Magic," 304–5, and Sanzo, "Magic and Communal Boundaries," 227–29. For the argument that clerics are involved in spells and amulets, see Luijendijk, "Gospel Amulet," 428–29. For a discussion of this phenomenon more generally, see Frankfurter, "Dynamics of Ritual Expertise."

Chapter 4

1. *Moralia* I.140d. Greek and English translation: Pomeroy, *Plutarch's "Advice,"* 20 (Greek), 7 (English).

2. And in most cases, the wife would remain outside the *familia* of her husband. By the time Plutarch is writing, most marriages recorded in Roman law were without *manus*, meaning that the wife did not technically join the husband's *familia* or come under his power; she stayed under her father's power. See J. Gardner, *Family and Familia*, 209–10; Treggiari, *Roman Marriage*, 32–35.

3. Sessa makes the point that although the head of the household is in charge, dependents often implement the rituals: *Formation of Papal Authority*, 12 (and notes cited there). We find instances of husbands directing wives in matters of domestic cult in

the comedy of Plautus, *Trinummus*, lines 39–42, and *Rudens*, lines 1206–1208 (my thanks to Mandy Wall for these references). For the expectation that enslaved household members would prepare for and enact domestic worship, see the discussion of Cato below. For the ways women might become ritual agents through daily tasks such as weaving or grinding, see Frankfurter, "'As I Twirl This Spindle.'"

4. See Crenshaw, "Demarginalizing." See also discussion and critique in Hancock, "Intersectionality"; Hancock, "Multiplication"; McCall, "Complexity of Intersectionality"; and Nash, "Re-thinking Intersectionality." Among the suggestions in these essays is the important call to move away from essentializing identities by thinking in terms of interlocking and multiplicative models of intersectionality rather than additive ones. I agree with Brooten and Shaner that this can be usefully applied to the ancient world if contextualized carefully. Brooten, "Enslaved Women," and Shaner, *Enslaved Leadership*.

5. The status of a wife in a marriage could vary widely depending on a number of factors: whether she is under the power of her husband or father, the size of her dowry, the position of her natal family, or whether she has legal independence when entering the marriage. See Treggiari, *Roman Marriage*; Dixon, *Roman Mother*; J. Gardner, *Family and Familia*; Saller, *Patriarchy, Property and Death*.

6. "Intimate outsider" is a phrase used by Stichele and Penner in *Contextualizing Gender*, 70. Working with a similar understanding related just to slaves, Harrill uses the term "domestic enemy" in *Slaves in the New Testament*, 145–63. Also on the *Controversiae*, see Connolly, "Mastering Corruption"; Parker, "Loyal Slaves"; P. Clark, "Women, Slaves."

7. Connolly, "Mastering Corruption."

8. Bell, *Ritual Theory*. Bell uses "ritualization" instead of "ritual" to signal a more open and dynamic way of understanding ritual. It is more of a process than a clearly bounded event, and it involves the privileging of certain daily activities in a particular context.

9. Bell, *Ritual Theory*, 204.

10. Bell, *Ritual Theory*, 216.

11. Castelli also makes this point in "Interpretations of Power," 203.

12. Bell, *Ritual Theory*, 211. She talks about this as "misrecognition" (108–10, 114–17). See also the work of de Certeau, *Practice of Everyday Life*.

13. Schüssler Fiorenza, "Exploring," 17 (emphasis in original).

14. Schüssler Fiorenza, "Exploring," 17 (emphasis in original).

15. Schüssler Fiorenza, "Exploring," 17.

16. The idea of multiple selves has been explored by different scholars. Meeks borrows the phrase "status inconsistency" from sociologists to discuss a similar phenomenon (*First Urban Christians*, 22–23). More recently, see Lahire, "From the Habitus to Heritage," 348; Rebillard, "Material Culture." See also Rebillard's *Christians and Their Many Identities*. For my own previous work on multiple identities, see Johnson Hodge, *If Sons, Then Heirs*, 117–35, and "Apostle to the Gentiles."

17. Butler, *Bodies That Matter*, 95.

18. Butler, *Bodies That Matter*, 108.

19. A. Allen, *Power of Feminist Theory*, 72.

20. For a volume that explores similar interactions between power and ritual in households and other contexts, see Dillon, Eidinow, and Maurizio, *Women's Ritual Competence*.

21. V. Brown, "Social Death," 1246. Brown objects to Patterson's notion of "social death" as a description of slave existence: "Surely they must have found some way to turn the 'disorganization, instability, and chaos' of slavery into collective forms of belonging and striving, making connections when confronted with alienation and finding dignity in the face of dishonor" (1236; Brown quotes Trevor Burnard, *Mastery, Tyranny, and Desire* [Chapel Hill: University of North Carolina Press, 2009], 179). I am grateful for Shaner's *Enslaved Leadership*, which led me to Brown's work and other sources in this discussion.

22. W. Johnson, "On Agency." Johnson challenges the notion that enslaved people could have something like "agency," to the extent that agency entails something like free will to act or an autonomous notion of the self. He also critiques the use of "agency" with respect to Black slaves as a white framing: white scholars give slaves their agency.

23. V. Brown, "Social Death," 1231–32.

24. V. Brown, "Social Death," 1241.

25. V. Brown, "Social Death," 1246.

26. These scholars draw upon anthropological approaches to space such as

those explored in Bourdieu, "Berber House," and Lefebvre, *Production of Space*.

27. Cooper, "Closely Watched Households," 9.

28. Sessa, "Christianity and the *Cubiculum*," 176.

29. Treggiari, *Roman Marriage*, 169; J. Clarke, *Houses of Roman Italy*, 10; Harmon, "Family Festivals," 1599–1600. See Pomeroy's important caution about conflating Athenian and late-Republican evidence, especially regarding the issue of whether brides left the gods of their natal households (presumably their fathers') in order to pledge loyalty to their husbands' gods (*Families*, 70–71).

30. McNamara, "Gendering Virtue," 154–55. See also MacDonald, *Early Christian Women*, 49–126.

31. Orr, "Roman Domestic Religion"; Harmon, "Family Festivals," 1595.

32. See Lott, *Neighborhoods of Augustan Rome*; Flower, *Dancing Lares*; Tybout, "Domestic Shrines," 370; Beard, North, and Price, *Religions of Rome*, 184–85. On the relationship between the imperial cult and households, see Gradel, *Emperor Worship*, 198–212.

33. We find this thinking in Plato (*Laws* 3.690a–d) and Aristotle (*Politics* 1.1260a 9–14). See Balch, *Let Wives Be Submissive*, 63–116, for how later moralists continue this thinking.

34. Pomeroy, *Xenophon*, 69–73.

35. Greek and translation from Pomeroy, *Xenophon*, 138–39.

36. Similar elite values are expressed centuries after Xenophon by Hierocles, a second-century CE Stoic proponent of marriage, who argues that "the beauty of a household consists in the yoking together of a husband and wife who are united to each other by fate, are consecrated to the gods who preside over weddings, births and hearths ... who exercise appropriate rule over their household and servants, take care in rearing their children, and pay attention to the necessities of life" (*On Duties: On Marriage* 4.22.21–24); translation from *Moral Exhortation* (Malherbe), 102. Greek (in Stobaeus): Wachsmuth and Hense, *Ioannis Stobaei Anthologium*. In this passage, Hierocles focuses less on gender hierarchy in order to foreground the notion of unity of the husband and wife—a unity determined by fate and consecrated by the gods—in all facets of household life. See Sessa, *Formation of Papal Authority*, 9–14, for a discussion of the importance of household management and the development of the position of Christian bishops.

37. Reay, "Agriculture." Reay calls this dynamic "masterly extensability" (339).

38. Latin and English translation (amended) from Cato and Varro, *On Agriculture* (Hooper, LCL 283), 123–25.

39. Elsewhere Cato counsels limitations on the religious activities of the *vilicus* as well: "He must not get involved in any religious activities except those at the crossroads during the festival of the Compitalia, and those at the household hearth" (*De agricultura* 5). Latin: Cato and Varro, *On Agriculture* (Hooper, LCL 283), 14–16; translation: Wiedemann, *Greek and Roman Slavery*, 149. See also Columella, who writes about the *vilicus*: "He must not make any religious sacrifices except if the master has told him to" (*De re rustica* 1.8.5). Columella continues by counseling the *vilicus* to forbid fortune tellers and sorcerers from coming on the farm, calling these "silly superstition" (1.8.6). Latin: Columella, *On Agriculture* (Ash, LCL 361), 86–87. Translation: Wiedemann, *Greek and Roman Slavery*, 142.

40. Padilla Peralta discusses this tension in "Slave Religiosity," 333.

41. Cooper describes the importance of the reciprocal (if asymmetrical) power in the Roman household in "Closely Watched Households," 7. See Kraemer, *Unreliable Witnesses*, 267 and passim, for a similar assessment of how gender and religion intersect.

42. This is an interesting encounter to think about, because Paul is a Jew writing to non-Jews about interactions with the god of Israel and how this affects their daily lives (especially as they await the return of the messiah). In chapter 1, I discuss Jewish households and the extent to which they might be similar or different from other types of households. See also Hezser, *Oxford Handbook*; Magness, *Stone and Dung*; Satlow, *Jewish Marriage in Antiquity*.

43. See my study of Paul's influence on later writers on this topic: Johnson Hodge, "Mixed Marriage."

44. For a discussion of the interpretive options, see Johnson Hodge, "Married to an Unbeliever," and the scholarship cited there.

45. Castelli, "Paul on Women and Gender." See also the studies by M. Mitchell (*Paul and the Rhetoric*, esp. 121–23) and Nasrallah (*Ecstasy of Folly*, 78–79).

46. On the issue of slave marriage and family ties, see Glancy, *Slavery in Early Christianity*, 28, 45–46; Edmondson, "Slavery and the Roman Family"; Treggiari, "*Contubernales* in *CIL* 6"; Martin, *Slavery as Salvation*, 2–7; and Flory, "Family in *Familia*."

47. "20 ἕκαστος ἐν τῇ κλήσει ᾗ ἐκλήθη ἐν ταύτῃ μενέτω. 21 Δοῦλος ἐκλήθης ; μή σοι μελέτω · ἀλλ' εἰ καὶ δύνασαι ἐλεύθερος γενέσθαι, μᾶλλον χρῆσαι." Translation amended from NRSV.

48. Harrill, *Manumission of Slaves*; Glancy, *Slavery in Early Christianity*, 67–69; Shaner, *Enslaved Leadership*, 44–66.

49. Shaner encourages readers to think about how enslaved believers—who occupy complicated subject positions—would have heard this Pauline passage; see *Enslaved Leadership*, 44–56.

50. Nasrallah suggests that this slave market language might have prompted some to see their owners as commodities: "You Were Bought," 73.

51. It is ironic that 1 Corinthians serves as a resource for later Christian intellectuals who forbid marriage with an unbeliever. To do so, they draw from the notion of contagious pollution in 1 Cor 6, as well as from Paul's advice to widows in 7:39, to reframe mixed marriage as *porneia* (Johnson Hodge, "Mixed Marriage").

52. Note that the author does not make explicit that the slaves being addressed are in non-Christian households, but most assume this to be the case. Johnson Hodge, "'Holy Wives,'" 10.

53. *Hypotassō* also occurs in 3:5, 3:22, and 5:5. As Elliott points out, this is a "term of thematic significance" in this letter: *1 Peter*, 486.

54. Whether this verse hints at physical danger for the wife of an unbeliever is debated. For example, see Schüssler Fiorenza, who argues that this verse has the wife's safety in mind (*In Memory of Her*, 262). Elliott disagrees (*1 Peter*, 584).

55. MacDonald's discussion of this passage has been helpful to me: *Early Christian Women*, 195–204. Thinking along the same lines, she uses the phrase "quiet evangelist" (195).

56. A. Allen, *Power of Feminist Theory*, 72.

57. Johnson Hodge, "Mixed Marriage," 234–37.

58. Latin: *À son épouse* (Munier). Translation amended from Le Saint, *Tertullian*, 28.

59. I have discussed this issue elsewhere: Johnson Hodge, "Married to an Unbeliever" and "'Holy Wives.'" Daniel Ullucci points out that the head of the household is one kind of religious expert. The householder would have been responsible for overseeing the religious practices of the household, thus maintaining the reciprocal relationship between the gods and that household group and all of its production ("Toward a Typology," 96–97).

60. Johnson Hodge, "Daily Devotions," 52–53.

61. As I discuss in the introduction, it is tricky to glean historical evidence for daily practices from moralists and other intellectuals whose goal is to persuade rather than to describe. I maintain it is possible to do so carefully, taking into account the rhetorical aims of the author.

62. "[3] *Latebisne tu, cum lectulum, cum corpusculum tuum signas, cum aliquid immundum flatu explodis, cum etiam per noctem exurgis oratum? Et non magiae aliquid uideberis operari? Non sciet maritus quid secreto ante omnem cibum gustes? Et si sciuerit panem, non illum credet esse, qui dicitur?* [4] *Et haec ignorans quisque rationem simpliciter sustinebit sine gemitu, sine suspicione panis an ueneni?*" Latin: *À son épouse* (Munier). Translation: Le Saint, *Tertullian*, 30.

63. For a helpful source on gesture in the Roman period, especially as it is used in ritual and healing, see Corbeill, *Nature Embodied*. See also my discussion of prayer and gesture in chapter 2. Other sources on ancient gesture are Bremmer and Roodenburg, *Cultural History of Gesture*; Clark, Foster, and Hallett, *Kinesis*; and Boschung, Shapiro, and Wascheck, *Bodies in Transition*.

64. Dix imagines that a slave would have to keep the bread on his person, perhaps in a pocket: *Detection of Aumbries*, 11.

65. Le Saint, *Tertullian*, 129n117. See chapter 2.

66. *Apostolic Tradition* 41.17. Latin: Tidner, *Didascaliae apostolorum*, 146–47. Translation: Bradshaw, Johnson, and Phillips, *Apostolic Tradition*, 198, 200. See discussion in chapter 2.

67. Water is associated with a variety of actions in early Christian baptism, such as ushering in the holy spirit, cleansing of sins, purifying the initiate, exorcising unwanted spirits, protecting the body of the believer, and offering new life (harking back to Genesis). See Jensen, "Baptismal Rites and

Architecture," 118–24, on the symbolism of water specifically. Jensen cites Tertullian's *De baptismo*, which argues for the necessity of water for an authentic baptism. See also Burns and Jensen, *Christianity in Roman Africa*, 165–231.

68. Note that elsewhere Tertullian objects strenuously to women (who might use Thecla's example in the Acts of Paul) baptizing themselves (*Bapt.* 17).

69. The eucharist was not uniform in the early centuries of its practice, although there were some elements that were fairly consistent (McGowan, *Ancient Christian Worship*, 19–64). See also D. Smith, *From Symposium to Eucharist*; Smith and Taussig, *Meals*; Taussig, *In the Beginning*; and my discussion in chapter 2.

70. Borrowing a concept from anthropology, Corbeill refers to apotropaic gestures as "participatory," which signals that they are understood to influence reality (*Embodied Nature*, 31).

71. Greek: Lipsius and Bonnet, *Acta apostolorum apocrypha*, 1:250.

72. Tertullian also mentions that this gesture is used to protect against the sting of a scorpion (*Scorp.* 1.3). See chapter 3 for further discussion.

73. Latin: Tidner, *Didascaliae apostolorum*, 149–50. Translation: Bradshaw, Johnson, and Phillips, *Apostolic Tradition*, 216.

74. It is also possible that these are concerns shared more by the intellectuals trying to create boundaries around Christianity (see chapter 3). We find a similar sentiment expressed in a story told by Justin Martyr, in which a Christian wife struggles in her marriage to a non-Christian husband. She eventually divorces him, according to Justin, so that she does not have to "participate in his wrongful and impious acts by continuing to live with him by sharing his table and his bed" (*Second Apology* 2.1–6). Greek: Goodspeed, *Die ältesten Apologeten*, 79. English translation amended from Falls, *Saint Justin Martyr*, 120. Note also the *Apostolic Tradition*, which recommends moving to another room for your nocturnal prayers if your spouse is an unbeliever (41:11–12).

75. *Epistle to the Ephesians* 20.2: "φάρμακον ἀθανασίας, ἀντίδοτος τοῦ μὴ ἀποθανεῖν." Greek and English translation: *Apostolic Fathers*, vol. 1 (Lake, LCL 24), 194 (Greek), 195 (English). Bradshaw notes that this language might echo that found in "magical papyri" (Bradshaw, Johnson, and Phillips, *Apostolic Tradition*, 181). For more on the relationship between Christian and non-Christian protective language, see chapter 3.

76. Latin: Tidner, *Didascaliae apostolorum*, 143. Translation: Bradshaw, Johnson, and Phillips, *Apostolic Tradition*, 180.

77. Latin: PL 4:480. Translation: *ANF* 5:444.

78. Bradshaw, Johnson, and Phillips, *Apostolic Tradition*, 181; Bowes, *Private Worship*, 77.

79. *Oration to Gorgonia* 18 (*Oration* 8.18). Other fourth- and fifth-century authors also refer to the bread as protective. Ambrose recounts a believer using the bread for help in a shipwreck; note that the story depends upon the assumption that people will have the bread with them (*De excessu fratris sui Satyri* 1.43). Augustine describes how the bread is used to rid a house of evil spirits (*De civitate Dei* xxii.8). See Dix, *Detection of Aumbries*, 52–53, and Freestone, *Sacrament Reserved*, 25n2.

80. My thanks to Katherine Shaner for this observation about self-administering the bread.

81. Bell, *Ritual Theory*, 216.

82. Bell, *Ritual Theory*, 204.

83. Joshel, *Work, Identity*, 3–24; Joshel and Petersen, *Material Life*, 1–23; Forsdyke, *Slaves and Slavery*; Padilla Peralta, "Slave Religiosity." I am especially indebted to Katherine Shaner's *Enslaved Leadership* for offering a model for handling slavery in Christian contexts (xx–xxi and passim).

84. For example, Celsus writes in the second century: "Their injunctions are like this. 'Let no one educated, no one wise, no one sensible draw near. For these abilities are thought by us to be evils. But as for anyone ignorant, anyone stupid, anyone uneducated, anyone who is a child, let him come boldly.' By the fact that they themselves admit that these people are worthy of their God, they show that they want and are able to convince only the foolish, dishonorable and stupid, and only slaves, women and little children" (Origen, *Cels.* 3.44; Celsus's work, *The True Doctrine*, is preserved in Origen's third-century refutation). Greek: Koetschau, *Origenes Werke*, 239–40. Translation: *Contra Celsum* (Chadwick), 158. This accusation is reminiscent of the stereotypes about slaves and wives found in

the *Controversiae* literature discussed earlier in the chapter.

85. See Col 3:22–25; Eph 6:5–8; 1 Tim 6:1–2; Titus 2:9–10.

86. Greek and English translation from Bradshaw, Johnson, and Phillips, using the Sahidic version here (*Apostolic Tradition*, 82; Bradshaw discusses the complexity of this version of the text on p. 8). See the similar advice given in *Apostolic Constitutions* 8.32.26. A non-Christian parallel to this is found in Aelius Marcianus (third century), *Digest* 47.22.3.2, which states that a slave could be a member of a collegium with the owner's consent (cited by North, "Ritual Activity of Roman Slaves," 73). The *Apostolic Constitutions* also advises giving slaves time to rest on the Sabbath (8.33).

87. Indeed, the advent of Christianity does not change much about the institution of slavery, which was entrenched in the economy and social hierarchies of the Roman world. See Glancy, "Slavery and the Rise."

88. Although see evidence cited by North and McKeown for slave membership in collegia, specifically one document (*CIL* XIV 2112 II.1–5) that grants the collegium the right to give a funeral for an enslaved member even if the masters do not relinquish the body: North, "Ritual Activity of Roman Slaves," 74, and McKeown, "Magic, Religion," 290.

89. Bömer, *Untersuchungen über die Religion der Sklaven*.

90. Bodel, "Cicero's Minerva"; North, "Ritual Activity of Roman Slaves" (note North's disagreement over whether slaves had their own *Di Manes*, 77–79); McKeown, "Magic, Religion"; Eidinow, *Oracles, Curses, and Risk*; Harrill, "Servile Functionaries"; Bakker, *Living and Working*, 118–33, 195–203, 243–50; Dorcey, *Cult of Silvanus*; Forsdyke, *Slaves and Slavery*, 181–88. Padilla Peralta argues for a specific "slave religiosity," shaped both by involvement in the rituals of the master and by the restrictions placed on enslaved people ("Slave Religiosity").

91. McKeown, "Magic, Religion," 290.

92. Foss, "Watchful *Lares*," 218; Tybout, "Domestic Shrines," 367–70; George, "*Servus* and *Domus*," 316–17; George, "Slavery and Roman Material Culture," 391; George, "Lives of Slaves," 540; George, "Repopulating the Roman House," 316–17; Edmondson, "Slavery and the Roman Family," 344–45; Bodel, "Cicero's Minerva." Others have argued, however, that family members may have come to the service areas to worship, so the religious practices in the household were not necessarily segregated (Balch, "Rich Pompeian Houses"). Joshel and Petersen describe a shrine possibly dedicated by a slave in the garden of the House of Sutoria Primigenia in Pompeii (I.13.2), which held a statuette of Minerva with an inscription on its base. The authors observe that this is not in a service area but next to a dining area, which would have been used by the slave owner and his guests. They note, however, that there is disagreement over whether the inscription refers to an enslaved person (*Material Life*, 78). Temporal considerations also figure into this discussion, as slaves had access to different spaces when owners were not at home. See Joshel and Petersen, *Material Life*, 191–95.

93. Foss, "Watchful *Lares*," 211–16.

94. Bodel, "Cicero's Minerva," 265.

95. See Allison's cautions about this theory in *Pompeian Households*, 144–45, 155. On how slaves related to household space, see George, "Domestic Architecture."

96. V. Brown, "Social Death."

97. Hodkinson and Geary, *Slaves and Religions*, 8. See also Bodel, "Cicero's Minerva," 251.

98. Forsdyke describes a variety of ways that enslaved people in Greece participated in household rituals (*Slaves and Slavery*, 181–84).

99. Padilla Peralta considers this option as well ("Slave Religiosity," 338).

100. Latin: *Annales* (Fisher). Translation: Church, Brodribb, and Bryant, *Complete Works of Tacitus*.

101. Latin: CSEL 20. English translation amended from *ANF* 3:71 (Thelwall). On decorating with wreaths, lanterns, and garlands as a domestic religious practice, see chapter 2.

102. Latin: Dale, *Synod of Elvira*, 327. English translation amended from Maguire, "Canons of the Council."

103. Harrill, *Slaves in the New Testament*, 145–63; Glancy, "Slavery and the Rise," 468–76. At times Christian writers defended the integrity of slaves (Athenagoras, *Legatio pro Christianis* 35.3), while at other times Christian writers complain of betrayal by slaves (Justin, *Second Apology* 12.4; Tertullian, *Nat.* 1.7.14–17). See Harrill, *Slaves in the New Testament*, 153–57.

104. Possible references to enslaved believers with unbelieving masters include 1 Pet

2:18–25 and 1 Tim 6:1–2, which advise that special attention is warranted when slaves have believing masters, therefore implying that there are also slaves without believing masters (Shaner, *Enslaved Leadership*, 102–3). In addition, in *Idol.* 17.1, Tertullian asks what enslaved believers should do if they are in a position of having to attend their masters at a sacrifice. He proceeds to describe which actions constitute idolatry and which can be performed safely. And Celsus levels an intriguing accusation against Christians that might indicate the activity of enslaved believers: he refers to various kinds of workers (in leather and wool, also fullers, possibly slaves?) who refuse to speak to their elders and masters but who try to win over children and women (Origen, *Cels.* 55).

105. Glancy, *Slavery in Early Christianity*, 9–29.

106. There are several references to secret, unseen, or deceptive worship in non-Christian sources. Pliny refers to surreptitiously pouring a libation under the table at a banquet after someone has spoken an unlucky word (*Natural History* 28.24; also mentioned in chapter 2). Horace, complaining about deception and dishonesty, gives the example of someone praying to certain gods out loud (Janus, Apollo), while issuing a private prayer under his breath (to Laverna, the goddess of thieves) (*Epistle* 16.60–62). For more examples, see Bowes, *Private Worship*, 47, 240n182.

107. Hodkinson and Geary, *Slaves and Religions*, 14.

108. Hodkinson and Geary, *Slaves and Religions*, 16–17.

109. Hodkinson and Geary, *Slaves and Religions*, 17–18.

110. Hodkinson and Geary, *Slaves and Religions*, 17. For a similar phenomenon in American slavery, see Raboteau, *Slave Religion*, 211–88. See also Hicks, *Reclaiming Spirit*.

111. Orsi expresses a similar idea in his essay on lived religion: "Human beings at work on the world in the available religious idioms of their time and place are doing what they can with what they have at hand. Just as faith does not eliminate pain or death but renders them endurable . . . neither does religious practice obliterate social contradiction or liberate humans absolutely from their place in particular social, political, and domestic arrangements. Rather, religion enables them to do what they can in and through these realities" ("Everyday Miracles," 16).

112. Origen, *Cels.* 3.44 and 3.55.

Chapter 5

1. See the introduction.

2. The Martyrdom of Polycarp refers to Polycarp as the "father of the Christians" (12.2). For the way that martyrologies contribute to the construction of Christian identity, see Lieu, *Christian Identity*, 253–59.

3. P. Brown, *Cult of the Saints*, 37.

4. This argument has parallels to the work of David Brakke on the political maneuvering of bishops in the fourth century (including over ascetic practices). See Brakke, *Athanasius and the Politics* and "Canon Formation."

5. Associations also took responsibility for funding and organizing funerals. See Kloppenborg, *Christ's Associations*, 266–67.

6. This paragraph relies on Toynbee, *Death and Burial*, 43–50. See also King, *Ancient Roman Afterlife*. Denzey focuses on evidence for burials of women in *Bone Gatherers*, 17–20. Jewish burial practices shared many of the features described here (Hachlili, *Jewish Funerary Customs*, 514–16). For a study on how tombs interact with the Roman landscape, see Emmerson, *Life and Death*.

7. Hope, "Roof over the Dead"; Wallace-Hadrill, "Housing the Dead"; Jensen, "Dining with the Dead," 117; P. Brown, *Cult of the Saints*, 31; Yasin, "Funerary Monuments," 436–39. For a study of Roman banquets, see Dunbabin, *Roman Banquet*. See Bodel's caution that architecturally, tombs were not like households: "From Columbaria to Catacombs," 190–91.

8. Stirling, "Archaeological Evidence"; Jensen, "Dining with the Dead," 117; Lindsay, "Eating with the Dead"; Hoskins Walbank, "Unquiet Graves."

9. Latin and English translation: Ovid, *Fasti* (Frazer, LCL 253), 95–97.

10. Toynbee, *Death and Burial*, 61–64; Denzey, *Bone Gatherers*, 96–97; Tulloch, "Women Leaders," 168.

11. Toynbee, *Death and Burial*, 35–39; Rives, *Religion in the Roman Empire*, 50–52; Février, "Le culte des morts," for Roman evidence of third-century dining (218) and for dining at tombs (passim); Jastrzebowska, *Untersuchungen zum christlichen Totenmahl*, for meals at Christian sites; MacMullen, *Second*

Church, 77, 110–11, and passim; Jensen, "Dining with the Dead"; and Lindsay, "Eating with the Dead."

12. Stirling, "Archaeological Evidence"; Jensen, "Dining with the Dead"; MacMullen, *Second Church*, 24 and passim. Remains of cooking vessels and ash piles may indicate that meals took place in Jewish graves, although scholars disagree on this (Hachlili, *Jewish Funerary Customs*, 382–83, 440–50). I am grateful to Ross Kraemer for fruitful conversation about Jewish practices.

13. For these tubes, see Février, "Le culte des morts," 218; Jastrzebowska, *Untersuchungen zum christlichen Totenmahl*, 206.

14. Lucian, *Mourning* 9. Greek and translation: Lucian, *Anacharsis or Athletics* . . . (Harmon, LCL 162), 118–19. Jensen makes the point that mourners (and partiers) understood that they were sharing their feast with the departed ("Dining with the Dead," 116). Hoskins Walbank comments that one common theme across time and grave types is the "communality both among the living and between the living and the dead" ("Unquiet Graves," 278).

15. This inscription is treated by some scholars as Christian and by others as non-Christian. The confusion stems in part from the fact that it was originally published in Ernest Diehl's catalogue of Christian inscriptions (*ILCV* 1570; translation is from MacMullen, *Second Church*, 58). Jensen gives Latin and Greek ("Dining with the Dead," 124–25). Eastman uses this inscription as part of a framework for understanding burial practices, including Christian ones, in *Paul the Martyr*, 75–84. A similar confusion (or debate) occurs in discussions of the *Aberkios* inscription. See G. Johnson, *Early-Christian Epitaphs*, 41, 64–67.

16. MacMullen, *Christianity and Paganism*, 110–11 and 219n23. Hope, "Roof over the Dead"; MacMullen, *Second Church*, 160n33 and more generally on 23–25; Jensen, "Dining with the Dead," 126. For a collection of inscriptions from the mid-fourth century and later that refer to *mensae*, see *ILCV* 3710–26. These are discussed in Trombley, *Hellenic Religion*, 68–69, including note 290.

17. Peter Brown says that burial practices enjoyed a "massive stability" in the Mediterranean region (*Cult of the Saints*, 24). Salzman argues that they are a part of the "religious *koine*" shared by Christ followers and others ("Religious *Koine*"). MacMullen refers to everyday practices as an "unbroken flow" (*Second Church*, 50). Archaeological finds of glass at a site in Tunisia indicate that Christians continued the drinking practices of their non-Christian neighbors. See Sterrett-Krause, "Drinking with the Dead?" (thanks to Ellen Perry for this reference).

18. This phenomenon can make it difficult to sort out what is Christian evidence and what is not (as in the Aelia Secundula inscription discussed above), especially since, in the early period, Christ followers do not necessarily mark their graves differently than anyone else; see Kloppenborg, *Christ's Associations*, 265–67, 274–77. Kloppenborg comments that before the end of the second century CE, graves of Christ followers are "epigraphically invisible" (265), and notes that the same phenomenon is true for Jewish burials (416n2). This may have been an arena of life in which such a demarcation was less relevant, or perhaps membership in the cult of Christ was less well defined for ancient people than we assume it to be (see chapter 3 for more discussion). See Öhler, "Graeco-Roman Associations," 87–88. In the third century we begin to see "lightly" Christianized burial inscriptions marked with crosses or the *chi-rho* symbol (Kloppenborg, *Christ's Associations*, 274). A striking set of evidence clearly identifies burials as Christian, even as it imitates traditional grave-marking with epigraphy and iconography: the third-century "Christians for Christians" epitaphs from Phrygia. See G. Johnson, *Early-Christian Epitaphs*; Gibson, *"Christians for Christians"*; Tabbernee, *Montanist Inscriptions*.

19. Février, "Le culte des morts"; Jensen, *Understanding Early Christian Art*, 52–59; Jensen, "Dining with the Dead," 123–24.

20. Although see the recent assessments of this by Bodel, "From Columbaria to Catacombs"; Rebillard, *Care of the Dead*; Denzey Lewis, "Reinterpreting 'Pagans' and 'Christians'"; and Denzey Lewis, *Early Modern Invention*. For a response defending the traditional view, see Nicolai, "Padre Umberto M. Fasola."

21. For a catalogue of these, see Jastrzebowska, "Les scènes de banquet." Dating these frescoes is difficult. They have traditionally been located somewhere in the third century, although some scholars argue for the fourth century

for some of them. For discussion of the Marcellino and Pietro paintings, see Zimmermann, "Werkstattgruppen römischer Katakombenmalerei," and Deckers, "Wie genau ist eine Katakombe."

22. Examples are found in the catacomb of Marcellino and Pietro, in the Greek Chapel in the Priscilla catacomb, and in the Callistus catacomb.

23. Some of these scenes have traditionally been interpreted as depicting the eucharist or an *agape* meal, as is evident in their designations: "Chapel of the Sacraments" (in the Callistus catacomb) and "Fractio Panis" ("the breaking of the bread" in the Priscilla catacomb). See Jastrzebowska, "Les scènes de banquet," 8ff for a history of this scholarship. Jensen argues that these scenes are better understood as traditional memorial meals ("Dining with the Dead," 124). For a discussion of gestures and toasting, see Tulloch, "Women Leaders," 183–91, and sources cited there. For the role of women in these paintings, see Tulloch and also Denzey, *Bone Gatherers*.

24. For evidence in the catacomb of Marcellino and Pietro, see Tulloch, "Women Leaders," 173–74. Meals were perhaps more common aboveground, near tombs; many of these sites have not survived to us (MacMullen, "Christian Ancestor Worship," 607).

25. Sarcophagus of Lot, discussed in Bisconti and Nicolai, "Riti e corredi funerari," 1. In the fifth-century tomb of a certain Limenius in a Christian cemetery in Cornus, Sardinia, a fragment of a bronze tube was found that is thought to be a similar libation tube. See Giuntella, Borghetti, and Stiaffini, *Mensae e riti funerari*, 34–35.

26. Nicolai, Bisconti, and Mazzoleni, *Christian Catacombs of Rome*, 79, 83 (here Bisconti).

27. Tulloch, "Women Leaders," 171–72.

28. King, *Ancient Roman Afterlife*; Toynbee, *Death and Burial*, 35–39; Rives, *Religion in the Roman Empire*, 19.

29. MacMullen, *Second Church*, 76. For a third-century example, see the stele of Licinia Amias (*ICUR* 4246; *ILCV* 1611B), online at https://commons.wikimedia.org/wiki/File:Stele_Licinia_Amias_Terme_67646.jpg.

30. See Jensen, "Dining with the Dead," 122n26 for a history of this term.

31. Text and translation: #37 in Snyder, *Ante Pacem*, 222, 211 (for date). See the Epigraphic Database Bari, where this inscription is identified as EDB7082 (Trismegistos 296859; *ICUR* 13886), https://www.edb.uniba.it/epigraph/7082.

32. Février, "Le culte des morts," 259. An alternative translation is "Januaria, be refreshed and pray for us."

33. I assume this inscription is considered Christian because of its location in the Callistus catacomb. Its date is unknown, although Février says it is attached to "primitive galleries" in this catacomb ("Le culte des morts," 259). See above for the debate about the dating of the catacombs.

34. Latin: CSEL 76, 63 64. Translation amended from *ANF* 4 (Thelwall). (Note that the numbering system used here places the excerpt at 10.5.) Jensen observes that Tertullian may have introduced the phrase "*refrigerium interim*" ("Dining with the Dead," 122n26).

35. Latin: *De corona* (Fontaine). Translation: *ANF* 3 (Thelwall).

36. Jensen, "Dining with the Dead," 122. What exactly we mean by "the church" is worth thinking about in this time period. Were communal gatherings taking place in households? In dedicated structures like Dura Europos?

37. Rebillard, *Care of the Dead*, 154.

38. Latin: Weeber, *Quintus Septimius Tertullianus*. Translation: *ANF* 3 (Thelwall). See also *Apol.* 13 for further discussion (and derision) of the view that the dead are deities.

39. MacMullen translates this phrase "snacks and stews" (*Second Church*, 160n33).

40. Latin: CSEL 20, 134–43. Translation amended from Tertullian, *On the Testimony of the Soul* (Howe). See also *Res.* 1, where Tertullian mocks people for believing that the dead are sentient beings who appreciate these feasts.

41. Tertullian refers to singing songs for the martyrs (*Scorp.* 7.2).

42. *Ecclesiastical History* 7.11.10. Greek: Eusebius, *Ecclesiastical History*, vol. 2 (Oulton, LCL 265), 158, with translation on 159.

43. *Ecclesiastical History* 7.13. Greek: Eusebius, *Ecclesiastical History*, vol. 2 (Oulton, LCL 265), 171. See 9.2 for another imperial restriction, about fifty years later. MacMullen dates this to 311 CE (*Second Church*, 10, 146n28).

44. Canon 34. Latin: Dale, *Synod of Elvira*. Translation: Maguire, "Canons of the Council." See Rebillard, *Care of the Dead*, 144, for a discussion of these canons. The Council of Elvira dates to between 295 and 314 CE.

45. Canon 35. Latin: Dale, *Synod of Elvira*.

46. This usage of *koimeterion*, a term originally associated with sleep, to refer to death also signals a reframing by Christians of death as a temporary rest rather than a final state. See Rebillard, *Care of the Dead*, 1–7, 144, and his earlier study, "Κοιμητήριον et Coemeterium."

47. Greek: *Apostolic Fathers*, vol. 2 (Lake, LCL 25), 312–45. Translation: Ehrman, *After the New Testament*, 35–35.

48. For a collection of these stories, many of which were authored or compiled later than our time period but record stories from the second, third, and fourth centuries, see Musurillo, *Acts of the Christian Martyrs*. For a discussion of these stories, see Rebillard, *Care of the Dead*, 95–96.

49. Greek: Klostermann, *Origenes Werke III*, 25. Translation: Origen, *Homilies on Jeremiah and I Kings 28* (J. C. Smith), 34.

50. *Praeparatio evangelica* 13.11.2. Greek: Mras, *Eusebius Werke*, 190. Translation: Gifford, *Eusebii Pamphili Evangelicae*. Cited by Rebillard, *Care of the Dead*, 100 (Rebillard's translation: "It is also our custom to gather at their tombs, to say prayers, to honor their blessed souls, certain that these gestures on our part are the right ones").

51. For a consideration of similar themes in the third-century Coptic Apocalypse of Elijah, see Frankfurter, "Cult of the Martyrs."

52. Latin: CSEL 3.2, 583. Translation: G. W. Clarke, *Letters of St. Cyprian*, 3:55.

53. Latin: CSEL 3.2, 503. Translation of *Epistle* 12: G. W. Clarke, *Letters of St. Cyprian*, 1:82. Gregory of Nyssa mentions similar commemorations in his Life of Gregory Thaumaturgus (*Vita Gregorii Thaumaturgi*, PG 46:953).

54. Jensen, "Dining with the Dead," 128; G. W. Clarke, *Letters of St. Cyprian*, 1:252–53n15, and bibliography cited there.

55. Translation: G. W. Clarke, *Letters of St. Cyprian*, 1:52, and notes on 147ff.

56. Rebillard, *Care of the Dead*, 155. Clarke's notes on this text seem to concur. See G. W. Clarke, *Letters of St. Cyprian*, 1:159n24.

57. Rebillard, *Care of the Dead*, 155.

58. Cyprian came to his position as bishop with little ecclesiastical experience but with all of the resources of the educated elite. Thus in his quick rise to clerical office (Cyprian converted to Christianity in 245 or 246, was quickly made a presbyter, and then was voted bishop in 248), as well as in his administration as bishop, he was able to mobilize these advantages to fashion himself as a patron. See Brent, *Cyprian and Roman Carthage*, 2–3, 70–75 (on patronage). See also Rapp, *Holy Bishops*, 89–92.

59. Cyprian of course becomes a martyr himself under the persecution of Valerian in 258 CE. A later account describes the elaborate funeral procession that followed his death (Acts of St. Cyprian 5.6; Latin and English translation from Musurillo, *Acts of the Christian Martyrs*). See also Yasin, *Saints and Church Spaces*, 61–62. In a sermon on the occasion of Cyprian's feast day, Augustine mentions with disapprobation the rowdy behavior (singing and dancing) that took place in all-night commemorations of the martyr (*Sermones* 311.5).

60. White, *Social Origins*, 2:240–42. See also Jensen, "Dining with the Dead," 128; MacMullen, *Second Church*, 57; Février, "Le culte des martyrs," 209–10; Marcillet-Jaubert, *Les inscriptions d'Altava*, 32–35 (= no. 19), and plates 7–9. Note that Février uses Marcillet-Jaubert's reconstruction. White has reconstructed it differently, identifying several as bishops.

61. Latin from White, *Social Origins*, 2:240–41.

62. White, *Social Origins*, 2:241–42. This represents White's changes to the earlier published version in Marcillet-Jaubert, *Les inscriptions d'Altava*, 32–34 (= no. 19), and plates 7–9.

63. I am relying here on White, *Social Origins*, 2:240–42.

64. MacMullen, *Second Church*, 57. MacMullen explains that *pie zezes*, here a transcription of the Greek, is a "universal salutation" (159n20).

65. White, *Social Origins*, 2:241n185, citing Marcillet-Jaubert, *Les inscriptions d'Altava*, 32–33. Marcillet-Jaubert, in turn, cites an earlier study by Dölger (*ΙΧΘΥΣ*, 5:74, 83) for support in reading this as a "standard formula in Christian funerary reference."

66. See Dunbabin, *Roman Banquet*, chapter 4.

67. According to White, the inscription uses a Greek *sigma* with a bar, which is indicated in the Latin above as a "Z" and is an abbreviation for *zaconus*, which means *diaconus* (*Social Origins*, 241n188).

68. Based on photographs, White has reconstructed the "Ep" with the names to suggest that this is a group of clerics (White, *Social Origins*, 2:241n188).

69. White suggests that these names possibly represent a dominant family going back to the third century (*Social Origins*, 2:241–42nn188–89).

70. White, *Social Origins*, 2:241n188.

71. White, *Social Origins*, 2:242n189.

72. White is skeptical that this is the traditional basilica form of fourth-century churches, though, because it is too early for the use of this term (*Social Origins*, 2:242).

73. For a helpful glossary of these terms, which are not used in a uniform manner across sites, see Krautheimer, *Early Christian and Byzantine Architecture*, 359–63.

74. Yasin, "Reassessing Salona's Churches," 75, including note 36.

75. For a description of the tomb, see Brøndsted, "La basilique." See Dyggve, *History of Salonitan Christianity*, fig. IV 12b, for his reconstruction of the "room." For inscriptions in the basilica, see Gauthier, Marin, and Prévot, *Salona IV*.

76. Another possibility is that these rectangular holes are for practices related to the production of secondary relics (or *brandea*), in which small boxes would be lowered through the hole in order to absorb some of the holiness of the body of the special dead. See Eastman, *Paul the Martyr*, 61. I am grateful to Daniel Ullucci for this reference.

77. See Brøndsted, "La basilique," 141. See also Dyggve, *History of Salonitan Christianity*, 102. Dyggve calls the tomb a triclinium (108; figs. V 27, V 12 D, IV 12b; in this last figure he places the triclinium tomb in an enclosed area, and on p. 102 he says that the grave consisted of "an ordinary masonry room with a large tessella that served as sacrificial table").

78. Brøndsted, "La basilique," 177–80; Dyggve, *History of Salonitan Christianity*, 102. Who these four are—or whether there were actually four, or whether they existed at all—is hard to determine. As Yasin explains, part of the problem is that we have conflicting and late literary (Martyrology of Jerome, sixth century) and iconographic (oratory of San Venanzio in Rome, seventh century) sources and little to no corroboration from the Kapljuč site itself ("Reassessing Salona's Churches," 69–72).

79. Yasin, "Reassessing Salona's Churches," 83.

80. Brøndsted, "La basilique," 179; Dyggve, *History of Salonitan Christianity*, 108.

81. Brøndsted, "La basilique," 139; Yasin, "Reassessing Salona's Churches," 82n52.

82. See Brøndsted, "La basilique," 117–18, for a description of how we can tell that the church floor mosaic is placed around the *mensa* slab. See also Marin, "L'inhumation privilégiée," 222.

83. Marin, "L'inhumation privilégiée," 222. See also Yasin, "Reassessing Salona's Churches," 82.

84. Dyggve, *History of Salonitan Christianity*, 108 and note 28. Daniel Ullucci suggests the possibility that legs might have been used to support a low railing, rather than a table or altar, so that the hole was still accessible (personal communication).

85. Marin, "L'inhumation privilégiée," 222.

86. Delehaye, "Nouvelles fouilles à Salone," 83n54.

87. Yasin, "Reassessing Salona's Churches," 89.

88. From Yasin, "Reassessing Salona's Churches," 75n37: "Asterius is included among the group of Dalmatian martyrs depicted in the mosaic from the S. Venanzio oratory.... He is thought to have been a priest based on the ecclesiastical garb he wears in the mosaic, in contrast to the four soldier-companions attired in military gear." Yasin argues that the claim that his tomb lies below the altar of the Kapljuč basilica has been made with no real evidence and that the area under the altar does not look much like a grave at all (79–82).

89. Yasin, "Reassessing Salona's Churches," 83. The inscription reads: "a vow made to the martyr Asterius (*vot / um fecit ad ma / rtirem Asterium*)." It is labeled as mosaic no. 5 (Brøndsted, "La basilique," 118–19; inscr. no. 65 in Gauthier et al., *Salona IV*, 1:243–44). Others, too, have suggested the connection between the inscription and Tomb G—see Gauthier et al., *Salona IV*, 1:16, 101, and 244.

90. Yasin carefully sifts through the implications of the Asterius votive inscription ("Reassessing Salona's Churches," 83, 86) and notes that we have no literary record of this saint (83).

91. We have a *terminus ante quem* of 385 for the construction of the basilica in the form of a funerary inscription (mosaic no. 15) that records a consular date of 385 CE. See Brøndsted, "La basilique," 122–23; inscr. no. 89 in Gauthier et al., *Salona IV*, 1:290–92; and Yasin, "Reassessing Salona's Churches," 76 and note 39.

92. Dyggve says Tomb G is "pre-Edict of Milan" (*History of Salonitan Christianity*, 107).

93. Brøndsted speculates that it could be before Diocletian ("La basilique," 142); Yasin, "Reassessing Salona's Churches," 83n54.

94. The literature on this site is vast. I list here several works that have been useful to me: Tolotti, *Memorie degli apostoli*; Styger, "Il monumento apostolico"; Styger, "Die erste Ruhestätte"; Spera, "Christianization of Space"; Jastrzebowska, *Untersuchungen zum christlichen Totenmahl*; Snyder, *Ante Pacem*, 180–89; Eastman, *Paul the Martyr*. For an exhibition catalogue featuring this site, see Donati, *Pietro e Paolo*.

95. Eastman explains that at the time, *ad catacumbas* referred to this specific place, and only later did it come to designate underground tombs (*Paul the Martyr*, 71). See also Denzey Lewis, *Early Modern Invention*, 198; Bodel, "From Columbaria to Catacombs," 197–99. According to Barbara Borg, there was an aboveground cemetery here in the second half of the first century, while the use of the tunnels belonging to the mine began at the turn of the second century. See Borg, *Crisis and Ambition*, 150; Borg, "Peter and Paul."

96. Borg, *Crisis and Ambition*, 150.

97. These are identified in Borg, *Crisis and Ambition*, as Mausoleum X (150–54), Y (118, 153, 156–57), and Z (157, 242, 264). Borg illustrates that one of these tombs changed from a family structure to a communal one (150ff). Kjærgaard, "'Memoria Apostolorum,'" 59 and 65; Bodel, "From Columbaria to Catacombs," 200; Nicolai, Bisconti, and Mazzoleni, *Christian Catacombs of Rome*, 14 (here Bisconti). On the Christian symbols, see Spera, "Christianization of Space," 26, and Flexsenhar, *Christians in Caesar's Household*, 115–20.

98. Eastman, *Paul the Martyr*, 72; Styger, "Il monumento apostolico," 48–49.

99. See Styger, "Il monumento apostolico," for a detailed description (painting, 55–57; benches, 53–55).

100. Styger, "Il monumento apostolico," 54–55; Jastrzebowska, *Untersuchungen zum christlichen Totenmahl*, 67–81; Kjærgaard, "'Memoria Apostolorum,'" 60, and fig. 1 on 61; MacMullen, "Christian Ancestor Worship," 604; Nicolai, "L'organizzazione dello spazio funerario," 49. For other examples of wells (non-Christian) from Isola Sacra, see Calza, *La necropoli*, 56–57. Kjærgaard describes a well at the site: "Towards the middle of the third century the area was levelled, in which process both the pozzolana quarry and the hypogaea were filled in with earth. However, a stairway was also added so that it remained possible to fetch water from the depths of the quarry" ("'Memoria Apostolorum,'" 59). Denzey Lewis refers to fountains (*Early Modern Invention*, 199). See Borg, "Peter and Paul," for the argument that the basin at the bottom of the staircase, the "scala del pozzo," served a religious function.

101. Styger, "Il monumento apostolico," 57–89; Mazzoleni, "Pietro e Paolo," 67–72, and 180 for photo of inscriptions (catalogue nos. 107, 108). Inscriptions in *ICUR* 12907–13096; *refrigerium* in inscriptions 12932 (https://www.edb.uniba.it/epigraph/26590), 12974 (https://www.edb.uniba.it/epigraph/26679), and 12981 (https://www.edb.uniba.it/epigraph/26693) at the Epigraphic Database Bari. Trout, "Saints, Identity," 302n12 and 176. Snyder lists 13 of the inscriptions in *Ante Pacem*, 251–58 (and reports that there are 222 in the covered *triclia* and an additional 5 or so on the stairway). La Piana reports 191 inscriptions: see "Tombs of Peter and Paul," 78.

102. One graffito is critical for the *triclia*'s dating: "Celerinus / 9th of August / A.D. 260" (Snyder, *Ante Pacem*, 255). See Styger, "Il monumento apostolico," 68; Marichal, "La date des graffiti," Celerinus on 134. (Borg cautions that this dating by Marichal is not certain; see "Peter and Paul," 46.)

103. Styger, "Il monumento apostolico," 58 (in Greek; inscription found in Tav. I); trans. in Snyder, *Ante Pacem*, 252.

104. Styger, "Il monumento apostolico," 58 (Tav. I); trans. in Snyder, *Ante Pacem*, 251.

105. This graffito is in Greek. Styger, "Il monumento apostolico," 60 (Tav. II); trans. in Snyder, *Ante Pacem*, 252–53 (Snyder notes that Grossi Gondi argues that *anagismois* would be equivalent to *refrigerium*: "Di un graffito greco").

106. Styger, "Il monumento apostolico," 61 (Tav. II); trans. amended from Snyder, *Ante Pacem*, 253.

107. Styger, "Il monumento apostolico," 68 (Tav. X, #42); trans. in Snyder, *Ante Pacem*, 254.

108. Styger, "Il monumento apostolico," 60 (Tav. I; not listed in Snyder, *Ante Pacem*; cited by Eastman, *Paul the Martyr*, 87; note 42 has Greek).

109. MacMullen conjures these scenes at martyr shrines in *Second Church*, 44, 61, 77.

110. See Stern's *Writing on the Wall* for an argument that writing graffiti is a form of devotion (35–79) and that it accompanied other mortuary practices for Jews and others (80–140).

111. Eastman, *Paul the Martyr*, 86–88.

112. There have been theories, both in antiquity and in modern scholarship, that the relics of Peter and Paul were translated to this site for a period of time. See La Piana, "Tombs of Peter and Paul." Eastman argues that there is not enough evidence that people in the third century thought there might be relics at this site; this theory began in the sixth century (*Paul the Martyr*, 72, 94–113). See also Denzey Lewis, *Early Modern Invention*, 200–206, for a discussion of these theories. Lewis's study as a whole argues that, contrary to popular scholarly opinion, relics were not in fact the determining factor in cult practice in late antique Rome. But see also the recent work of Barbara Borg, who is exploring the possibility that people in the second and third centuries may have believed the martyrs' remains were *ad catacumbas*. Key to her theory is that the staircase and shallow basin were preserved at every phase of this site's development, while nothing else survived. See Borg, "Peter and Paul," and her monograph in progress. I am grateful for personal communication with Borg regarding her work.

113. Much traditional scholarship has assumed a centralized and coordinated "church" in Rome by the third century, an organization that was in charge of Christian cemeteries (e.g., Kjærgaard, "'Memoria Apostolorum,'" 65). This view has been fueled by the famous line from Hippolytus that Zephyrinus called Callistus back from exile and gave him a *koimeterion* (*Refutation* 9.12). See Rebillard, *Care of the Dead*, 2–7, for a quick overview of this evidence and a refutation of the idea that this meant the "church" was in charge of the catacombs. See also Brent, *Hippolytus and the Roman Church*; Denzey Lewis, "Reinterpreting 'Pagans.'"

114. Borg, *Crisis and Ambition*, 80.

115. Borg, *Crisis and Ambition*, 153; Mausoleum X was originally used by a single family (150–53).

116. Borg, "Peter and Paul," 50. With this observation, Borg refutes the theory that Christians may have secretly worshiped at this site during the Valerian persecution.

117. M. Johnson, "Christian Burial Practices"; Bodel, "From Columbaria to Catacombs."

118. Spera, "Christianization of Space," 26: a fresco of the "Gadarene madman" from Matthew on the hypogeum for Clodius Hermes and images of anchors and fish on epitaphs.

119. Spera, "Christianization of Space," 26, 28: "That the immediate area was not as yet monopolized by Christian structures is revealed by the dedication of three marble altars, two to the God Attis and one to Jupiter by the *vir clarissimus* [28] and *augur* Lucius Cornelius Scipio Orphitus, organizer of a *taurobolium* and a *criobolium* in A.D. 295." In note 26 Spera lists the inscriptions: *CIL* 6.505 = 30781, 506 = 30782, 402.

120. Unless Barbara Borg's theory is correct that the site of veneration was the staircase and basin, the one feature that was preserved even after the huge basilica structure was built (Borg, "Peter and Paul").

121. For a comprehensive study of this structure, see Nieddu, *La Basilica Apostolorum*.

122. Nieddu, *La Basilica Apostolorum*, 107–18.

123. Spera, "Christianization of Space," 32.

124. Krautheimer, *Corpus Basilicarum Christianarum Romae*; Nieddu, *La Basilica Apostolorum*.

125. Hellström, "Form and Function," 301–2.

126. They had largely disappeared from the Roman landscape by the eighth century. See Denzey Lewis, *Early Modern Invention*, 316; Krautheimer, "Mensa-coemeterium-martyrium," 24.

127. MacMullen makes this point, and in characteristic fashion, he does some math to impress upon us how much attention was devoted to what he argues is "ancestor worship" in the funerary basilicas: "The six cemetery churches with room for some twelve thousand outside the walls could accommodate about the same number of

persons as all of the basilicas put together, both the Lateran and the titular, inside the city. The new building program thus constituted a hugely generous opening up of built space to some particular form of worship ("Christian Ancestor Worship," 601).

128. Krautheimer, *Early Christian and Byzantine Architecture*, 17–44, esp. 31–32; MacMullen, *Second Church*, 8–89. For a helpful description of these buildings and summaries of the scholarship, see Aulbach and Gorski, "Circiform Basilicas of Rome."

129. MacMullen, *Second Church*, 82; Denzey Lewis, *Early Modern Invention*, 317; Borg, "Late Antique Funerary Landscape," 241.

130. Denzey Lewis, *Early Modern Invention*, 318–19 (and 314–19 on this basilica); Hellström, "Form and Function," 299–300.

131. Krautheimer, "Mensa-coemeterium-martyrium," 22.

132. Borg, "Peter and Paul."

133. Nieddu, *La Basilica Apostolorum*, 116n489; Hellström, "Form and Function," 300, including note 32.

134. Kjærgaard has studied the patterns of destruction of specific parts of the *triclia* complex and argues that those most connected with Christian cult were destroyed differently—as if intentionally—than the rest of the site, which seems to have been filled in by the basilica ("'Memoria Apostolorum,'" 67). Eastman, assuming that the basilica was constructed by and for Christians, makes the point that the filling in of the *triclia* complex was an act of suppression of rival cult space. He notes that the *triclia* complex was known to hold non-Christian graves as well, so the building of the huge basilica over it effectively quashed those other cult practices (*Paul the Martyr*, 92–93).

135. Nieddu, *La Basilica Apostolorum*, 98; Kjærgaard, "'Memoria Apostolorum,'" 71–72 (with rubbing of the monogram by the author). Kjærgaard is confident in dating the building to the reigns of Constantine or one of his sons.

136. Kjærgaard, "'Memoria Apostolorum,'" 71.

137. Krautheimer, "Mensa-coemeterium-martyrium," 22; Helström, "Form and Function," 295.

138. Hellström, "Form and Function," 296. Hellström also mentions the "absence of Chi-Rho symbols" among the graffiti in the Memoria Apostolorum as evidence that the space was covered over, presumably to prepare for the basilica, at a date before the *chi-rho* comes into use; it is typically considered to be a Constantinian-period innovation (296; see also Nieddu, *La Basilica Apostolorum*, 142). Kjærgaard, however, says a *chi-rho* symbol was found at the site ("'Memoria Apostolorum,'" 70). See Nicolai, Bisconti, and Mazzoleni, *Christian Catacombs of Rome*, for an image of an "incised Christogram" from the "Catacomb of S. Sebastiano" (168, fig. 169, marking the grave of Vincentia). Neither of these sources lists a date or find spot.

139. Hellström, "Form and Function," 294–95. Hellström also offers evidence for a possible early date (ranging from late third century to 325 CE) for the Via Labicana basilica (295). Borg offers her view of the dating in "Late Antique Funerary Landscape," 239.

140. Hellström, "Form and Function," 296. Nieddu argues for the early Constantine period, based on the same comparison with the Maxentian villa (*La Basilica Apostolorum*, 140–43). Krautheimer comments that the basilica is clearly early fourth century: it could be from 320 or possibly prior to 313 (the latter date orally suggested by a scholar). See Krautheimer, "Mensa-coemeterium-martyrium," 22.

141. Spera, "Christianization of Space," 30; Hellström, "Form and Function," 301; Borg, *Crisis and Ambition*, 80.

142. Borg documents this in the first through the early third century (*Crisis and Ambition*, 159). If this is true, then the cult of Peter and Paul was taking place on imperial property.

143. Hellström, "Form and Function," 308.

144. Hellström, "Form and Function," 309.

145. Hellström, "Form and Function," 308. See Borg's assessment of this theory in "Late Antique Funerary Landscape," 239–40.

146. Spera comments that the basilica was built at the same time as the Maxentian complex, which included a villa, circus, and mausoleum of Romulus (and her comment might be based on that same evidence of the building features and forms). See "Christianization of Space," 31. I am grateful to Ellen Perry for conversations about the relationship between building techniques and possible patronage.

147. Krautheimer describes the donations to other funerary basilicas (though not the one on Via Appia) made by Constantine and later

emperors as recorded in the *Liber Pontificalis*: altars, chalices, pitchers, altar vessels. See "Mensa-coemeterium-martyrium," 24–26.

148. Denzey Lewis, *Early Modern Invention*, 302.

149. I am intrigued by Borg's recent theory that the preservation of the staircase and basin signals some connection to earlier cult practices at this site ("Late Antique Funerary Landscape"), and I look forward to her development of this argument. For the various places in Rome where Peter and Paul were honored, see Eastman, *Paul the Martyr*, and Denzey Lewis, *Early Modern Invention*. For the relationship between saints and church architecture more generally, see Yasin, *Saints and Church Spaces*.

150. See Kjærgaard, "'Memoria Apostolorum,'" 73–74.

151. As Bowes writes about Rome, for example: "Fragmentary sources from Rome help us reconstruct a city jostling with competing groups and no unified, powerful, singular church" (*Private Worship*, 52).

152. Ullucci, "Toward a Typology"; Wendt, *At the Temple Gates*; Stowers, "Why Expert"; Eyl, *Signs, Wonders, and Gifts*. See two volumes of essays on this topic: Rosenblum, Vuong, and DesRosiers, *Religious Competition in the Third Century CE*, and DesRosiers and Vuong, *Religious Competition in the Greco-Roman World*.

153. See Stowers, *History and the Study* and *Christian Beginnings*, as well as the discussion of his theory in the introduction.

154. Eshleman, *Social World of Intellectuals*; Marx-Wolf, *Spiritual Taxonomies*. We could add scribes, artisans, and others to this list.

155. Salzman, *Making of a Christian Aristocracy*, 43–48.

156. Ullucci, "Spiritual Offerings," 11n23 (unpublished manuscript). I am grateful to Ullucci for making this work available ahead of publication.

157. We have already encountered some of these experts in previous chapters: the literate producer who excels in intellectual skills such as interpretation and argument (chaps. 2, 3, and 4), the artisan or scribe who excels in crafting gems or amulets (chap. 3), and the ritual expert who oversees exchanges with the gods (chaps. 2 and 3).

158. Osiek, "Roman and Christian Burial Practices," 269. Of course, this is also one of Peter Brown's main arguments in *Cult of the Saints*.

159. Kalleres, *City of Demons*; Marx-Wolf, *Spiritual Taxonomies*.

160. Eshleman, *Social World of Intellectuals*, 102.

161. Here, I echo MacMullen's basic claim in *Second Church*.

162. Frankfurter, "Where the Spirits Dwell," 37.

163. Frankfurter, "Where the Spirits Dwell," 37.

164. Ullucci, "Spiritual Offerings," 18. See also Maier, "Heresy, Households," 223.

165. See Yasin, "Reassessing Salona's Churches" (arguing against the ubiquitously accepted model of evolution of martyr cult: graves, to martyr grave, to small shrines, to cult centers, to basilicas), and Denzey Lewis, *Early Modern Invention* (arguing that at least in Rome, the cult of the saints did not depend on relics and the inherent holiness of bodies).

166. Denzey Lewis, *Early Modern Invention*, 182.

167. Stowers, "Why Expert," 148.

168. Stowers also discusses a variety of experts in this formative period of the third century (*History and the Study*, chap. 8).

169. P. Brown, *Cult of the Saints*, 37; Rebillard, *Care of the Dead*, 146–47; Spieser, "Ambrose's Foundations." Augustine describes the incident involving Monica in *Confessions* 6.2.2.

170. P. Brown, *Cult of the Saints*, 37; Spieser, "Ambrose's Foundations," 9; Rebillard, *Care of the Dead*, 146–47.

171. Damasus famously mounts a campaign to promote the cult of the martyrs in Rome (Nicolai, Bisconti, and Mazzoleni, *Christian Catacombs of Rome*, 49–59, here Nicolai; Denzey Lewis, *Early Modern Invention*, 90–120). Augustine, although he worked to ban banquets for martyrs, acknowledges the importance of care of the ordinary dead to families and suggests that meals and offerings at tombs be allowed (Epistle 26.6); see Rebillard, *Care of the Dead*, 147–49; MacMullen, *Second Church*, 61–62. John Chrysostom strategically moved the communal service to a cemetery church outside the city walls of Antioch for Good Friday (Spieser, "Ambrose's Foundations," 9). Chrysostom also refers to a conflict between two Christian sects that played out in the form of covering over the burials of one group with the burials of the other (Mayer, "Late Antique Church," 168–70; my thanks to Sarah Porter for this reference). Bishops and others seek

to be buried near martyrs: Meletius (Spieser, "Ambrose's Foundations," 9); Alexander in Tipasa (Février, "Le culte des martyrs," 191–215, Tipasa on 191–204; Jensen, "Dining with the Dead," 126–27); Paulinus of Nola (Trout, *Paulinus of Nola*).

172. Rebillard demonstrates that while church officials had some success with commemorations of the special dead (the martyrs), they did not control burial practices for the ordinary dead for centuries after Constantine. It seems that Christians continued to honor their deceased family members in traditional ways. See Rebillard, *Care of the Dead*.

173. Bowes, *Private Worship*; Frankfurter, *Christianizing Egypt*; Maier, "Heresy, Households."

Conclusion

1. Lactantius: *Divine Institutes* 4.27. Tertullian: *Cor.* 3; Latin: *De corona* (Fontaine), and English translation amended from *ANF* 3 (Thelwall). Chrysostom: *Homily 12 on 1 Corinthians*, section 14. See chapters 2 and 3 above for discussions of signing.

2. Meeks, *First Urban Christians*.

3. In fact, the seeds of this book were planted in a graduate seminar on ancient households with Stowers in the mid-1990s.

4. Two of my early teachers, Bernadette Brooten and Elisabeth Schüssler Fiorenza, have been influential here. Many other scholars have influenced my thinking as well, including Elizabeth Castelli, Karen King, Ross Kraemer, Amy-Jill Levine, and Amy Richlin, to name just a few.

5. Trouillot, *Silencing the Past*, 27.

6. Petersen discusses her goal of seeking to "re-see" women in her work on Pompeii ("Pompeian Women," 14).

7. Quote from Frankfurter, *Christianizing Egypt*, 6.

8. Denzey Lewis, *Early Modern Invention*, 373.

9. See 1 Cor 7 and 11, for example. See also Pliny's correspondence with Trajan, which famously mentions the torture of two enslaved women he calls *ministrae* (Letter 10.96).

10. See the study by Cianca, *Sacred Ritual*.

11. The work of other scholars also supports this view: Michael Flexsenhar, David Frankfurter, Lucy Grig, Nicola Denzey Lewis, Bruce Longenecker, and Stanley Stowers, among others.

12. Boin, *Ostia in Late Antiquity*, 37.

13. Boin, *Ostia in Late Antiquity*, 35.

BIBLIOGRAPHY

Selected Primary Sources

Acts of John, Acts of Paul, Acts of Peter
Greek: Lipsius, Richard Adelbert, and Max Bonnet, eds. *Acta apostolorum apocrypha post Constantinum Tischendorf.* 2 vols. Leipzig: H. Mendelssohn, 1891–1903.
English translation: Hennecke, Edgar. *New Testament Apocrypha.* Edited by Wilhelm Schneemelcher. Vol. 2, *Writings Related to the Apostles, Apocalypses and Related Subjects.* English translation by R. McL.Wilson. Rev. ed. Louisville, KY: John Knox Press, 1992.

Acts of St. Cyprian
Latin and English translation: Musurillo, Herbert, ed. and trans. *Acts of the Christian Martyrs.* Oxford: Clarendon Press, 1972.

Acts of the Christian Martyrs
English translation: Musurillo, Herbert, ed. and trans. *Acts of the Christian Martyrs.* Oxford: Clarendon Press, 1972.

Acts of Thecla
Greek: Lipsius, Richard Adelbert, and Max Bonnet, eds. *Acta apostolorum apocrypha post Constantinum Tischendorf.* 2 vols. Leipzig: H. Mendelssohn, 1891–1903.
English translation: Ehrman, *After the New Testament.*
English translation: Hennecke, Edgar. *New Testament Apocrypha.* Edited by Wilhelm Schneemelcher. Vol. 2, *Writings Related to the Apostles, Apocalypses and Related Subjects.* English translation by R. McL.Wilson. Rev. ed. Louisville, KY: John Knox Press, 1992.

Apostolic Constitutions
Greek: von Funk, F. X. *Didascalia et Constitutiones apostolorum.* Vol. 1. Paderborn: Ferdinand Schoeningh, 1905.
Greek: Metzger, Marcel, ed. and trans. *Les Constitutions apostoliques.* Vol. 1. Sources chrétiennes 320. Paris: Cerf, 1985.
English translation: Yasin, "Funerary Monuments."

Apostolic Tradition
Latin: Tidner, Erik, ed. *Didascaliae apostolorum, Canonum ecclesiasticorum, Traditionis apostolicae versiones Latinae.* TU 75. Berlin: Akademie, 1963.
Original language and English translation: Bradshaw, Johnson, and Phillips, *Apostolic Tradition.*

Apuleius
Latin and English translation: Apuleius. *The Golden Ass: Being the Metamorphoses of Lucius Apuleius.* Translated by W. Adlington. Revised by Stephen Gaselee. LCL 44. New York: G. P. Putnam's Sons; London: William Heinemann, 1924.

Athanasius
De amuletis
Greek: PG 26:1320.

Cato
De agricultura
Latin and English translation: Cato and Varro. *On Agriculture.* Translated by William David Hooper. Revised by Harrison Boyd Ash. LCL 283. Cambridge, MA: Harvard University Press, 1934.
English translation: Wiedemann, *Greek and Roman Slavery.*

Celsus, Aulus Cornelius (first-century medical writer)
Latin and English translation: Celsus. *De medicina.* Translated by W. G. Spencer. Vol. 2. LCL 304. Cambridge, MA: Harvard University Press, 1961.

Celsus (second-century critic of Christianity)
Contra Celsum
Greek: Koetschau, P., ed. *Origenes Werke.* GCS 3. Leipzig: Hinrichs' Buchhandlung, 1899.

English translation: Origen. *Contra Celsum*. Edited and translated by Henry Chadwick. Cambridge: Cambridge University Press, 1965.
English translation: *ANF* 4. Translated by A. Cleveland Coxe.

Chrysostom, John
Contra Judaeos et gentiles quod Christus sit deus
Greek: PG 48.
English translation: Jensen, *Cross*.
Homily on 1 Corinthians
Greek: PG 61:106.
English translation: Schaff, Philip, ed. *Nicene and Post-Nicene Fathers, First Series*. Vol. 12. Translated by Talbot W. Chambers. Buffalo, NY: Christian Literature Publishing, 1889. Revised and edited for New Advent by Kevin Knight. https://www.newadvent.org/fathers/220112.htm.
Homily 54 on Matthew
Greek: PG 58.
English translation: Schaff, Philip, ed. *Nicene and Post-Nicene Fathers, First Series*. Vol. 10. Translated by George Prevost. Revised by M. B. Riddle. Buffalo, NY: Christian Literature Publishing, 1888. Revised and edited for New Advent by Kevin Knight. https://www.newadvent.org/fathers/200154.htm.

Cicero
De legibus
Latin: Cicero. *De legibus*. Edited by Georges de Plinval. Paris: Belles Lettres, 1959.
English translation: Bodel, "Cicero's Minerva," 250.
On His House
Latin: Cicero. "On His House." In *Orations*, edited by Albert Clark. Oxford: Clarendon Press, 1909.
English translation: Treggiari, *Roman Social History*, 80–81.

Columella
De re rustica (On Agriculture), Volume 1
Latin and English translation: Lucius Junius Moderatus Columella. *On Agriculture*. Volume 1, *Books 1–4*. Translated by Harrison Boyd Ash. LCL 361. Cambridge, MA: Harvard University Press, 1941.

Coptic Apocalypse of Peter
English translation: Ehrman, *After the New Testament*, 229. [Ehrman uses the translation of James Brashler in *Nag Hammadi Codex VII (NHS XXX)*, edited by Birger Pearson (Leiden: E. J. Brill, 1996).]

Council of Laodicea
Greek: Mansi, J. D. *Sacrorum Conciliorum Nova Amplissima Collectio*. Vol. 2, col. 570. Florence: Antonio Zatta, 1859. Documenta Catholica Omnia. https://www.documentacatholicaomnia.eu/01_50_1692-1769-_Mansi_JD.html.
English translation: Schaff, Philip, and Henry Wace, eds. *The Seven Ecumenical Councils*. Vol. 14 of *The Nicene and Post-Nicene Fathers, Second Series*. Edinburgh: T&T Clark, 1994–98.

Cyprian
De dominica oratione
Latin: PL 4:521, col. 519–44.
English translation: *ANF* 5. Translated by Philip Schaff.
English translation: Saint Cyprian. *Treatises*. Translated by Roy Ferrari. Fathers of the Church 36. Washington, DC: Catholic University of America Press, 1958.
De lapsis
Latin: PL 4.
Latin: Hartel, W., ed. *S. Thasci Caecili Cypriani Epistulae*. CSEL 3.2. New York: Johnson, 1965. Orig. pub. 1871.
English translation: *ANF* 5. Revised and edited for New Advent by Kevin Knight. https://www.newadvent.org/fathers/050703.htm.
Epistle 4
Latin: PL 4. [Freestone cites this passage as *Epistle 5* (24).]
English translation: *ANF* 5. Translated by Robert Ernest Wallis. Revised and edited for New Advent by Kevin Knight. https://www.newadvent.org/fathers/050604.htm.
English translation [listed as Epistle 5]: Donna, Rose Bernard, ed. *Saint Cyprian, Letters (1–81)*. Fathers of the Church 51. Washington, DC: Catholic University of America Press, 1964.
Epistle 12
Latin: Hartel, W., ed. *S. Thasci Caecili Cypriani Epistulae*. CSEL 3.2. New York: Johnson, 1965. Orig. pub. 1871.
Latin: Diercks, G. F. *Epistulae*. Corpus Christianorum Series Latina 3B-C. Turnhout: Brepols, 1994–96.
English translation: G. W. Clarke, *Letters of St. Cyprian*, vol. 1.

Epistle 39
Latin: Hartel, G., ed. *S. Thasci Caecili Cypriani Epistulae*. CSEL 3.2. New York: Johnson, 1965. Orig. pub. 1871.
English translation: G. W. Clarke, *Letters of St. Cyprian*, vol. 3.
Letter to Demetrianus
Latin: Hartel, W., ed. *S. Thasci Caecili Cypriani Epistulae*. CSEL 3.1. Vienna: C. Gerold's Sons, 1868–71.
English translation: *ANF* 5. Translated by Robert Ernest Wallis. Revised and edited for New Advent by Kevin Knight. https://www.newadvent.org/fathers/050705.htm.
Letter to Jubaianus (73.9)
Latin: Hartel, W., ed. *Cyprian: Opera Omnia*. CSEL 3.1 Vienna: C. Gerold's Sons, 1868–71.
English translation: Donna, Rose Bernard. *Saint Cyprian: Letters (1–81)*. Fathers of the Church 51. Washington, DC: Catholic University of America Press, 1964. [Note that this letter is numbered as 72.9 by the New Advent catalog, https://www.newadvent.org/fathers/050672.htm.]

Eusebius
Ecclesiastical History
Greek and English translation: Eusebius. *Ecclesiastical History*. Volume 2. Translated by J. E. L. Oulton. LCL 265. Cambridge, MA: Harvard University Press, 1932.
Praeparatio evangelica
Greek: Mras, K., ed. *Eusebius Werke: Achter Band. Die Praeparatio Evangelica*. GCS 21. Berlin: Akademie, 1956, 190.
English translation: Gifford, E. H., ed. *Eusebii Pamphili Evangelicae preparationis libri XV*. Oxford: Oxford University Press, 1903.

Galen
On the Natural Faculties
Greek and English translation: Galen. *On the Natural Faculties*. Translated by Arthur John Brock. LCL 71. New York: G. P. Putnam's Sons, 1916.

Hierocles
On Duties: On Marriage
Greek (in Stobaeus): Wachsmuth, C., and O. Hense, eds. *Ioannis Stobaei Anthologium*. 5 vols. Berlin: Weidmann, 1974.

English translation: Malherbe, Abraham J. *Moral Exhortation, A Greco-Roman Sourcebook*. Philadelphia: Westminster Press, 1986.

Hippolytus (attributed)
Appendix to the Works of Hippolytus (or *Elucidations*)
Greek: PG 10.
English translation: *ANF* 5.

Ignatius of Antioch
Epistle to the Ephesians
Greek and English translation: *The Apostolic Fathers, Volume I: I Clement. II Clement. Ignatius. Polycarp. Didache. Barnabus*. Translated by Kirsopp Lake. LCL 24. Cambridge, MA: Harvard University Press, 1998.

Julius Africanus
Cesti
English translation: Thee, *Julius Africanus*.
Chronographiae
Greek and English translation: Julius Africanus. *Chronographiae*. In *Iulius Africanus Chronographiae: The Extant Fragments*. Translated by William Adler. Edited by Martin Wallraff. New York: De Gruyter, 2007.

Justin Martyr
Second Apology
Greek: Goodspeed, Edgar J. *Die ältesten Apologeten*. Göttingen: Vandenhoeck and Ruprecht, 1984.
English translation: Falls, Thomas B. *Saint Justin Martyr*. Fathers of the Church 6. New York: Christian Heritage, 1948.

Lucian
Mourning
Greek and English translation: Lucian. *Anacharsis or Athletics. . . .* Translated by A. M. Harmon. Cambridge, MA: Harvard University Press, 1961.

Martyrdom of Polycarp
Greek and English translation: *The Apostolic Fathers, Volume II: The Shepherd of Hermas. The Martyrdom of Polycarp. The Epistle to Diognetus*. Translated by Kirsopp Lake. LCL 25. Cambridge, MA: Harvard University Press, 1997. Orig. pub. 1913.
English translation: Ehrman, *After the New Testament*.

Minucius Felix
Octavius
Latin and English translation: Tertullian, Minucius Felix. *Apology. De spectaculis*.

BIBLIOGRAPHY

Novatian
De spectaculis
Latin: Hartel, W., ed. *S. Thasci Caecili Cypriani Opera Omnia.* Vol. 3, part 3, *Appendix, "Opera Spuria."* Vienna: C. Gerold's Sons, 1871.
English translation: *ANF* 5.

Origen
Contra Celsum
Greek: Koetschau, P., ed. *Origenes Werke.* GCS 3. Leipzig: Hinrichs' Buchhandlung, 1899.
English translation: Origen. *Contra Celsum.* Translated by Henry Chadwick. Cambridge: Cambridge University Press, 1965.
De oratione
Greek: Koetschau, P., ed. *Origenes Werke.* GCS 3. Leipzig: Hinrichs' Buchhandlung, 1899.
Homily on Jeremiah
Greek: Klostermann, Erich, ed. *Origenes Werke.* Vol. 3. GCS 6. Leipzig: J. C. Hinerichs'sche Buchhandlung, 1901.
English translation: Origen. *Homilies on Jeremiah and I Kings 28.* Translated by John Clark Smith. Fathers of the Church 97. Washington, DC: Catholic University of America Press, 1998.

Ovid
Fasti
Latin and English translation: Ovid. *Fasti.* Translated by James G. Frazer. LCL 253. Cambridge, MA: Harvard University Press, 1949.
Metamorphoses
Latin and English translation: Apuleius. *The Golden Ass: Being the Metamorphoses of Lucius Apuleius.* Translated by W. Adlington. Revised by S. Gaselee. LCL 44. New York: G. P. Putnam's Sons; London: William Heinemann, 1924.

Plato
Laws
Greek: Burnet, John, ed. *Platonis Opera.* Oxford: Oxford University Press, 1903.
English translation: Bury, R. G., ed. *Plato in Twelve Volumes.* Vols. 10 and 11. Cambridge, MA: Harvard University Press; London: William Heinemann, 1967, 1968.
Minucius Felix: Octavius. Translated by T. R. Glover and Gerald H. Rendall. LCL 250. Cambridge, MA: Harvard University Press, 1977.

Plautus
Trinummus (also known as "Three Bob Day")
Latin and English translation: Plautus. *Stichus. Trinummus (Three Bob Day). Truculentus. The Tale of a Travelling Bag. Fragments.* Translated by Paul Nixon. LCL 328. Cambridge, MA: Harvard University Press, 1938.

Pliny the Elder
Natural History
Latin and English translation: Pliny. *Natural History, Volume VIII: Books 28–32.* Translated by W. H. S. Jones. LCL 18. Cambridge, MA: Harvard University Press, 1963.

Pliny the Younger
Epistle 10
Latin available on Perseus: https://www.perseus.tufts.edu/hopper/text?doc=Plin.+Ep.+10.96.

Plutarch
Moralia
Greek and English translation: Pomeroy, Sarah B., ed. *Plutarch's "Advice to the Bride and Groom" and "A Consolation to His Wife": English Translations, Commentary, Interpretive Essays and Bibliography.* New York: Oxford University Press, 1991.

Synod of Elvira
Latin: Dale, A. W. W. *The Synod of Elvira and Christian Life in the Fourth Century.* New York: Macmillan, 1882.
English translation: "The Canons of the Council of Elvira." Translated by Andrew Maguire. Early Church Texts. https://earlychurchtexts.com/.
Latin and French translation and notes: von Hefele, Karl Joseph. *Histoire des conciles d'après les documents originaux.* Paris: Letouzey, 1907.

Tacitus
Annals
Latin: Cornelius Tacitus. *Annales.* Edited by Charles Dennis Fisher. Oxford: Clarendon Press, 1906.
English translation: Church, Alfred John, William Jackson Brodribb, and Sara Bryant, eds. *Complete Works of Tacitus.* New York: Random House, 1942.

Tertullian
For Latin text and English translations of all Tertullian's works, see The Tertullian Project, https://www.tertullian.org.

Ad uxorem
Latin: Tertullian. *À son épouse*. Edited and translated by Charles Munier. Sources chrétiennes 273. Paris: Cerf, 1980.
English translation: Le Saint, *Tertullian*.
English translation: *ANF* 4, 39–49. Translated by S. Thelwall.

Adversus Marcionem
Latin and English translation (amended): Tertullian. *Adversus Marcionem*. Edited and translated by E. Evans. Oxford: Clarendon Press, 1972.

Apology
Latin: Tertullian, Minucius Felix. *Apology. De spectaculis. Minucius Felix: Octavius*. Translated by T. R. Glover and Gerald H. Rendall. LCL 250. Cambridge, MA: Harvard University Press, 1977.
English translation: *ANF* 3, 37. Translated by S. Thelwall.

De anima
Latin: Tertullian. *De anima*. Edited with a commentary by J. H. Waszink. Amsterdam, 1947.
English translation: *ANF* 3. Translated by P. Holmes.

De baptismo
Latin and English: *Tertullian's Homily on Baptism*. Edited with an introduction, translation, and commentary by Ernest Evans. London: SPCK, 1964.

De corona (or *De corona militis*)
Latin: Tertullian. *De corona*. Edited by J. Fontaine. Paris: Presses Universitaires de France, 1966.
English translation: *ANF* 3. Translated by S. Thelwall.

De idolatria
Latin: Reifferscheid, A., and Georg Wissowa, eds. *Quinti Septimi Florentis Tertulliani Opera*. CSEL 20. Vienna: F. Tempsky, 1890.
English translation: *ANF* 3. Translated by S. Thelwall.

De monogamia
Latin: Tertullian. *Ad martyras, Ad Scapulam. . . .* Edited by V. Bulhart. CSEL 76. Vienna: Hoelder-Pichler-Tempsky, 1957.
English translation: *ANF* 4. Translated by S. Thelwall.

De oratione
Latin and English translation: Evans, E., ed. and trans. *Tertullian's Tract on the Prayer*. London: SPCK, 1953.
English translation: *ANF* 3. Translated by S. Thelwall.

De spectaculis
Latin: Weeber, Karl-Wilhelm, ed. *Quintus Septimius Tertullianus*. Stuttgart: Reclam, 1988.
English translation: *ANF* 3. Translated by S. Thelwall.

De testimonio animae
Latin: Reifferscheid, A., and Georg Wissowa, eds. *Quinti Septimi Florentis Tertulliani Opera*. CSEL 20. Vienna: F. Tempsky, 1890.
English translation: Tertullian. *On the Testimony of the Soul*. Translated by Q. Howe. 2007. The Tertullian Project: https://www.tertullian.org/articles/howe_testimonio_animae.htm.

On Chastity
Latin: Tertullian. *Exhortation à la chasteté*. Edited by Claudio Moreschini. Translated by Jean-Claude Fredouille. Sources chrétiennes 319. Paris: Cerf, 1985.
English translation: *ANF* 4. Translated by S. Thelwall.

Tibullus
Latin and English translation: Catullus, Tibullus. *Catullus, Tibullus, Pervigilium Veneris*. Translated by F. W. Cornish, J. P. Postgate, J. W. Mackail. Revised by G. P. Goold. LCL 6. Cambridge, MA: Harvard University Press, 1988.

Xenophon
Oeconomicus
Greek and English translation: Pomeroy, *Xenophon*.

Secondary Sources

Adams, Edward. *The Earliest Christian Meeting Places: Almost Exclusively Houses?* London: Bloomsbury T&T Clark, 2013.

Adler, William. "The Cesti and Sophistic Culture in the Severan Age." In *Die Kestoi des Julius Africanus und ihre Überlieferung*, edited by Martin Wallraff, 1–15. New York: De Gruyter, 2007.

Allen, Amy. *The Power of Feminist Theory: Domination, Resistance, Solidarity*. Boulder, CO: Westview Press, 1999.

Allen, Marti Lu. "The Terracotta Figurines from Karanis: A Study of Technique,

Style, and Chronology in Fayoumic Coroplastics." PhD diss., University of Michigan, 1985.

Allison, Penelope. *Pompeian Households: An Analysis of the Material Culture*. Los Angeles: Cotsen Institute of Archaeology, 2004.

——. "Roman Households: An Archaeological Perspective." In *Roman Urbanism: Beyond the Consumer City*, edited by H. M. Parkins, 112–46. London: Routledge, 1997.

Archer, Leonie. "The Role of Jewish Women in the Religion, Ritual, and Cult of Graeco-Roman Palestine." In *Images of Women in Antiquity*, edited by Averil Cameron and Amélie Kuhrt, 273–87. Detroit: Wayne State University Press, 1983.

Argetsinger, Kathryn. "Birthday Rituals: Friends and Patrons in Roman Poetry and Cult." *Classical Antiquity* 23 (1992): 175–93.

Arnal, William. "The Collection and Synthesis of 'Tradition' and the Second Century Invention of Christianity." *Method and Theory in the Study of Religion* 23 (2011): 193–215.

Aulbach, Louis F., and Linda C. Gorski. "The Circiform Basilicas of Rome." *Journal: Houston Archaeological Society* 140 (2019): 99–122.

Aune, David E. "Magic in Early Christianity." In *Apocalypticism, Prophecy, and Magic in Early Christianity: Collected Essays*, edited by David E. Aune, 368–420. Tübingen: Mohr Siebeck, 2006.

Bakker, Jane Theo. *Living and Working with the Gods: Studies of Evidence for Private Religion and Its Material Environment in the City of Ostia (100–500 AD)*. Dutch Monographs on Ancient History and Archaeology 12. Amsterdam: J. C. Gieben, 1994.

Balch, David L. *Let Wives Be Submissive: The Domestic Code in 1 Peter*. Chico, CA: Scholars Press, 1981.

——. "Rich Pompeian Houses, Shops for Rent, and the Huge Apartment Building in Herculaneum as Typical Spaces for Pauline House Churches." *Journal for the Study of the New Testament* 27, no. 1 (2004): 39–40.

Barton, Carlin A., and Daniel Boyarin. *Imagine No Religion: How Modern Abstracts Hide Ancient Realities*. New York: Fordham University Press, 2016.

Beard, Mary, John North, and Simon Price. *Religions of Rome*. Vol. 1, *A History*. Cambridge: Cambridge University Press, 1998.

Bell, Catherine. *Ritual Theory, Ritual Practice*. New York: Oxford University Press, 1992.

Benga, Daniel. "'Defining Sacred Boundaries': Processes of Delimitation from the Pagan Society in Syrian Christianity According to the *Didascalia Apostolorum*." *Zeitschrift für antikes Christentum* 17, no. 3 (2013): 526–59.

Bernstein, Frances. "Pompeiian Women." In *The World of Pompeii*, edited by John J. Dobbins and Pedar W. Foss, 526–37. New York: Routledge, 2007.

Berry, Joanne. "Household Artefacts: Towards a Re-interpretation of Roman Domestic Space." In *Domestic Space in the Roman World*, edited by Ray Laurence and Andrew Wallace-Hadrill, 183–96. Journal of Roman Archaeology Supplementary Series 22. Portsmouth, RI: Journal of Roman Archaeology, 1997.

Betz, Hans Dieter, ed. *The Greek Magical Papyri in Translation*. Chicago: University of Chicago Press, 1986.

Bisconti, Fabrizio, and V. Fiocchi Nicolai. "Riti e corredi funerari." In *Christiana loca: Lo spazio cristiano nella Roma del primo millennio*, vol. 2, edited by L. Pani Ermini, 61–96. Rome: Fratelli Palombi, 2000.

Blumell, Lincoln H., and Thomas A. Wayment, eds. *Christian Oxyrhynchus: Texts, Documents, and Sources*. Waco, TX: Baylor University Press, 2015.

Boak, Arthur E. R., and Enoch Peterson. *Karanis: Topographical and Architectural Report of Excavations During the Seasons 1924–28*. Ann Arbor: University of Michigan Press, 1931.

Bodel, John. "Cicero's Minerva, *Penates*, and the Mother of the *Lares*: An Outline of Roman Domestic Religion." In *Household and Family Religion in Antiquity*, edited by John Bodel and Saul M. Olyan, 248–75. Malden, MA: Blackwell, 2008.

———. "From Columbaria to Catacombs." In *Commemorating the Dead: Texts and Artifacts in Context*, edited by Laurie Brink and Deborah Green, 177–242. New York: De Gruyter, 2008.

Bohak, Gideon. *Ancient Jewish Magic*. Cambridge: Cambridge University Press, 2008.

Boin, Douglas. *Coming Out Christian in the Roman World: How the Followers of Jesus Made a Place in Caesar's Empire*. New York: Bloomsbury, 2015.

———. *Ostia in Late Antiquity*. Cambridge: Cambridge University Press, 2013.

Bömer, Franz. *Untersuchungen über die Religion der Sklaven in Griechenland und Rom*. Stuttgart: Steiner, 1990.

Bonner, Campbell. *Studies in Magical Amulets, Chiefly Graeco-Egyptian*. Ann Arbor: University of Michigan Press, 1950.

Borg, Barbara E. *Crisis and Ambition: Tombs and Burial Customs in Third-Century AD Rome*. Oxford: Oxford University Press, 2013.

———. "The Late Antique Funerary Landscape of Rome: 3rd to 4th c. AD." In *Burial and Memorial in Late Antiquity*, vol. 2, *Regional Perspective*, edited by Alexandra Dolea and Luke Lavan, 222–47. Leiden: Brill, 2024.

———. "Peter and Paul *ad catacumbas*: A Pozzolana Mine Reconsidered." In *The Economy of Death: New Research on Collective Burial Spaces in Rome from the Late Republic to the Late Roman Time*, edited by Norbert Zimmermann and Thomas Fröhlich, 45–58. Heidelberg: Propylaeum, 2022.

Boschung, Dietrich, Alan Shapiro, and Frank Wascheck, eds. *Bodies in Transition: Dissolving Boundaries of Embodied Knowledge*. Paderborn: Wilhelm Fink, 2015.

Bourdieu, Pierre. "The Berber House." In *Rules and Meanings: The Anthropology of Everyday Knowledge*, edited by Mary Douglas, 98–110. New York: Penguin, 1973.

Boustan, Ra'anan, and Joseph E. Sanzo. "Christian Magicians, Jewish Magical Idioms, and the Shared Magical Culture of Late Antiquity." *Harvard Theological Review* 110, no. 2 (2017): 217–40.

Bowes, Kim. "At Home." In *A Companion to the Archaeology of Religion in the Ancient World*, edited by Rubina Raja and Jörg Rüpke, 209–19. Malden, MA: Blackwell, 2015.

———. *Private Worship, Public Values, and Religious Change in Late Antiquity*. Cambridge: Cambridge University Press, 2008.

Boyarin, Daniel. *Border Lines: The Partition of Judaeo-Christianity*. Philadelphia: University of Pennsylvania Press, 2006.

Boyce, George K. *Corpus of the Lararia of Pompeii*. Memoirs of the American Academy in Rome 24. Rome: American Academy of Rome, 1937.

Bradshaw, Paul F. *Daily Prayer in the Early Church: A Study of the Origin and Early Development of the Divine Office*. New York: Oxford University Press, 1982.

———. *The Search for the Origins of Christian Worship: Sources and Methods for the Study of Early Liturgy*. 2nd ed. Oxford: Oxford University Press, 2002.

Bradshaw, Paul F., Maxwell Johnson, and L. Edward Phillips. *The Apostolic Tradition: A Commentary*. Hermeneia. Minneapolis: Fortress, 2002.

Brakke, David. *Athanasius and the Politics of Asceticism*. Oxford: Clarendon Press, 1995.

———. "Canon Formation and Social Conflict in Fourth-Century Egypt: Athanasius of Alexandria's Thirty-Ninth 'Festal Letter.'" *Harvard Theological Review* 87, no. 4 (1994): 395–419.

Brashear, William M. "The Greek Magical Papyri: An Introduction and Survey; Annotated Bibliography (1928–1994)." In *Aufstieg und Niedergang der römischen Welt*, part 2, vol. 18/55, edited by Wolfgang Haas, 3380–684. Berlin: De Gruyter, 1995.

Bremmer, Jan N. "Urban Religion, Neighbourhoods and the Early Christian Meeting Places." *Religion in the Roman Empire* 6, no. 1 (2020): 48–74.

Bremmer, Jan, and Herman Roodenburg, eds. *A Cultural History of Gesture*. Ithaca: Cornell University Press, 1992.

Brent, Allen. *Cyprian and Roman Carthage*. Cambridge: Cambridge University Press, 2010.

———. *Hippolytus and the Roman Church in the Third Century: Communities in Tension Before the Emergence of a Monarch-Bishop*. New York: Brill, 1995.

Brøndsted, Johannes. "La basilique des cinq martyrs à Kapljuč." In *Recherches à Salone*, edited by Ejnar Dyggve, 35–186. Copenhagen: J. H. Schultz, 1928.

Brooten, Bernadette J. "Enslaved Women in Basil of Caesarea's Canonical Letters: An Intersectional Analysis." In *Doing Gender, Doing Religion*, edited by Ute Eisen, Christine Gerber, and Angela Standhartinger, 325–55. Tübingen: Mohr Siebeck, 2013.

Brown, Peter. *The Cult of the Saints: Its Rise and Function in Latin Christianity*. Chicago: University of Chicago Press, 1981.

Brown, Vincent. "Social Death and Political Life in the Study of Slavery." *American Historical Review* (2009): 1231–49.

Brussière, Jean, and Birgitta Lindros Wohl. *Ancient Lamps in the J. Paul Getty Museum*. Los Angeles: Getty Publications, 2017.

Buell, Denise. "Embodied Temporalities: Health, Illness, and the Matter of Feminist Biblical Interpretation." In *The Bible and Feminism: Remapping the Field*, edited by Yvonne Sherwood and Anna Fisk, 454–76. Oxford: Oxford University Press, 2017.

Burns, J. Patout, Jr., and Robin M. Jensen. *Christianity in Roman Africa: The Development of Its Practices and Beliefs*. Grand Rapids, MI: Eerdmans, 2014.

Butler, Judith. *Bodies That Matter: On the Discursive Limits of "Sex."* New York: Routledge, 1993.

Calza, Guido. *La necropoli del Porto di Roma nell'Isola Sacra*. Rome: La Libreria dello Stato, 1940.

Castelli, Elizabeth. "Interpretations of Power in 1 Corinthians." *Semeia* 54 (1991): 197–222.

———. "Paul on Women and Gender." In *Women and Christian Origins*, edited by Ross Shepard Kraemer and Mary Rose D'Angelo, 226–30. New York: Oxford University Press, 1999.

Chancey, Mark, and Eric M. Meyers. "How Jewish Was Sepphoris in Jesus' Time?" *Biblical Archaeology Review* 26, no. 4 (2000): 18–33.

Chapman, David W. *Ancient Jewish and Christian Perceptions of Crucifixion*. Grand Rapids, MI: Baker, 2010.

Chepel, Elena. "Invocations of the Blood of Christ in Greek Magical Amulets." *Scrinium* 13 (2017): 53–71.

Chowdharay-Best, George. "Notes on the Healing Properties of Saliva." *Folklore* 86, no. 3 (1975): 195–200. https://www.jstor.org/stable/1260235.

Cianca, Jenn. *Sacred Ritual, Profane Space: The Roman House as Early Christian Meeting Place*. Montreal: McGill-Queen's University Press, 2018.

Clark, Christina A., Edith Foster, and Judith P. Hallett, eds. *Kinesis: The Ancient Depiction of Gesture, Motion, and Emotion; Essays for Donald Lateiner*. Ann Arbor: University of Michigan Press, 2015.

Clark, Patricia. "Women, Slaves, and the Hierarchies of Domestic Violence: The Family of St. Augustine." In *Women and Slaves in Greco-Roman Culture: Differential Equations*, edited by Sandra R. Joshel and Sheila Murnaghan, 109–29. New York: Routledge, 1998.

Clarke, George W. *The Letters of St. Cyprian of Carthage*. Vols. 1 and 3. Ancient Christian Writers 43, 44. New York: Newman Press, 1984–89.

Clarke, John R. *The Houses of Roman Italy 100 BC–AD 250: Ritual, Space, and Decoration*. Berkeley: University of California Press, 1991.

Cohen, Shaye J. D. "From Permission to Prohibition: Paul and the Early Church on Mixed Marriage." In *Paul's Jewish Matrix*, edited by Thomas G. Casey and Justin Taylor, 259–91. Rome: G&B; Mahwah, NJ: Paulist, 2011.

Concannon, Cavan W. *Assembling Early Christianity: Trade, Networks, and the Letters of Dionysius of Corinth*. Cambridge: Cambridge University Press, 2017.

Connolly, Joy. "Mastering Corruption: Constructions of Identity in Roman Oratory." In *Women and Slaves in Greco-Roman Culture: Differential Equations*, edited by Sandra R. Joshel and Sheila Murnaghan, 130–51. New York: Routledge, 1998.

Conway, Colleen. *Behold the Man: Jesus and Greco-Roman Masculinity*. Oxford: Oxford University Press, 2008.

Cook, John Granger. "Crucifixion as a Spectacle." *Novum Testamentum* 54 (2012): 68-100.

———. *Crucifixion in the Mediterranean World*. Tübingen: Mohr Siebeck, 2014.

Cooper, Kate. "Closely Watched Households: Visibility, Exposure and Private Power in the Roman Domus." *Past and Present* 197 (2007): 3–33.

Corbeill, Anthony. *Nature Embodied: Gesture in Ancient Rome*. Princeton, NJ: Princeton University Press, 2004.

Cotter, Wendy. *Miracles in Greco-Roman Antiquity: A Sourcebook for the Study of New Testament Miracle Stories*. London: Routledge, 1999.

Crenshaw, Kimberlé. "Demarginalizing the Intersection of Race and Sex: A Black Feminist Critique of Antidiscrimination Doctrine, Feminist Theory, and Antiracist Politics." *University of Chicago Legal Forum*, 1989, 139–67.

Davidson, Ivor J. *The Birth of the Church: From Jesus to Constantine AD 30–312*. Grand Rapids, MI: Baker, 2004.

De Bruyn, Theodore. "Appeals to Jesus and the One 'Who Heals Every Illness and Every Infirmity' (Matt 4:23, 9:35) in Amulets in Late Antiquity." In *The Reception and Interpretation of the Bible in Late Antiquity*, edited by Lorenzo DiTommaso and Lucian Turcescu, 65–81. Boston: Brill, 2008.

———. *Making Amulets Christian: Artifacts, Scribes, Contexts*. Oxford: Oxford University Press, 2017.

De Bruyn, Theodore, and Jitse Dijkstra. "Greek Amulets and Formularies from Egypt Containing Christian Elements: A Checklist of Papyri, Parchments, Ostraka, Tablets." *Bulletin of the American Society of Papyrologists* 48 (2011): 163–216.

de Certeau, Michel. *The Practice of Everyday Life*. Vol. 1. Translated by S. F. Rendall. Berkeley: University of California Press, 1984.

Deckers, Johannes Georg. "Wie genau ist eine Katakombe zu datieren? Das beispiel SS. Marcellino e Pietro." In *Memoriam Sanctorum Venerantes: Miscellanea in onore di Monsignor Victor Saxer*, 217–38. Vatican City: Pontificio Istituto di Archeologia Cristiana, 1992.

Deissman, Adolf. *Light from the East: The New Testament Illustrated by Recently Discovered Texts of the Graeco-Roman World*. Translated by Lionel R. M. Strachan. New York: Hodder and Stoughton, 1910.

Delehaye, Hippolyte. "Nouvelles fouilles à Salone." *Analecta Bollandiana* 47 (1929): 77–88.

Denzey, Nicola. *The Bone Gatherers: The Lost Worlds of Early Christian Women*. Boston: Beacon, 2007.

Denzey Lewis, Nicola. *Early Modern Invention of Late Antique Rome*. Cambridge: Cambridge University Press, 2020.

———. "Popular Christianity and Lived Religion in Late Antique Rome: Seeing Magic in the Catacombs." In *Locating Popular Culture in the Ancient World*, edited by Lucy Grig, 257–76. Cambridge: Cambridge University Press, 2015.

———. "Reinterpreting 'Pagans' and 'Christians' from Rome's Late Antique Mortuary Evidence." In *Pagans and Christians in Late Antique Rome: Conflict, Competition, and Coexistence in the Fourth Century*, edited by Michele Renee Salzman, Marianne Sághy, and Rita Lizzi Testa, 273–90. Cambridge: Cambridge University Press, 2015.

Denzey Lewis, Nicola, Georgia Frank, David Frankfurter, Lucy Grig, and William Klingshern. "Viewpoint Essays." *Studies in Late Antiquity* 5, no. 1 (2021): 103–60.

Derchain, Philippe. "Die älteste Darstellung des Gekreuzigten auf einer magischen Gemme des 3. Jahrhunderts." In *Christentum am Nil*, edited by K. Wessel, 109–13. Recklinghausen: Bongers, 1964.

DesRosiers, Nathaniel P., and Lily C. Vuong, eds. *Religious Competition in the Greco-Roman World*. Atlanta: SBL Press, 2016.

Dieleman, Jacco. "The Greco-Egyptian Magical Papyri." In *Guide to the Study of Magic*, edited by David Frankfurter, 283–32. Leiden: Brill, 2019.

Dillon, Matthew, Esther Eidinow, and Liza Maurizio, eds. *Women's Ritual Competence in the Greco-Roman*

Mediterranean. London: Routledge, 2017.
Dix, Gregory. *A Detection of Aumbries*. Westminster: Dacre, 1954.
———. *Shape of the Liturgy*. Westminster: Dacre, 1945.
Dixon, Suzanne. *The Roman Family*. Baltimore, MD: Johns Hopkins University Press, 1992.
———. *The Roman Mother*. Norman: University of Oklahoma Press, 1988.
Dölger, Franz Joseph. *Lumen Christi*. Translated from German to French by Marc Zemb. Paris: Éditions du Cerf, 1958.
Donati, Angela. *Pietro e Paolo: La storia, il culto, la memoria nei primi secoli*. Milan: Electa, 2000.
Dorcey, P. F. *The Cult of Silvanus: A Study in Roman Folk Religion*. Columbia Studies in the Classical Tradition 20. Leiden: Brill, 1992.
Dunbabin, Katherine M. D. *The Roman Banquet: Images of Conviviality*. Cambridge: Cambridge University Press, 2003.
Dyggve, Ejnar. *History of Salonitan Christianity*. Oslo: H. Aschehoug, 1951.
Eastman, David. *Paul the Martyr: The Cult of the Apostle in the Latin West*. Atlanta: Society of Biblical Literature, 2011.
Edmondson, Jonathan. "Slavery and the Roman Family." In *The Cambridge World History of Slavery*, vol. 1, *The Ancient Mediterranean World*, edited by Keith Bradley and Paul Cartledge, 337–61. Cambridge: Cambridge University Press, 2011.
Ehrman, Bart D. *After the New Testament: A Reader in Early Christianity*. New York: Oxford University Press, 1999.
Eidinow, Esther. *Oracles, Curses, and Risk Among the Ancient Greeks*. Oxford: Oxford University Press, 2007.
Eitrem, Samson. *Some Notes on the Demonology of the New Testament*. Oslo: Universitetsforlaget, 1996.
Elliott, John H. *1 Peter: A New Translation with Introduction and Commentary*. The Anchor Bible. New York: Doubleday, 2000.
Emmerson, Allison L. C. *Life and Death in the Roman Suburb*. Oxford: Oxford University Press, 2020.

Eshel, Hanan. "They're Not Ritual Baths." *Biblical Archaeology Review* 26, no. 4 (2000): 42–45.
———. "We Need More Data." *Biblical Archaeology Review* 26, no. 4 (2000): 49–50.
Eshleman, Kendra. *The Social World of Intellectuals in the Roman Empire: Sophists, Philosophers, and Christians*. Cambridge: Cambridge University Press, 2012.
Eyl, Jennifer. *Signs, Wonders, and Gifts: Divination in the Letters of Paul*. New York: Oxford University Press, 2019.
Faraone, Christopher A. *The Transformation of Greek Amulets in Roman Imperial Times*. Philadelphia: University of Pennsylvania Press, 2018.
Faraone, Christopher A., and Dirk Obbink, eds. *Magika Hiera: Ancient Greek Magic and Religion*. New York: Oxford, 1991.
Février, Paul-Albert. "Le culte des martyrs en Afrique et ses plus anciens monuments." *Corsi di Cultura sull'Arte Ravennate e Bizantina* 17 (1970): 191–215.
———. "Le culte des morts dans les communautés chrétiennes durant le IIIe siècle." In Atti del IX Congresso Internazionale di Archeologia Cristiana, Roma, 21–27 settembre 1975. 1, I Monumenti Cristiani Precostantiniani, 211–74. Vatican City: Pontificio Istituto de Archeologia Cristiana, 1978.
Fine, Steven. "Jewish Art and Biblical Exegesis in the Greco-Roman World." In *Picturing the Bible: The Earliest Christian Art*, edited by J. Spier, 24–49. New Haven, CT: Yale University Press, 2007.
Finney, Paul Corby. "Images on Finger Rings and Early Christian Art." In *Studies on Art and Archeology in Honor of Ernst Kitzinger on His Seventy-Fifth Birthday*, edited by William Tronzo and Irving Lavin, 181–86. Dumbarton Oaks Papers 41. Washington, DC: Dumbarton Oaks Research Library and Collection, 1987.
Flexsenhar, Michael, III. *Christians in Caesar's Household: The Emperors' Slaves in the Making of Christianity*. University Park: Penn State University Press, 2019.
Flory, M. B. "Family in *Familia*: Kinship and Community in Slavery." *American*

Journal of Ancient History 3 (1978): 78–95.

Flower, Harriet I. *The Dancing Lares and the Serpent in the Garden: Religion and the Roman Street Corner.* Princeton, NJ: Princeton University Press, 2017.

Forsdyke, Sara. *Slaves and Slavery in Ancient Greece.* Cambridge: Cambridge University Press, 2021.

Foss, Pedar. "Watchful *Lares*: Roman Household Organization and the Rituals of Cooking and Eating." In *Domestic Space in the Roman World: Pompeii and Beyond*, edited by Ray Laurence and Andrew Wallace-Hadrill, 197–218. Journal of Roman Archaeology Supplementary Series 22. Portsmouth, RI: Journal of Roman Archaeology, 1997.

Frank, Georgia. *Unfinished Christians: Ritual Objects and Silent Subjects in Late Antiquity.* Philadelphia: University of Pennsylvania Press, 2023.

Frankfurter, David. "Ancient Magic in a New Key: Refining an Exotic Discipline in the History of Religions." In *Guide to the Study of Ancient Magic*, edited by David Frankfurter, 3–20. Religions in the Graeco-Roman World 189. Leiden: Brill, 2019.

———. "'As I Twirl This Spindle . . .': Ritualization and the Magical Efficacy of Household Tasks in Western Antiquity." *Preternature* 10, no. 1 (2021): 117–39.

———. "Beyond Magic and Superstition." In *Late Ancient Christianity*, edited by Virginia Burrus, 255–84. A People's History of Christianity 2. Minneapolis: Fortress, 2005.

———. *Christianizing Egypt: Syncretism and Local Worlds in Late Antiquity.* Princeton, NJ: Princeton University Press, 2018.

———. "The Cult of the Martyrs in Egypt Before Constantine: The Evidence of the Coptic 'Apocalypse of Elijah.'" *Vigiliae Christianae* 48, no. 1 (1994): 25–47.

———. "Dynamics of Ritual Expertise in Antiquity and Beyond: Towards a New Taxonomy of 'Magicians.'" In *Magic and Ritual in the Ancient World*, edited by Paul Mirecki and Marvin W. Meyer, 159–78. Leiden: Brill, 2002.

———, ed. *Guide to the Study of Ancient Magic.* Religions in the Graeco-Roman World 189. Boston: Brill, 2019.

———. "Healing Spells." In *Ancient Christian Magic: Coptic Texts of Ritual Power*, edited by Marvin W. Meyer and Richard Smith. Princeton, NJ: Princeton University Press, 1994, 79–82.

———. "Narrating Power: The Theory and Practice of the Magical *Historiola* in Ritual Spells." In *Ancient Magic and Ritual Power*, edited by Marvin W. Meyer and Paul Mirecki, 457–76. Leiden: Brill, 1995.

———. *Religion in Roman Egypt: Assimilation and Resistance.* Princeton, NJ: Princeton University Press, 1998.

———. "Religious Practice and Piety." In *The Oxford Handbook of Roman Egypt*, edited by Christina Riggs, 319–36. New York: Oxford University Press, 2012. DOI: 10.1093/oxfordhb/9780199571451.013.0021.

———. "Restoring 'Syncretism' in the History of Early Christianity." *Studies in Late Antiquity* 5, no. 1 (2021): 128–38.

———. "The Spaces of Domestic Religion in Late Antique Egypt." *Archiv für Religionsgeschichte* 18–19, no. 1 (2017): 7–23.

———. "Where the Spirits Dwell: Possession, Christianization, and Saints' Shrines in Late Antiquity." *Harvard Theological Review* 103, no. 1 (2010): 27–46.

Frankfurter, David, and Zsuzsanna Varhelyi, eds. "Sacra Privata: Domestic Religion in Greco-Roman Antiquity and Early Christianity." Special issue, *Archiv für Religionsgeschichte* 18–19, no. 1 (2017).

Freestone, W. H. *The Sacrament Reserved.* Milwaukee: Young Churchman, 1917.

Frenschkowski, Marco. "Domestic Religion, Family Life and the Apocryphal Acts of the Apostles." *Archiv für Religionsgeschichte* 18–19, no. 1 (2017): 123–55.

Fröhlich, Thomas. *Lararien- und Fassadenbilder in den Vesuvstädten. Untersuchunges sur 'volkstümlichen' pompejanishcen Malerei.* RömMitt-Erg 32. Mainz: P. von Zabern, 1991.

Fugger, Verena. "Shedding Light on Early Christian Domestic Cult: Characteristics and New Perspectives in the Context of Archaeological Findings." *Archiv für Religionsgeschichte* 18–19, no. 1 (2017): 201–35.

Gager, John G., ed. *Curse Tablets and Binding Spells from the Ancient World*. New York: Oxford University Press, 1992.

Galor, Katharina. "The Stepped Water Installations of the Sepphoris Acropolis." In *The Archaeology of Difference: Gender, Ethnicity, and the Other in Antiquity*, edited by D. Edwards and C. McCollough, 205–17. Boston: American Schools of Oriental Research, 2007.

Gardner, Gregg E. "City of Lights: The Lamps of Roman and Byzantine Jerusalem." *Near Eastern Archaeology* 77, no. 4 (2014): 284–90.

Gardner, Jane. *Family and Familia in Roman Law and Life*. Oxford: Clarendon Press, 1998.

Gasparini, Valentino, Maik Patzelt, Rubina Raja, Anna-Katharina Rieger, Jörg Rüpke, and Emiliano Urciuoli, eds. *Lived Religion in the Ancient Mediterranean World*. Berlin: De Gruyter, 2020.

Gauthier, N., E. Marin, and F. Prévot, eds. *Salona IV: Inscriptions de Salone chrétienne IVe–VIIe siècles*. Collection de l'École française de Rome 194/4. Rome: École française de Rome, 2010.

Gazda, Elaine. *Guardians of the Nile: Sculptures from Karanis in the Fayoum (c. 250 BC–AD 450)*. Ann Arbor: Kelsey Museum of Archaeology; University of Michigan Press, 1978.

George, Michele. "Domestic Architecture and Household Relations: Pompeii and Roman Ephesos." *Journal for the Study of the New Testament* 27, no. 1 (2004): 7–25.

———. "The Lives of Slaves." In *The World of Pompeii*, edited by Pedar Foss and John J. Dobbins, 538–49. London: Routledge, 2007.

———. "Repopulating the Roman House." In *The Roman Family in Italy—Status, Sentiment, Space*, edited by B. Rawson and P. Weaver, 299–319. Oxford: Clarendon Press, 1997.

———. "Servus and Domus: The Slave in the Roman House." In *Domestic Space in the Roman World: Pompeii and Beyond*, edited by Ray Laurence and Andrew Wallace-Hadrill, 15–24. Journal of Roman Archaeology Supplementary Series 22. Portsmouth, RI: Journal of Roman Archaeology, 1997.

———. "Slavery and Roman Material Culture." In *The Cambridge World History of Slavery*, vol. 1, *The Ancient Mediterranean World*, edited by Keith Bradley and Paul Cartledge, 385–413. Cambridge: Cambridge University Press, 2011.

Giacobello, Frederica. *Larari pompeiani: Iconografia e culto dei Lari in ambito domestico*. Milan: LED, 2008.

Gibson, Elsa. *The "Christians for Christians" Inscriptions of Phrygia*. Missoula, MT: Scholars Press, 1978.

Giuntella, Anna Maria, Giuseppina Borghetti, and Daniela Stiaffini. *Mensae e riti funerari in Sardegna: La testimonianza di Cornus*. Mediterraneo tardoantico medievale: Scavi e ricerche 1. Taranto: Scorpione, 1985.

Glancy, Jennifer. "Slavery and the Rise of Christianity." In *The Cambridge World History of Slavery*, vol. 1, *The Ancient Mediterranean World*, edited by Keith Bradley and Paul Cartledge, 456–81. Cambridge: Cambridge University Press, 2011.

———. *Slavery in Early Christianity*. New York: Oxford University Press, 2002.

Goldenberg, Robert. "The Jewish Sabbath in the Roman World Up to the Time of Constantine the Great." *Aufstieg und Niedergang der Römischen Welt* 2.19.1 (1979): 414–47.

Grabar, André. *The Beginnings of Christian Art, 200–395*. London: Thames and Hudson, 1977.

Gradel, Ittai. *Emperor Worship and Roman Religion*. Oxford: Clarendon Press, 2002.

Graf, Fritz. "The Christian Transformation of Magic." In *Mito y magia en Grecia y Roma*, edited by E. Suárez de la Torre and A. Pérez Jiménez, 299–310. Barcelona: Portico, 2013.

———. *Magic in the Ancient World*. Reprint edition. Cambridge, MA: Harvard University Press, 1999.

Grantham, Billy J. "Faunal Remains." In *Sepphoris III: The Architecture, Stratigraphy, and Artifacts of the Western Summit of Sepphoris, Volume 2*, edited by Eric M. Meyers, Carol L. Meyers, and Benjamin D. Gordon, 871–88. University Park, PA: Eisenbrauns, 2018.

Grossi Gondi, G. Felice. "Di un graffito greco nella triclia di S. Sebastiano sull'Appia." *Nuovo bullettino di archeologia cristiana* 28 (1922): 27–31.

Hachlili, Rachel. *Jewish Funerary Customs, Practices and Rites in the Second Temple Period*. Leiden: Brill, 2004.

Hadley, James Thomas. "Early Christian Perceptions of Sacred Spaces." *Revue de la culture matérielle* 80–81 (2014–15): 89–107.

Hallett, Judith. "The Eleven Elegies of the Augustan Poet Sulpicia." In *Women Writing Latin: From Roman Antiquity to Early Modern Europe*, edited by L. J. Churchill, P. R. Brown, and J. E. Jeffrey, 1:45–84. New York: Routledge, 2002.

Hancock, Ange-Marie. "Intersectionality as a Normative and Empirical Paradigm." *Politics and Gender* 3, no. 2 (2007): 248–54.

———. "When Multiplication Doesn't Equal Quick Addition: Examining Intersectionality as a Research Paradigm." *Perspectives on Politics* 5, no. 1 (2007): 63–79.

Harley-McGowan, Felicity. "The Constanza Carnelian and the Development of Crucifixion Iconography in Late Antiquity." In *Gems of Heaven: Recent Research on Engraved Gemstones in Late Antiquity c. 200–600*, edited by Chris Entwhistle and Noël Adams, 214–20. London: British Museum, 2012.

———. "Images of the Crucifixion in Late Antiquity: The Testimony of Engraved Gems." PhD diss., University of Adelaide, 2001.

———. "Jesus the Magician: A Crucifixion Amulet and Its Date." In *Magical gems in Their Contexts: Proceedings of the International Workshop Held at the Museum of Fine Arts, Budapest, 16–18 February 2012*, edited by Kata Endreffy, Árpád M. Nagy, and Jeffrey Spier, 103–16, plates 348–49. Rome: "L'Erma" di Bretschneider, 2019.

———. "Picturing the Passion." In *The Routledge Handbook of Early Christian Art*, edited by Robin M. Jensen and Mark D. Ellison, 290–307. New York: Routledge, 2018.

Harley-McGowan, Felicity, and Jeffrey Spier. "Magical Amulet with Crucifixion." In *Picturing the Bible: The Earliest Christian Art*, edited by Jeffrey Spier, 228–29. Fort Worth, TX: Kimbell Art Museum, 2007.

Harmon, Daniel P. "The Family Festivals of Rome." *Aufstieg und Niedergang der römischen Welt* 2.16.2 (1978): 1595–1600.

Harrill, J. Albert. *Manumission of Slaves in Early Christianity*. Tübingen: Mohr Siebeck, 1995.

———. "Servile Functionaries or Priestly Leaders? Roman Domestic Religion, Narrative Intertextuality, and Pliny's Reference to Slave Christian *Ministrae* (Ep. 10,96,8)." *Zeitschrift für die neutestamentliche Wissenschaft* 97, nos. 1–2 (2006): 111–30.

———. *Slaves in the New Testament: Literary, Social, and Moral Dimensions*. Minneapolis: Fortress, 206.

Hawley, Richard. "Lords of the Rings: Ring-Wearing, Status, and Identity in the age of Pliny the Elder." In *Vita Vigilia Est: Studies in Honor of Barbara Levick*, edited by Edward Bispham, Greg Rowe, and Elaine Matthews, 103–11. Supplement edition 100. London: Institute of Classical Studies, 2007.

Hellström, Monica. "On the Form and Function of Constantine's Circiform Funerary Basilicas in Rome." In *Pagans and Christians in Late Antique Rome: Conflict, Competition, and Coexistence in the Fourth Century*, edited by Michele Renee Salzman, Marianne Sághy, and Rita Lizzi Testa, 291–313. Cambridge: Cambridge University Press, 2015.

Hezser, Catherine, ed. *The Oxford Handbook of Jewish Daily Life in Roman Palestine*. Oxford: Oxford University Press, 2010.

Hicks, Derek S. *Reclaiming Spirit in the Black Faith Tradition*. New York: Palgrave, 2012.

Hijmans, Steven. "Language, Metaphor, and the Semiotics of Roman Art: Some Thoughts on Reading the Mosaics of Mausoleum M in the Vatican Necropolis." *Bulletin Antieke Beschaving* 75 (2000): 147–64.

Hodkinson, Stephen, and Dick Geary, eds. *Slaves and Religions in Graeco-Roman*

Antiquity and Modern Brazil. Newcastle upon Tyne: Cambridge Scholars Publishing, 2012.

Hope, Valerie. "A Roof over the Dead: Communal Tombs and Family Structure." In *Domestic Space in the Roman World*, edited by Ray Laurence and Andrew Wallace-Hadrill, 69–90. Journal of Roman Archaeology Supplementary Series 22. Portsmouth, RI: Journal of Roman Archaeology, 1997.

Hoskins Walbank, Mary. "Unquiet Graves: Burial Practices of the Roman Corinthians." In *Urban Religion in Roman Corinth: Interdisciplinary Approaches*, edited by Daniel Schowalter and Steven Friesen, 249–80. Cambridge, MA: Harvard University Press, 2005.

Husselman, Elinor. *Karanis Excavations of the University of Michigan in Egypt, 1928–1935: Topography and Architecture; A Summary of the Reports of the Director, Enoch E. Peterson*. Ann Arbor: University of Michigan Press, 1979.

Hvalvik, Reidar. "Praying with Outstretched Hands: Nonverbal Aspects of Early Christian Prayer and the Question of Identity." In *Early Christian Prayer and Identity Formation*, edited by Reidar Hvalvik and Karl Olav Sandnes, 57–90. Tübingen: Mohr Siebeck, 2014.

Jastrzebowska, Elisabeth. "Les scènes de banquet dans les peintures et sculptures chrétiennes des IIIe et IVe siècles." *Recherches augustiniennes* 14 (1979): 3–90.

———. *Untersuchungen zum christlichen Totenmahl aufgrund der Monumente des 3. und 4. Jahrhunderts unter der Basilika des Hl. Sebastian in Rom*. Frankfurt am Main: P. Lang, 1981.

Jensen, Robin M. "Baptismal Rites and Architecture." In *Late Ancient Christianity*, edited by Virginia Burrus, 117–44. A People's History of Christianity 2. Minneapolis: Fortress, 2005.

———. *The Cross: History, Art, and Controversy*. Cambridge, MA: Harvard University Press, 2017.

———. "Dining with the Dead: From the Mensa to the Altar in Christian Late Antiquity." In *Commemorating the Dead: Texts and Artifacts in Context—Studies of Roman, Jewish, and Christian Burials*, edited by Laurie Brink and Deborah Green, 107–43. New York: De Gruyter, 2008.

———. *Understanding Early Christian Art*. New York: Routledge, 2000.

Johnson, Gary J. *Early-Christian Epitaphs from Anatolia*. Atlanta, GA: Scholars Press, 1995.

Johnson, Mark J. "Christian Burial Practices of the Fourth Century: Shared Tombs?" *Journal of Early Christian Studies* 5, no. 1 (1997): 37–59.

Johnson, Walter. "On Agency." *Journal of Social History* 37, no. 1 (2003): 113–24.

Johnson Hodge, Caroline. "Apostle to the Gentiles: Constructions of Paul's Identity." *Biblical Interpretation* 13, no. 3 (2005): 270–88.

———. "Daily Devotions: Stowers's Modes of Religion Meet Tertullian's ad Uxorem." In *"The One Who Sows Bountifully": Essays in Honor of Stanley K. Stowers*, edited by Caroline Johnson Hodge, Saul M. Olyan, Daniel Ullucci, Emma Wasserman, 43–54. Providence, RI: Brown Judaic Studies, 2013.

———. "'Holy Wives' in Roman Households: 1 Peter 3:1–6." *Journal of Interdisciplinary Feminist Thought* 4, no. 1 (2010). https://digitalcommons.salve.edu/jift/vol4/iss1/1.

———. *If Sons, Then Heirs: A Study of Kinship and Ethnicity in the Letters of Paul*. New York: Oxford University Press, 2007.

———. "Married to an Unbeliever: Households, Hierarchies and Holiness in 1 Corinthians 7:12–16." *Harvard Theological Review* 103, no. 1 (2010): 1–25.

———. "Mixed Marriage in Early Christianity: Trajectories from Corinth." In *Corinth in Contrast: Studies in Inequality*, edited by Steven J. Friesen, Sarah A. James, and Daniel N. Schowalter, 117–244. Boston: Brill, 2014.

———. "Ritual Epicleses in the Greek Acts of Thomas." In *The Apocryphal Acts of the Apostles: Harvard Divinity School Studies*, edited by François Bovon, Ann Graham Brock, and Christopher R. Matthews, 171–204. Cambridge, MA: Harvard University Center for the Study of World Religion, 1998.

———. "'Wife, Pray to the Lar': Wives, Slaves, and Worship in Roman Households." In *The Struggle over Class: Socioeconomic Analysis of Ancient Jewish and Christian Texts, Writings from the Greco-Roman World Supplement Series*, edited by G. Anthony Keddie, Michael A. Flexsenhar III, and Steven J. Friesen, 73–94. Atlanta: Society of Biblical Literature Press, 2021.

Johnson Hodge, Caroline, Saul M. Olyan, Daniel Ullucci, and Emma Wasserman, eds. *Essays in Honor of Stanley K. Stowers*. Providence, RI: Brown Judaic Studies, 2013.

Johnston, Sarah Iles. *Restless Dead: Encounters Between the Living and the Dead in Ancient Greece*. Berkeley: University of California Press, 1999.

Jones, Brice. *New Testament Texts on Greek Amulets from Late Antiquity*. London: T&T Clark, 2016.

Joshel, Sandra R. *Work, Identity, and Legal Status at Rome: A Study of the Occupational Inscriptions*. Norman, OK: University of Oklahoma Press, 1992.

Joshel, Sandra R., and Lauren Hackworth Petersen. *The Material Life of Roman Slaves*. Cambridge: Cambridge University Press, 2017.

Kalleres, Dayna. *City of Demons: Violence, Ritual, and Christian Power in Late Antiquity*. Berkeley: University of California Press, 2015.

King, Charles W. *The Ancient Roman Afterlife: Di Manes, Belief, and the Cult of the Dead*. Austin: University of Texas Press, 2020.

Kjærgaard, Jørgen. "From 'Memoria Apostolorum' to Basilica Apostolorum: On the Early Christian Cult-Centre on the Via Appia." *Analecta Romana Instituti Danici* 13 (1984): 59–68.

Kloppenborg, John S. *Christ's Associations: Connecting and Belonging in the Ancient City*. New Haven, CT: Yale University Press, 2019.

Kokkinia, Christina. "A Roman Financier's Version of Euergetism: C. Vibius Salutaris and Ephesos." *Tekmeria* 14 (2019): 215–52. DOI: 10.12681/tekmeria.17405.

Kotansky, Roy D. "An Early Christian Gold Lamella for Headache." In *Magic and Ritual in the Ancient World*, edited by Paul Mirecki and Marvin Meyer, 37–46. Leiden: Brill, 2002.

———. "Greek Exorcistic Amulets." In *Ancient Magic and Ritual Power*, edited by Marvin W. Meyer and Paul Mirecki, 243–77. Leiden: Brill, 1995.

———. *Greek Magical Amulets: The Inscribed Gold, Silver, Copper, and Bronze Lamellae. Part 1: Published Texts of Known Provenance*. Opladen: Westdeutcher Verlag, 1994.

———. "Incantations and Prayers on Inscribed Greek Amulets." In *Magika Hiera: Ancient Greek Magic and Religion*, edited by Christopher A. Faraone and Dirk Obbink, 107–37. New York: Oxford University Press, 1991.

———. "The Magic 'Crucifixion Gem' in the British Museum." *Greek, Roman, and Byzantine Studies* 15 (2017): 631–59.

———. "Two Amulets in the Getty Museum: A Gold Amulet for Aurelia's Epilepsy; An Inscribed Magical-Stone for Fever, 'Chills,' and Headache." *J. Paul Getty Museum Journal* 8 (1980): 181–88.

Kraemer, Ross Shepard. "On the Meaning of the Term 'Jew' in Greco-Roman Inscriptions." *Harvard Theological Review* 82, no. 1 (1989): 35–53.

———. *Unreliable Witnesses: Religion, Gender, and History in the Greco-Roman Mediterranean*. New York: Oxford University Press, 2011.

Krautheimer, Richard, ed. *Corpus Basilicarum Christianarum Romae*. Vatican City: Pontificio Istituto de Archeologia Cristiana: 1937–80.

———. *Early Christian and Byzantine Architecture*. Baltimore, MD: Penguin, 1965.

———. "Mensa-coemeterium-martyrium." *Cahiers archéologiques* 11 (1960): 15–40.

Lahire, Bernard. "From the Habitus to an Individual Heritage of Dispositions: Towards a Sociology at the Level of the Individual." *Poetics* 31, nos. 5–6 (2003): 329–55.

La Piana, George. "The Tombs of Peter and Paul Ad Catacumbas." *Harvard Theological Review* 14 (1921): 53–94.

Lapp, Eric C. "Lamps." In *Sepphoris in Galilee: Crosscurrents of Culture*, edited by Rebecca Martin Nagy, 217–25. Raleigh: North Carolina Museum of Art; Winona Lake, IN: Eisenbrauns, 1996.

———. *Sepphoris II: The Clay Lamps from Ancient Sepphoris; Light Use and Regional

Interactions. University Park, PA: Eisenbrauns, 2015.
Larson, Jennifer. *Understanding Greek Religion: A Cognitive Approach*. London: Routledge, 2016.
Latour, Bruno. *The Pasteurization of France*. Cambridge, MA: Harvard University Press, 1993.
Lefebvre, Henri. *The Production of Space*. Oxford: Blackwell, 1991.
Le Saint, William P. *Tertullian: Treatises on Marriage and Remarriage; To His Wife, An Exhortation to Chastity, Monogamy*. Ancient Christian Writers 13. New York: Newman Press, 1951.
Lieu, Judith M. *Christian Identity in the Jewish and Graeco-Roman World*. New York: Oxford University Press, 2004.
———. "Household and Family in Diaspora Judaism." *Archiv für Religionsgeschichte* 18–19, no. 1 (2017): 75–90.
Lindsay, Hugh. "Eating with the Dead: The Roman Funerary Banquet." In *Meals in a Social Context: Aspects of the Communal Meal in the Hellenistic and Roman World*, edited by Inge Nielsen and Hanne Sigismund Nielsen, 67–80. Mediterranean Antiquity 1. Aarhus: Aarhus University Press, 1988.
Longenecker, Bruce W. *The Cross Before Constantine: The Early Life of a Christian Symbol*. Minneapolis: Fortress, 2015.
———. *The Crosses of Pompeii: Jesus-Devotion in a Vesuvian Town*. Minneapolis: Fortress, 2016.
Lott, J. Bert. *The Neighborhoods of Augustan Rome*. Cambridge: Cambridge University Press, 2004.
Love, Edward. *Code-Switching with the Gods: The Bilingual (Old Coptic-Greek) Spells of PGM IV (P. Bibliothèque Nationale Supplément Grec. 574) and Their Linguistic, Religious, and Socio-Cultural Context in Late Roman Egypt*. Berlin: Walter de Gruyter, 2016.
Luijendijk, AnneMarie. "A Gospel Amulet for Joannia (P.Oxy. VIII 1151)." In *Daughters of Hecate: Women and Magic in the Ancient World*, edited by Kimberly B. Stratton with Dayna S. Kalleres, 425–30. New York: Oxford University Press, 2014.
MacDonald, Margaret Y. *Early Christian Women and Pagan Tradition: The Power of the Hysterical Woman*. Cambridge: Cambridge University Press, 1996.
Mack, Burton. *Myth of Innocence: Mark and Christian Origins*. Philadelphia: Fortress, 1988.
MacMullen, Ramsay. "Christian Ancestor Worship in Rome." *Journal of Biblical Literature* 129, no. 3 (2010): 597–613.
———. *Christianity and Paganism in the Fourth to Eighth Centuries*. New Haven, CT: Yale University Press, 1997.
———. *Christianizing the Roman Empire (A.D. 100–400)*. New Haven, CT: Yale University Press, 1984.
———. *The Second Church: Popular Christianity A.D. 200–400*. Atlanta: Society of Biblical Literature, 2009.
Magness, Jodi. *Stone and Dung, Oil and Spit: Jewish Daily Life in the Time of Jesus*. Grand Rapids, MI: Eerdmans, 2011.
Maguire, Eunice Dauterman, Henry P. Maguire, and Maggie J. Duncan-Flowers. *Art and Holy Powers in the Early Christian House*. Urbana: University of Illinois Press, 1989.
Maguire, Henry. "Magic and the Christian Image." In *Early Byzantine Magic*, edited by Henry Maguire, 51–71. Washington, DC: Dumbarton Oaks, 1995.
Maier, Harry O. "Heresy, Households, and the Disciplining of Diversity." In *Late Ancient Christianity*, edited by Virginia Burrus, 213–33. A People's History of Christianity 2. Minneapolis: Fortress, 2005.
Maravela, Anastasia. "Christians Praying in a Graeco-Egyptian Context: Intimations of Christian Identity in Greek Papyrus Prayers." In *Early Christian Prayer and Identity Formation*, edited by Reidar Hvalvik and Karl Olav Sandnes, 291–324. Tübingen: Mohr Siebeck, 2014.
Marcillet-Jaubert, Jean. *Les inscriptions d'Altava*. Aix-en-Provence: Editions Ophrys, 1968.
Marcus, Joel. *Mark 1–8: A New Translation with Introduction and Commentary*. Anchor Bible. New York: Doubleday, 2002.
Marichal, M. Robert. "La date des graffiti de la triclia de Saint-Sebastien et leur place dans l'histoire de l'écriture latine." *Recherches de science religieuse* 36 (1962): 111–54.

Marin, Emilio. "L'inhumation privilégiée à Salone." In *L'inhumation privilégiée du VIe au VIIIe siècle en Occident: Actes du colloque tenu à Créteil les 6–18 Mars 1984*, edited by Y. Duval and J. C. Picard, 221–29. Paris: de Boccard, 1986.

Marshall, F. H. *Catalogue of the Finger Rings, Greek, Etruscan, and Roman, in the Departments of Antiquities, British Museum*. London: The Trustees, 1907.

Martin, Dale. *Slavery as Salvation: The Metaphor of Slavery in Pauline Christianity*. New Haven, CT: Yale University Press, 1990.

Marx-Wolf, Heidi. *Spiritual Taxonomies and Ritual Authority: Platonists, Priests, and Gnostics in the Third Century C.E.* Philadelphia: University of Pennsylvania Press, 2016.

Maxwell, Jaclyn. "Lay Piety in the Sermons of John Chrysostom." In *Byzantine Christianity*, edited by Derek Krueger and Denis R. Janz, 19–38. Philadelphia: Fortress, 2010.

Mayer, Wendy. "The Late Antique Church at Qausīyeh Reconsidered: Memory and Martyr Burial in Syrian Antioch." In *Martyrdom and Persecution in Late Antique Christianity: Festschrift Boudewijn Dehandschutter*, edited by J. Leemans, 161–77. Leuven: Uitgeverij Peeters, 2010.

Mazzoleni, Danilo. "Pietro e Paolo nell'epigrafia cristiana." In *Pietro e Paolo: La storia, il culto, la memoria nei primi secoli*, edited by Angela Donati, 67–72. Milan: Electa, 2000.

McCall, Leslie. "The Complexity of Intersectionality." *Signs* 3 (2005): 1771–800.

McGowan, Andrew. *Ancient Christian Worship: Early Church Practices in Social, Historical, and Theological Perspective*. Grand Rapids, MI: Baker Books, 2014.

———. *Ascetic Eucharists: Food and Drink in Early Christian Ritual Meals*. Oxford: Clarendon Press, 1999.

McKay, Heather A. *Sabbath and Synagogue: The Question of Sabbath Worship in Ancient Judaism*. Boston: Brill, 2001.

McKeown, Niall. "Magic, Religion, and the Roman Slave: Resistance, Control, and Community." In *Slaves and Religions in Graeco-Roman Antiquity and Modern Brazil*, edited by Stephen Hodkinson and Dick Geary, 280-307. Newcastle upon Tyne: Cambridge Scholars Publishing, 2012.

McNamara, Jo Ann. "Gendering Virtue." In *Plutarch's "Advice to the Bride and Groom" and "A Consolation to His Wife": English Translations, Commentary, Interpretive Essays and Bibliography*, edited by Sarah B. Pomeroy, 151–61. New York: Oxford, 1991.

Meeks, Wayne. *First Urban Christians: The Social World of the Apostle Paul*. New Haven, CT: Yale University Press, 1983.

Meyer, Marvin W., and Richard Smith, eds. *Ancient Christian Magic: Coptic Texts of Ritual Power*. Princeton, NJ: Princeton University Press, 1994.

Meyers, Carol L., and Eric M. Meyers. "Image and Identity: Menorah Representations at Sepphoris." In *Viewing Ancient Judaism: Jewish Art and Archaeology in Honor of Rachel Hachlili*, edited by A. E. Killebrew and A. Segal, 385–400. Leiden: Brill, 2016.

Meyers, Eric M. "Aspects of Everyday Life in Roman Palestine with Special Reference to Private Domiciles and Ritual Baths." In *Jews in the Hellenistic and Roman Cities*, edited by J. R. Bartlett, 193–220. London: Routledge, 2002.

———. "The Ceramic Incense Shovels from Sepphoris: Another View." In *"I Will Speak the Riddles of Ancient Times": Archaeological and Historical Studies in Honor of Amihai Mazar on the Occasion of His Sixtieth Birthday*, edited by A. M. Maeir and P. de Miroschedji, 865–78. Winona Lake, IN: Eisenbrauns, 2006.

———. "Yes, They Are." *Biblical Archaeology Review* 26, no. 4 (2000): 46–51.

Milburn, Robert. *Early Christian Art and Architecture*. Berkeley: University of California Press, 1988.

Miner, Dorothy. *Early Christian and Byzantine Art*. Baltimore: Walters Art Gallery, 1947.

Mirecki, Paul, and Marvin Meyer, eds. *Magic and Ritual in the Ancient World*. Leiden: Brill, 2002.

Mitchell, Margaret M. *Paul and the Rhetoric of Reconciliation: An Exegetical Investigation of the Language and Composition of 1 Corinthians*. Louisville, KY: Westminster John Knox, 1991.

Mitchell, Stephen. "The Cult of Theos Hypsistos Between Pagans, Jews and Christians." In *Pagan Monotheism in Late Antiquity*, edited by Polymnia Athanassiadi and Michael Frede, 81–148. Oxford: Oxford University Press, 1999.

Moore, Stephen D. "'Oh Man, Who Art Thou?': Masculinity Studies and New Testament Studies." In *New Testament Masculinities*, edited by Stephen D. Moore and Janice Capel Anderson, 1–22. Semeia Studies 45. Atlanta: Society of Biblical Literature, 2003.

Moyer, Ian S., and Jacco Dieleman. "Miniaturization and the Opening of the Mouth in a Greek Magical Text (PGM XII.270–350)." *Journal of Ancient Near Eastern Religions* 3 (2003): 47–72.

Murray, Mary Charles. "Art and the Early Church: Major Pieces of Evidence." *Journal of Theological Studies* 28, no. 2 (1977): 303–45.

———. *Rebirth and Afterlife: A Study of the Transmutation of Some Pagan Imagery in Early Christian Funerary Art*. British Archaeological Reports. Oxford: Oxford University Press, 1981.

Nagy, Árpád M. "Engineering Ancient Amulets: Magical Gems of the Roman Imperial Period." In *The Materiality of Magic*, edited by Dietrich Boschung and Jan M. Bremmer, 211–19. Paderborn: Wilhelm Fink, 2015.

Nash, Jennifer C. "Re-thinking Intersectionality." *Feminist Review* 89, no. 1 (2008): 1–15.

Nasrallah, Laura Salah. *An Ecstasy of Folly: Prophecy and Authority in Early Christianity*. Cambridge, MA: Harvard University Press, 2003.

———. "The Work of Nails: Religion, Mediterranean Antiquity, and Contemporary Black Art." *Journal of the American Academy of Religion* 90 (2022): 356–76.

———. "You Were Bought with a Price: Freepersons and Things in 1 Corinthians." In *Corinth in Contrast: Studies in Inequality*, edited by Steven J. Friesen, Sarah A. James, and Daniel N. Schowalter, 54–73. Leiden: Brill, 2014.

Nicolai, Vincenzo Fiocchi. "L'organizzazione dello spazio funerario." In *Christiana loca: Lo spazio cristiano nella Roma del primo millennio*, ed. Letizia Pani Ermini, 1: 43–58. Rome: Fratelli Palombi, 2000–2001.

———. "Padre Umberto M. Fasola studioso degli antichi cimiteri cristiani: A proposito delle origini delle catacombe dei loro caratteri identitari." *Rivista di archeologia cristiana* 94 (2018): 99–137.

Nicolai, Vincenzo Fiocchi, Fabrizio Bisconti, and Danilo Mazzoleni. *The Christian Catacombs of Rome: History, Decoration, Inscriptions*. Regensburg: Schnell and Steiner, 2009.

Nieddu, Anna Maria. *La Basilica Apostolorum sulla via Appia e l'area cimiteriale circostante*. Monumenti di antichita cristiana 11.19. Rome: Vatican City, 2009.

Nilsson, Martin P. "Divine Service." *Harvard Theological Review* 38, no. 1 (1945): 63–69.

Nongbri, Brent. *Before Religion: A History of a Modern Concept*. New Haven, CT: Yale University Press, 2013.

North, J. A. "The Ritual Activity of Roman Slaves." In *Slaves and Religions in Graeco-Roman Antiquity and Modern Brazil*, edited by Stephen Hodkinson and Dick Geary, 68–93. Newcastle upon Tyne: Cambridge Scholars Publishing, 2012.

Ogden, Daniel, ed. *Magic, Witchcraft, and Ghosts in the Greek and Roman Worlds: A Sourcebook*. Oxford: Oxford University Press, 2002.

Öhler, Markus. "Das ganze Haus: Antike Alltagsreligiosität und die Apostelgeschichte." *Zeitschrift für die Neutestamentliche Wissenschaft* 102 (2011): 201–34.

———. "Graeco-Roman Associations, Judean Synagogues and Early Christianity in Bithynia-Pontus." In *Authority and Identity in Emerging Christianities in Asia Minor and Greece*, edited by Cilliers Breytenbach and Julien Ogereau, 62–88. Leiden: Brill, 2018.

Orr, David G. "Roman Domestic Religion: The Evidence of the Household Shrines." *ANRW* 2.16.2 (1978): 1569–75.

Orsi, Robert. "Everyday Miracles: The Study of Lived Religion." In *Lived Religion in America: Toward a History of Practice*, edited by David D. Hall, 3–21. Princeton, NJ: Princeton University Press, 1997.

Orsini, Pasquale, and Willy Clarysse. "Early New Testament Manuscripts and Their Dates: A Critique of Theological Paleography." *Ephemerides Theologicae Lovanienses* 88, no. 4 (2012): 443–74.

Osiek, Carolyn. "Roman and Christian Burial Practices and the Patronage of Women." In *Commemorating the Dead: Texts and Artifacts in Context—Studies of Roman, Jewish, and Christian Burials*, edited by Laurie Brink and Deborah Green, 243–70. New York: De Gruyter, 2008.

Padilla Peralta, Dan-el. "Slave Religiosity in the Roman Middle Republic." *Classical Antiquity* 36, no. 2 (2017): 317–69.

Parker, Holt. "Loyal Slaves and Loyal Wives." In *Women and Slaves in Greco-Roman Culture: Differential Equations*, edited by Sandra R. Joshel and Sheila Murnaghan, 152–73. New York: Routledge, 1998.

Peppard, Michael. *The World's Oldest Church*. New Haven, CT: Yale University Press, 2016.

Petersen, Lauren Hackworth. "Pompeian Women and the Making of a Material History." In *Women's Lives, Women's Voices: Roman Material Culture and Female Agency in the Bay of Naples*, edited by Brenda Longfellow and Molly Swetnam-Burland, 11–28. Austin: University of Texas Press, 2021.

Pomeroy, Sarah B. *Families in Classical and Hellenistic Greece: Representations and Realities*. Oxford: Clarendon Press, 1997.

———. *Xenophon: Oeconomicus; A Social and Historical Commentary*. Oxford: Clarendon Press, 1994.

Pulleyn, Simon. *Prayer in Greek Religion*. Oxford: Clarendon Press, 1997.

Raboteau, Albert J. *Slave Religion: The Invisible Institution in the Antebellum South*. New York: Oxford University Press, 2004.

Rapp, Claudia. *Holy Bishops in Late Antiquity: The Nature of Christian Leadership in an Age of Transition*. Berkeley: University of California Press, 2013.

Rathmayr, Elisabeth. "Götter- und Kaiserkult im Privatbereich Wohnbereich anhand von Skulpturen aus dem Hanghaus 2 in Ephesos." *Römische historische Mitteilungen* 48 (2006): 103–33.

———. *Hanghaus 2 in Ephesos: Die Wohneinheit 7: Baubefund, Ausstattung, Funde*. Textband 2. Wien: Verlag der Österreichischen Akademie der Wissenschaften, 2016.

———. "The Meaning and Use of Terracotta Figurines in the Terrace Houses in Ephesos." In *Religion in Ephesos Reconsidered: Archaeology of Spaces, Structures, and Objects*, edited by Daniel Schowalter, Stephen J. Friesen, Sabine Ladstätter, and Christine Thomas, 230–51. Leiden: Brill, 2020.

Reay, Brendon. "Agriculture, Writing, and Cato's Aristocratic Self-Fashioning." *Classical Antiquity* 24, no. 2 (2005): 331–61.

Rebillard, Éric. *Care of the Dead in Late Antiquity*. Ithaca, NY: Cornell University Press, 2009.

———. *Christians and Their Many Identities in Late Antiquity: North Africa, 200–450 CE*. Ithaca: Cornell University Press, 2012.

———. "Κοιμητήριον et Coemeterium: Tombe, tombe sainte, nécropole." *Mélanges de l'École française de Rome, Antiquité* 105, no. 2 (1993): 975–1001.

———. "Material Culture and Religious Identity." In *A Companion to the Archaeology of Religion in the Ancient World*, edited by Rubina Raja and Jörg Rüpke, 427–36. Malden, MA: Blackwell, 2015.

Reif, Stefan C. "Prayer and Liturgy." In *The Oxford Handbook of Jewish Daily Life in Roman Palestine*, edited by Catherine Hezser, 545–65. New York: Oxford, 2010.

Riggsby, Andrew. "'Public and Private' in Roman Culture: The Case of the Cubiculum." *Journal of Roman Archaeology* 10 (1997): 36–55.

Rives, James B. *Religion in the Roman Empire*. Malden, MA: Blackwell, 2007.

Rogers, Guy M. *The Sacred Identity of Ephesos: Foundation Myths of a Roman City*. London: Routledge, 1991.

Rosenblum, Jordan, Lily C. Vuong, and Nathaniel P. DesRosiers, eds., *Religious Competition in the Third Century CE: Jews, Christians, and the Greco-Roman*

BIBLIOGRAPHY

World. Göttingen: Vandenhoeck & Ruprecht, 2014.

Runesson, Anders. "Ekklesia." Bible Odyssey. https://www.bibleodyssey.org:443/tools/ask-a-scholar/ekklesia.

Rutgers, Leonard V. "Incense Shovels at Sepphoris?" In *Galilee Through the Centuries: Confluence of Cultures*, edited by Eric M. Meyers, 177–98. Winona Lake, IN: Eisenbrauns, 1999.

Saller, Richard. *Patriarchy, Property and Death in the Roman Family*. Cambridge: Cambridge University Press, 1994.

Salzman, Michele Renee. *The Making of a Christian Aristocracy: Social and Religious Change in the Western Roman Empire*. Cambridge, MA: Harvard University Press, 2004.

———. "Religious *Koine* and Religious Dissent in the Fourth Century." In *A Companion to Roman Religion*, edited by Jörg Rüpke, 109–25. Malden, MA: Blackwell, 2011.

Sanders, E. P. *Jewish Law from Jesus to the Mishnah: Five Studies*. London: SCM; Philadelphia: Trinity Press International, 1990.

———. *Judaism: Practice and Belief, 63 BCE–66 CE*. London: SCM; Philadelphia: Trinity Press International, 1992.

Sanzo, Joseph E. "Early Christianity." In *Guide to the Study of Ancient Magic*, edited by David Frankfurter, 198–239. Leiden: Brill, 2019.

———. "Jesus Among the Restless Dead." Paper presented at the North American Patristics Society annual conference at Oxford University, Oxford, UK, August 19–24, 2019.

———. "Magic and Communal Boundaries: The Problems with Amulets in Chrysostom, *Adv. Iud.* 8, and Augustine, *In Io. tra.* 7." *Henoch* 39 (2017): 227–46.

———. *Ritual Boundaries: Magic and Differentiation in Late Antique Christianity*. Berkeley: University of California Press, 2024.

———. *Scriptural Incipits on Amulets from Late Antique Egypt: Text, Typology, and Theory*. Tübingen: Mohr Siebeck, 2014.

Satlow, Michael L. *Jewish Marriage in Antiquity*. Princeton, NJ: Princeton University Press, 2001.

Schüssler Fiorenza, Elisabeth. "Exploring the Intersections of Race, Gender, Status, and Ethnicity in Early Christian Studies." In *Prejudice and Christian Beginnings: Investigating Race, Gender, and Ethnicity in Early Christian Studies*, edited by Laura Nasrallah and Elisabeth Schüssler Fiorenza, 1–23. Minneapolis: Fortress, 2009.

———. *In Memory of Her: A Feminist Theological Reconstruction of Christian Origins*. New York: Crossroad, 1983.

Sessa, Kristina. "Christianity and the *Cubiculum*: Spiritual Politics and Domestic Space in Late Antique Rome." *Journal of Early Christian Studies* 15, no. 2 (2007): 171–204.

———. *Daily Life in Late Antiquity*. Cambridge: Cambridge University Press, 2018.

———. *The Formation of Papal Authority in Late Antique Italy: Roman Bishops and the Domestic Sphere*. Cambridge: Cambridge University Press, 2012.

Shaner, Katherine A. *Enslaved Leadership in Early Christianity*. Oxford: Oxford University Press, 2018.

Sheckler, Allyson Everingham, and Mary Joan Winn Leith. "The Crucifixion Conundrum and the Santa Sabina Doors." *Harvard Theological Review* 103, no. 1 (2010): 67–88.

Smith, Dennis E. *From Symposium to Eucharist: The Banquet in the Early Christian World*. Minneapolis: Fortress, 2003.

Smith, Dennis E., and Hal Taussig. *Meals in the Early Christian World: Social Formation, Experimentation and Conflict at the Table*. New York: Palgrave Macmillan, 2012.

Smith, Jonathan Z. *Drudgery Divine: On the Comparison of Early Christianities and the Religions of Late Antiquity*. Chicago: University of Chicago Press, 1990.

———. "Trading Places." In *Ancient Magic and Ritual Power*, edited by Marvin W. Meyer and Paul Mirecki, 13–27. Leiden: Brill, 1995.

Smith, Morton. "Jewish Elements." In *Studies in the Cult of Yahweh*, vol. 2, *New Testament, Early Christianity, and Magic*, edited by Shaye J. D. Cohen, 242–56. Leiden: Brill, 1996.

Snyder, Graydon. *Ante Pacem: Archaeological Evidence of Church Life Before*

Constantine. Rev. ed. Macon, GA: Mercer, 2018.

Spera, Lucrezia. "The Christianization of Space along the Via Appia: Changing Landscape in the Suburbs of Rome." *American Journal of Archaeology* 107, no. 1 (2003): 23–43.

Spier, Jeffrey. *Late Antique and Early Christian Gems*. Wiesbaden: Reichert, 2007.

———. *Picturing the Bible: The Earliest Christian Art*. New Haven, CT: Yale University Press, 2007.

Spieser, Jean-Michel. "Ambrose's Foundations at Milan and the Question of Martyria." In *Urban and Religious Spaces in Late Antiquity and Early Byzantium*, edited by Jean-Michel Spieser, 1–12. Burlington, VT: Ashgate, 2001.

Stander, H. F. "Amulets and the Church Fathers." *Ekklesiastikos Pharos* 75, no. 2 (1993): 55–66.

Stern, Karen. "Vandals or Pilgrims? Jews, Travel Culture, and Devotional Practice in the Pan Temple of Egyptian El-Kanais." In *"The One Who Sows Bountifully": Essays in Honor of Stanley K. Stowers*, edited by Caroline Johnson Hodge, Saul M. Olyan, Daniel Ullucci, and Emma Wasserman, 177–88. Providence, RI: Brown Judaic Studies, 2013.

———. *Writing on the Wall: Graffiti and the Forgotten Jews of Antiquity*. Princeton, NJ: Princeton University Press, 2017.

Sterrett-Krause, Allison E. "Drinking with the Dead? Glass from Roman and Christian Burial Areas at Leptiminus (Lamta, Tunisia)." *Journal of Glass Studies* 59 (2017): 47–82.

Stichele, Caroline Vander, and Todd Penner. *Contextualizing Gender in Early Christian Discourse: Thinking Beyond Thecla*. New York: T&T Clark, 2009.

Stirling, L. "Archaeological Evidence for Food Offerings in the Grave of Roman North Africa." In *Daimonopylai: Essays in Classics and the Classical Tradition Presented to E. G. Berry*, edited by Rory B. Egan, Mark Joyal, and Edmund Grindlay Berry, 427–49. Winnipeg: University of Manitoba Center for Hellenic Civilization, 2004.

Stowers, Stanley. *Christian Beginnings: A Study in Ancient Mediterranean Religion*. Edinburgh: University of Edinburgh Press, 2024.

———. *History and the Study of Religion: The Ancient Mediterranean as a Test Case*. New York: Oxford University Press, 2024.

———. "Kinds of Myth, Meals and Power: Paul and the Corinthians." In *Redescribing Paul and the Corinthians*, edited by Ron Cameron and Merrill P. Miller, 105–50. Atlanta: Society of Biblical Literature, 2011.

———. "Locating the Religion of Associations." In *Re-Making the World: Categories and Early Christianity: Essays in Honor of Karen L. King*, edited by Taylor G. Petrey, Carly Daniel-Hughes, Benjamin Dunning, Laura Nasrallah, and AnneMarie Luijendijk, 301–24. Tübingen: Mohr Siebeck, 2019.

———. "The Religion of Plant and Animal Offerings Versus the Religion of Meanings, Essences and Textual Mysteries." In *Ancient Mediterranean Sacrifice: Images, Acts, Meanings*, edited by Jennifer Knust and Zsuzsa Varhelyi, 35–56. New York: Oxford University Press, 2011.

———. "Religion as a Social Kind." Paper presented at the Religion Before Religion symposium at Bowdoin College, Brunswick, ME, October 14–15, 2016.

———. "Theorizing the Religion of Ancient Households and Families." In *Household and Family Religion in Antiquity*, edited by John Bodel and Saul Olyan, 5–19. Malden, MA: Blackwell, 2008.

———. "Why 'Common Judaism' Does Not Look like Mediterranean Religion." In *Strength to Strength: Essays in Honor of Shaye J. D. Cohen*, edited by Michael L. Satlow, 235–55. BJS 363. Providence, RI: Brown Judaic Studies, 2018.

———. "Why Expert Versus Nonexpert Is Not Elite Versus Popular Religion: The Case of the Third Century." In *Religious Competition in the Greco-Roman World*, edited by Nathan DesRosiers and Lily C. Vuong, 139–53. Atlanta: Society of Biblical Literature, 2016.

Styger, Paul. "Die erste Ruhestätte der Apostelfürsten Petrus und Paulus an der Via Appia in Rom." *Zeitschrift für katholische Theologie* 45, no. 4 (1921): 549–72.

———. "Il monumento apostolico della via Appia." *Atti della Pontificia Accademia Romana di Archeologia, Dissertazioni* 2, no. 13 (1918): 48–98.

Tabbernee, William. *Montanist Inscriptions and Testimonia*. Washington, DC: Catholic University of America Press, 1996.

Taussig, Hal. *In the Beginning Was the Meal: Social Experimentation and Early Christian Identity*. Minneapolis: Fortress, 2009.

Thee, Francis C. R. *Julius Africanus and the Early Christian View of Magic*. Tübingen: Mohr Siebeck, 1984.

Tolotti, Francesco. *Memorie degli apostoli in catacumbas*. Vatican City: Pontificate Institute, 1953.

Tombs, David. "Crucifixion, State Terror, and Sexual Abuse." *Union Seminary Quarterly Review* 53, nos. 1–2 3 (1999): 89–108.

———. "Lived Religion and the Intolerance of the Cross." In *Lived Religion and the Politics of (In)Tolerance*, edited by R. Ruard Ganzevoort and Srdjan Sremac, 63–83. London: Palgrave Macmillan, 2017.

Trouillot, M.-R. *Silencing the Past: Power and the Production of History*. Boston: Beacon Press, 1995.

Toynbee, Jocelyn. *Death and Burial in the Roman World*. Ithaca, NY: Cornell University Press, 1971.

Treggiari, Susan. "*Contubernales* in CIL 6." *Phoenix* 35 (1981): 42–69.

———. *Roman Marriage: Iusti Coniuges From the Time of Cicero to the Time of Ulpian*. Oxford: Clarendon Press, 1991.

———. *Roman Social History*. London: Routledge, 2001.

Trnka-Amrhein, Yvona. "The Seal of the Living God: A Christian Amulet in the Chester Beatty Library." *Zeitschrift für Papyrologie und Epigraphik* 214 (2020): 87–108.

Trout, Dennis. *Paulinus of Nola: Life, Letters, and Poems*. Berkeley: University of California Press, 1999.

———. "Saints, Identity, and the City." In *Late Ancient Christianity*, edited by Virginia Burrus, 165–87. A People's History of Christianity 2. Minneapolis: Fortress, 2005.

Tulloch, Janet H. "Women Leaders in Funerary Banquets." In *A Woman's Place: House Churches in Earliest Christianity*, edited by Carolyn Osiek, Margaret MacDonald, and Janet H. Tulloch, 164–219. Minneapolis: Fortress, 2006.

Twelftree, Graham H. "Jesus the Exorcist and Ancient Magic." In *A Kind of Magic: Understanding Magic in the New Testament and Its Religious Environment*, edited by Michael Labahn and Bert Jan Lietaert Peerbolte, 57–86. London: T&T Clark, 2007.

Tybout, Richard A. "Domestic Shrines and 'Popular Painting': Style and Social Context." *Journal of Roman Archaeology* 9 (1996): 358–74.

Ullucci, Daniel. "Toward a Typology of Religious Experts in the Ancient Mediterranean." In *"The One Who Sows Bountifully": Essays in Honor of Stanley K. Stowers*, edited by Caroline Johnson Hodge, Saul M. Olyan, Daniel Ullucci, and Emma Wasserman, 80–103. Providence, RI: Brown Judaic Studies, 2013.

———. "Spiritual Offerings: Social Networks, Wealth, and the Spread of Early Christianity." Unpublished manuscript.

Van Andringa, William. *Quotidien des dieux et des hommes: La vie religieuse dans les cités du Vésuve à l'époque romaine*. Rome: École française de Rome, 2009.

Van der Horst, Pieter W. "The Great Magical Papyrus of Paris (PGM IV) and the Bible." In *A Kind of Magic: Understanding Magic in the New Testament and Its Religious Environment*, edited by Michael Labahn and Bert Jan Lietaert Peerbolte, 173–83. London: T&T Clark, 2007.

Van Straten, F. T. "Gifts for the Gods." In *Faith, Hope, and Worship: Aspects of Religious Mentality in the Ancient World*, edited by H. S. Versnel, 82–83, plates 7 and 8. Leiden: Brill, 1981.

Viladesau, Richard. *The Beauty of the Cross: The Passion of Christ in Theology and the Arts—From the Catacombs to the Eve of the Renaissance*. New York: Oxford University Press, 2006.

Wallace-Hadrill, Andrew. "Housing the Dead: The Tomb as House in Roman Italy." In *Commemorating the Dead: Texts and Artifacts in Context—Studies of Roman, Jewish, and Christian Burials*, edited by Laurie Brink and Deborah Green, 39–77. New York: De Gruyter, 2008.

Wallraff, Martin, ed. *Iulius Africanus Chronographiae: The Extant Fragments*. New York: De Gruyter, 2007.

Wasserman, Tommy. "P78 (Oxy. XXXIV 2684): The Epistle of Jude on an Amulet." *New Testament Manuscripts: Their Text and Their World*, edited by Thomas J. Kraus and Tobias Nicklas, 137–60. Leiden: Brill, 2006.

Wendt, Heidi. *At the Temple Gates: The Religion of Freelance Experts in the Roman Empire*. New York: Oxford University Press, 2016.

White, L. Michael. *Building God's House in the Roman World: Architectural Adaptation Among Pagans, Jews, and Christians*. Baltimore, MD: Johns Hopkins University Press, 1990.

———. *The Social Origins of Christian Architecture*. 2 vols. Valley Forge, PA: Trinity Press, 1996–97.

Wiedemann, Thomas. *Greek and Roman Slavery*. Baltimore, MD: Johns Hopkins University Press, 1981.

Wilburn, Andrew T. *Materia Magica: The Archaeology of Magic in Roman Egypt, Cyprus, and Spain*. Ann Arbor: University of Michigan Press, 2012.

Williams, Charles K, II. "Roman Corinth: The Final Years of Pagan Cult Facilities Along East Theater Street." In *Urban Religion in Roman Corinth: Interdisciplinary Approaches*, edited by Daniel L. Schowalter and Steven J. Friesen, 221–47. Cambridge, MA: Harvard University Press, 2005.

Yandek, Amy C. "Pagan Roman Religious Acculturation? An Inquiry into the Domestic Cult at Karanis, Ephesos and Dura-Europos: The First to Fifth Centuries CE." PhD diss., Temple University, 2013.

Yarbrough, O. Larry. "The Alexamenos Graffito Street Art in Ancient Rome." In *Engaging the Passion: Perspectives on the Death of Jesus*, edited by O. Larry Yarbough, 231–38. Minneapolis: Fortress, 2015.

Yasin, Ann Marie. "Funerary Monuments and Collective Identity: From Roman Family to Christian Community." *Art Bulletin* 87, no. 3 (2005): 433–57.

———. "Reassessing Salona's Churches: Martyrium Evolution in Question." *Journal of Early Christian Studies* 20, no. 1 (2012): 59–112.

———. *Saints and Church Spaces in the Late Antique Mediterranean: Architecture, Cult, and Community*. Cambridge: Cambridge University Press, 2009.

Zimmermann, Norbert. "Archaeological Evidence for Private Worship and Domestic Religion in Terrace House 2 at Ephesos." In *Religion in Ephesos Reconsidered: Archaeology of Spaces, Structures, and Objects*, edited by Daniel Schowalter, Stephen J. Friesen, Sabine Ladstätter, and Christine Thomas, 211–29. Leiden: Brill, 2020.

———. "Werkstattgruppen römischer Katakombenmalerei." In *Jarbuch für Antike Christentum*. Expanded vol. 35. Münster: Aschendorff, 2002.

Zimmermann, Norbert, Sabine Ladstätter, Mustafa Büyükkolancı, Renate Pillinger, Andreas Pülz, Barbara Tober, and Johannes Weber. *Wall Painting in Ephesos from the Hellenistic to the Byzantine Period*. Istanbul: Ege Yayınları, 2011.

Zissu, Boaz, and David Amit. "Common Judaism, Common Purity, and the Second Temple Period Judean Miqwa'ot (Ritual Immersion Baths)." In *Common Judaism: Explorations in Second-Temple Judaism*, edited by Wayne O. McCready and Adele Reinhartz, 47–62. Minneapolis: Fortress, 2011.

INDEX

1 Corinthians, 8, 36, 80–82, 84, 89
1 Peter, 72, 79, 82–84, 89, 91, 93
1 Thessalonians, 31
1 Timothy, 33

Acts of John, 48, 101
Acts of Paul, 34
Acts of Peter, 37
Acts of the Apostles, 35, 48, 55, 92
Acts of Thecla, 1, 87, 101
Adler, William, 54
Aelia Secundula, 97–98
afterlife, 30, 33
agriculture, 8, 18–19, 48, 77
altar, 14, 18, 20–23, 26–27, 31, 48–49, 52, 99, 102, 108–9, 112–14, 119
Ambrose, 96, 121
ancestors, 2, 7, 17, 20–21, 39, 55, 75, 90–91, 95
angels, 7, 29, 36, 43, 55–57
Aphrodite, 14–15, 18
apocalypse, 36, 57
Apostolic Tradition, 31–32, 34, 37–38, 41–42, 47, 86–89
Apuleius, 35
archaeology, 4, 17, 19–21, 26, 28, 31, 46, 93, 97, 101, 103, 107–14, 117, 125
artisans, 28
astrology, 70
Athanasius, 52
Augustine, 54, 121
Aulus Cornelius Celsus, 38–39, 52–53, 93
authentic religion, 5, 9

baptism, 2, 37–40, 56–57, 81, 86–88, 92, 99, 100, 125
    authority to perform, 81, 86
Basil of Caesarea, 42
basilica, 96, 103–9, 113–16, 119
    Apostolorum (Appia), 114–6
    circiform, 113
    funerary, 96, 115–6
    Praenestina, 115
    Tomb G, 114, 116, 119
Bell, Catherine, 73–74, 77, 79, 88, 91

birthday rituals, 31, 99
blessings, 7, 25, 41, 54, 69, 98, 111, 127
bloodstone gem, 59–63, 65, 68
Bodel, John, 90
Bömer, Franz, 89
Borg, Barbara, 112, 114
Boustan, Ra'anan, 59, 66
Bowes, Kim, 41, 46
breath, 37–39, 47, 52–53, 57, 86
British Museum, 59–60
Brown, Peter, 96, 121
Brown, Vincent, 75, 90
busts, 15, 20, 44
Butler, Judith, 75, 84

Callistus, 118
candomblé, 92
Carthage, 101–2
Cato, 16, 78–80, 82, 91, 93
Cesti, 54
Chepel, Elena, 56
chi ro, 45, 55, 57
childbirth, 14, 24, 51, 54
children, 11, 14, 16, 28, 31, 37, 47, 51, 53, 70, 80–81, 93, 122
    naming of, 47
    of a non-Christian parent, 51, 80–81
Christians, Christianity
    assimilation, adaptation of traditional rituals, 5, 10–12, 26, 28, 47, 51, 58, 58, 63, 66, 69–70, 76, 79, 96, 98, 118, 124–26
    boundaries of, 26, 50–52, 54, 58–59, 64, 66, 69, 98, 100, 124, 126
    diversity and fluidity of, 50–51, 58, 66, 68–69, 76, 96, 98
    doctrine, theology, 2, 9, 30, 32, 51, 64–65, 73, 99, 126
    domestic cult, 2–3, 5–6, 27–28, 31, 35, 41, 49–41, 72, 76, 86–87, 89, 124, 126; critique by literate producers, 35, 42, 47, 50, 54, 69, 73, 79–80, 86, 92, 100, 121, 124–25
    imagery, 3–4, 11, 33–34, 37, 39, 43–47, 49–53, 56, 63, 66, 68, 112, 124–25;

Christians, Christianity (*continued*)
  anchors, 45; crucifixion/cross, 59–64; doves, 45, 57; fish, 45; Good Shepherd, 45; ichthus, 44–45; ships, 45
  incantations, 52, 54
  interpretation, 9, 33, 72
  literate producers, 7–9, 12, 35, 37, 39–40, 42, 47, 50–52, 54, 59, 65, 68–70, 72–73, 79, 85, 93–95, 98–99, 117–18, 121, 124, 126
  non-monotheistic, 50, 58, 76
  "true" versus "erroneous"/"lax," 50, 68
  texts, 2, 9, 30, 42–43, 69, 72, 79–80, 89, 99
  worship, 39, 48, 100, 116
Chrysostom, John, 37, 43, 47, 53–54, 69, 122
church councils, 4, 42, 91, 100
church manuals, 4, 87, 89
Cicero, 17, 77
circumcision, 80
citizens/citizenship, 17
civic religion/cult, 9, 17–19, 21, 28, 39, 46, 77, 90
  rites, rituals, 8, 15–16, 77
civic, public spaces, 18, 27, 117–19
Clement of Alexandria, 33–34, 45
clothing, 23, 31, 35, 42, 96
cognitive science, 5, 7–8
coins, 33, 97–98
Columella, 77
community, 75, 124–25
comparative studies, 12
compita (crossroads), 24
Concannon, Cavan, 12
confession, confessor, *confessio*, 33, 40, 96, 102, 105, 120
Constantine, 3, 12, 27, 45, 69, 95, 114–16, 126
Constanza gem, 62–63
Controversiae, 72, 77
Cooper, Kate, 76
Corbeill, Anthony, 33
creative assemblage, 28, 37
creeds, 45
crucifixion, 37, 39, 44, 46, 56, 59–64, 66–68
  ritual use of materials, 67
cult of the dead, 95–96, 99–100, 106, 112, 116–17, 119–21, 125
cult of the genius, 76–77
curses, 49
Cyprian, 32–33, 36–37, 40, 42, 52, 88, 101–3, 105, 118
Cyril of Jerusalem, 57–58

death, dead, 16, 20, 24, 33–34, 56, 64, 67–68, 75, 95–121, 125
  anniversaries of, 97, 99–102
  communication with, 67, 75, 97–99
  cult of (*see* cult of the dead)
  divinization, *manes*, 98, 100, 118
  festivals of the dead, 95, 97, 100–102, 109, 111, 120–21; Parentalia, 97; singing and dancing, 97, 111
  good death, 67
  realm of, 20
  restless dead, 67–68
  social death, 75
  special dead, 101–2, 109–10, 112, 116, 118, 120 (*see also* martyrs)
  See also mortuary practices; tombs
de Bruyn, Theodore, 6, 43, 50
deities
  anthropomorphizing of, 30, 48
  engagement in history, 6, 50
  gifts and help from, 6, 8, 29–30, 35, 37, 51, 57, 67, 69–70
  gifts to, 7–8, 14, 25–26, 29–31, 48–50, 70 (*see also* offerings)
  human relationships/interactions with, 5–8, 15, 17, 26, 29, 32, 34–35, 47, 49–50, 53, 68, 70, 75–76, 79, 85, 93, 93, 98, 118, 127
  of household spaces, 7, 14, 16, 29 (*see also* household)
  local, regional, and foreign, 15, 21, 72–73, 79–80, 84
  revelatory messages from, 7
demons, devils, 29, 39, 51–53, 55–58, 87, 99, 118, 122
devotional practices. *See* religious practices
disability, 33, 38, 48, 55
divination, 53, 67
Dix, Gregory, 40
domestic cult. *See* household
dominus. *See* paterfamilias

Eastman, David, 111
ecclesiastical structures, authority, 3, 10, 40–41, 47, 52, 70, 87, 96, 101–5, 109, 112–14, 116–21
  bishops, 3, 10, 12, 37, 53, 96, 101–5, 117–21
  clergy, 41, 52, 70, 103–5, 112, 121
  deacons, 40, 102, 104–5
economic interests, 6–8, 14, 32, 44, 74, 77, 96, 102, 108, 112, 117, 120
Egypt, 11, 17–20, 26, 42–43, 119
  Christianity in, 11, 42–43, 119
  deities, 15, 18, 20
ekklesia, 2–3, 43, 81, 103

INDEX

elites/eliteism, 1, 12, 17, 19, 26, 72, 77–78, 89, 94, 96, 117
    writers, 26, 72, 89, 92, 96 (*see also* literate producers)
enslaved people, 3, 11–14, 16, 23, 26, 37, 41, 44, 47, 51, 53, 62, 70–86, 88–93, 109, 112, 124–25, 127
    abuse of, 91
    burial of, 109, 112
    Christians, 53, 70, 79, 81–83, 89–90, 124
    families, 90
    of Christian masters, 82, 89
    of non-Christian masters, 51, 70, 85, 89, 91
    slave market language, 82
    slaves of Christ, 82
    soma, 91
Ephesians, 31, 36
Ephesos, 17, 19–21, 25–26
    terrace houses, 19–21
Eshleman, Kendra, 118
Eucharist, 8, 37, 39–42, 52, 56, 76, 86–88, 91, 93, 99–100, 102, 114, 125
Eusebius, 100–1
evangelism, 83, 126
exorcism, 39, 42, 52–53, 56, 119, 126
Ezekiel, 36

fasting, 25, 33, 40–41
feminist theory, 11, 73–74, 93, 123
fertility, 16, 18, 26
    figures of, 18
figurines, 14, 18–19, 21, 23, 25
foreignness, 17, 71–72, 74, 76, 91
    foreign cults, 72
    foreign gods, 17, 71–72, 74, 76, 79–80
Foss, Pedar, 90
Foucault, Michel, 73
fragrance, 25
Frankfurter, David, 1, 11, 28, 44, 47, 58, 66, 69, 119
freeborn persons, 90
freedpersons, 23, 82, 109, 112
    burial of, 109, 112
funerary reliefs, 20

Galen, 38
Gallienus, 100
garlands, 48, 78, 91, 87
Gauls, 34
Geary, Dick, 90
Genesis, 46
genii, 21
genius loci, 20

gestures, 4, 7, 10, 14, 16, 23, 28–29, 33–39, 46–47, 49, 53, 70, 74, 85–88, 90–91, 93, 98, 122–23, 125
    Christian: blowing, 34, 37–39, 57, 76, 86–88, 81; finger rings, 44–46; kissing, 37; sealing oneself, 35–37, 39, 51, 53, 87; signing one's bed, 34, 86–87; sign of the cross, 27, 35–37, 47, 53, 57, 76, 87, 91, 106, 122; threshold prayers, 1, 27
    posture: directionality, 34; kneeling, 1, 33–34; for rituals, 49, 98; *orants*, 18, 33–34; outstretched hands, 34; prostration, 33; sitting, 33; standing, 33
    traditional: blowing, 16, 34–35, 37–39, 57, 76, 86–88, 91; blowing a kiss, 35; insufflation, 37–39, 86–87; secret gestures, 34, 86; signing oneself, 34–37, 39, 53, 85–88, 91, 95, 122; spitting, 37–38, 85; tongue clucking, 16, 34; touching the lips/face, 35
Gospel of John, 38
Gospel of Luke, 56
Gospel of Mark, 38, 43
Gospel of Matthew, 32, 43, 55
graffiti, 24, 95, 111–2
    Alexamenos graffito, 62–63
Greece, Greek, 7, 20, 36, 49, 55–56, 59, 67, 89, 93
    deities, 15, 18, 19–21, 25, 35
    Magical Papyri, 39, 44, 49, 56, 60, 67
Gregory of Nazianzus, 88

Harley-McGowan, Felicity, 63–66
healing and health, 6, 14, 26, 29, 35–36, 38–39, 42, 44, 47–48, 50, 52–59, 61, 66–69, 77, 86, 88, 111, 126–27
    illness, 17, 54–56, 67
    use of saliva, 37–39, 86
Hellström, Monica, 115
heresy, heretics, 35
Hippolytus, 37, 118
Hodkinson, Stephen, 90
holidays, 2, 13, 16, 78
    Kalends, 14, 16, 78, 110
holiness, 17, 80–82, 84, 88
    contagious, 80, 82
    of households, 17, 80–81
household
    and empire, 2, 77
    gods, 13, 16, 21, 29, 39, 46, 71–72, 76–79, 81, 85, 87–88, 90, 92
    hierarchy, 11, 16, 23, 26, 44, 47, 71–73, 75, 77–90, 92–93, 119, 125

household (*continued*)
    head of, 3, 7–8, 16, 21, 23, 39–41, 48, 51, 71–74, 76–79, 81–86, 91–93 (*see also* paterfamilias)
    management, 44, 73, 77–79, 82, 85, 119
    mixed, 72, 80, 82, 85–87, 93, 125–26
    shrines, 21, 31, 79, 90–92
    social networks of, 8, 71–73, 77–78, 80–82, 95
    spaces/"spatial grammar," 76, 90; atria, 21, 23, 31, 90, 114; bedrooms, 1, 27, 32, 38; dining rooms, 1, 109; doorways, 1–2, 7, 14, 20, 27, 58, 76; courtyards, 1, 20, 31; gardens, 23, 90; hearths, 2, 7, 17, 39, 47, 78, 91; kitchens, 16, 23, 27, 79, 90–92; pantries, 21; secret places (*cubicula*), 32–33, 71, 88; service areas, 79
    worship, 7, 15–21, 23, 28, 38, 71–72, 88, 121
hybridization, 69, 92, 126
hypogea, 112

iconography, 18, 25, 67–68
idols, idolatry, 51, 91, 99–100
Ignatius of Antioch, 88
incantations, 29, 33, 49, 52, 54
incarceration, 28, 40, 102
incense, 14, 18, 20, 24, 26, 31, 97
    burners, 18, 20
    shovels, 24–25
indigenous practices, 92
inscriptions, 20, 24, 26, 44–45, 54–55, 57, 63, 89, 98–99, 103–6, 108–10, 114, 116, 119, 121
    funerary, 89, 98–99, 104–5, 108
    Januarius, 103–6, 109, 114, 116–17, 119
    memoria, 103–5; Apostolorum, 109, 112–23, 116, 120
    votive, 26, 108
institutionalization of religious practices, 6, 9, 12, 42, 117, 119–21, 125–26
Irenaeus, 52
Isaiah, 43
Israel, 17, 25, 55, 57

Jensen, Robin, 99
Jerome, 42
Jesus, 24, 28–30, 32, 34–39, 43–47, 52–53, 55, 57–60, 62–68, 82–83
    imitation of, 83
    power of blood of, 36, 56
    power of name of, 29, 35–36, 46, 48, 52–53, 55, 59
Jews, Judaism, 24–26, 30, 36, 39, 46, 49–50, 52, 55, 59, 66, 68, 93, 117

boundaries of, 26, 52
daily and domestic life, 24–25
dietary restrictions, 25
"Ioudaioi," 26
literate producers, 24
ritual objects: crucifixion material, 67; *lulav*, 25; menorah, 25; phylactery, 55; *shofar*, 25
Sabbath, 25, 46
Shema, 29
synagogues, 24–25, 32
texts, 8, 25, 30; Mishnah, 24–25
Torah shrine, 25
Johnson, Walter, 75
Johnston, Sarah Iles, 67
Jonah, 46
Josephus, 25
judgment, 5, 36, 52–53
Julius Africanus, 54
Justin Martyr, 40, 52

Kalleres, Dayna, 118
Karanis, 17–20, 25–26
    North Temple, 19
Kotansky, Roy, 55–56, 60, 64–65
Kraemer, Ross, 26

Lactantius, 53, 122
lamps, 16, 18, 20–21, 25–26, 35, 46–48, 51, 99
lares, 21, 23–24, 77–78, 89, 91
Larson, Jennifer, 7
Latour, Bruno, 12
Leith, Mary Joan, 66
Lewis, Nicola Denzey, 120, 124
libations, 4, 15–16, 21, 23, 34, 97–98
    tubes in sarcophagi, 98
Liber Pontificalis, 114
Licinius, 115
literate producers, 7–9, 12, 17, 24, 27–28, 32–33, 35, 37, 39, 42, 47, 50, 54, 56, 58–59, 65, 69–70, 72–73, 79, 84–85, 89, 93, 95–96, 98, 121, 124 126
liturgy, 3, 27, 29–30, 40, 43–44, 56, 69, 126
Longenecker, Bruce, 64
Lord's Prayer, 29–30, 32, 43, 55–56
Lucian, 44, 97–98
luck, 16, 34, 45
Luijendijk, AnneMarie, 69

Mack, Burton, 123
MacMullen, Ramsey, 13, 54, 104
magic, magicians, 35, 39, 48–49, 52–54, 58–60, 62–66, 68, 70, 86, 88
    use by Christians, 65
    transcultural lingo, 58

Marcion, 36
marginalization, 11–12
Marin, Emilio, 107
marriage, 32, 41, 54, 71–72, 76–78, 80–82, 84–86, 99–100
    betrothal, 44, 87
    between a Christian and a non-Christian, 4, 32–34, 38–42, 72, 80–87, 126
    divorce, 80
    remarriage, 40–41, 99
    weddings, 51
    widow and widower duties, 99–100, 118
martyrs/martyrdom, 54, 95–96, 100–21, 125
    martyr-churches, 114
    cult of, 100–101, 105, 121
    relics of, 44, 96, 105, 111, 114, 121
    presbyter-martyrs, 108, 119
    soldier-martyrs, 106
Marx-Wolf, Heidi, 118
    Maxwell, Jaclyn, 47
McKeown, Niall, 89–90
meals, 2, 6–7, 9, 11, 16, 20, 25, 27, 31, 34, 39–41, 85–87, 97–99, 101–2, 104–5, 109–10, 112, 125
    See also ritual; tombs
Medusa, 25
mikva'ot. *See* stepped pools
mimicry, 23, 79
Minucius Felix, 27
miracles, 48, 52, 87
modes of religion, 5–10, 12–15, 17, 23, 26, 28–30, 39, 42, 52, 73, 85, 94–95, 110, 117, 124–26
money. *See* economic interests
mortuary practices, 12, 16, 75, 90, 95–121, 125
    care of the dead, 16, 95–98, 102, 113, 118
    Christian, 98–119
    cremation, 96
    See also tombs
mourning, 75, 90

niches, 14, 18, 20–23, 31, 91
    aediculae, 21–23
Novatian, 42

obedience, 12, 16, 76–78, 82–85, 88–89
offerings, 1–2, 4, 6–8, 10, 14–16, 18, 23–24, 26–29, 31, 39–40, 48–49, 69, 87, 90, 95, 97–102, 106, 109–113, 116, 118, 121, 124–25, 127
    of food and/or drink, 14–15, 18, 24, 31, 39, 87, 99, 102, 104, 106
    grave, 16, 95, 97–99, 101–2, 106, 109–11
    of incense, 14
    of plants and/or animals, 7, 18, 21, 39

official religion, rituals, 3–5, 9–10, 12, 16–17, 41, 46, 86, 92, 95, 109, 120
oil, 25, 37, 44, 97
Origen, 32–34, 36, 39, 52–54, 101
Osiek, Carolyn, 118
ouroboros, 57, 59
Ovid, 97

paterfamilias, 16, 23, 48, 71–74, 76–79, 81–85, 91–93
    emperor as, 77, 83
    as household priest, 40, 81
    related to gods, 21, 76
Patterson, Orlando, 75
patriarchal ideology, 11–12, 16–17, 71–73, 76, 79, 80–84, 88, 90, 92–93
    Christianity as disruptive of, 73
    and ritual, 73, 92
patrilocal marriage, 76
patronage system, 29, 89–90, 96, 102–5, 109, 111–12, 114–20, 126
    "spiritual patronage," 118
penates, 17, 21
persecution, 87, 102, 106, 108, 114, 125
Philodemus, 77
pietas, 33
pilgrims/pilgrimage, 96, 110–11, 116, 120
Plato, 17
Pliny the Elder , 16, 34–35, 37–38, 67
Plutarch, 16, 71–72, 74, 76, 79–80, 82, 93
politics, 12, 74–75, 77–78, 83, 117
    of survival, 75
    political power, 3, 9–10, 12, 17, 78, 83, 95, 102, 118, 121, 125
Polycarp, 101
Pompeii, 17, 21–26, 90
    house of Sutoria Primigenia, 23
    House of the Red Walls, 21–23
    Mt. Vesuvius, 20–21
    Via dell'Abbondanza, 23
popular religion, 5, 9, 12, 95, 103, 117–9
power, 7, 9–10, 16–17, 30, 35, 39, 43–44, 52, 55, 63–64, 68, 71–81, 84–85, 92–93, 95–96, 102–3, 108, 115–18, 121
    bodies as sites of, 73
    dynamics/structure, 10, 16–17, 71, 75, 79, 92
    negotiation, 76, 81, 93, 115, 119
    of supernatural beings, 1, 5, 14–15, 17, 20, 25–26, 29–30, 41, 47–58, 67–68, 76, 96, 98, 102, 111, 118, 121, 124
practice theory, 2–3, 74
praise, 7, 29
prayer, 4, 6–8, 10, 13–14, 18, 23, 25–35, 37, 39, 42–43, 46, 49, 56, 67–68, 77–78, 86, 90–91, 99, 101–2, 110–12, 124–25

prayer (*continued*)
  hours, 31
  nocturnal, 38–39
  physical aspects of, 33
  posture, 33–34 (*see also* gestures)
  private, 32–33, 86
pregnancy, 14, 16
priests/priestesses/priesthood, 17, 25, 28, 30, 40, 70
processions, 20–21, 96
prophecy, 36, 43
Psalms, 30, 43
Pseudo-Clementine, 67
purity, 24, 38–39, 52, 84, 86–88, 91

Rebillard, Éric, 99, 101–2
refrigerium, 98–99, 110
religion of everyday social exchange, 6–10, 13, 58, 68, 74, 93, 95, 121, 125–26
religious infidelity, 76
resurrection, 37, 39, 64, 67, 99
Revelation, Book of, 36
rituals
  ability to be adapted, co-opted, improvised, 1, 4–5, 10–17, 24–26, 28, 43, 47, 56, 66, 69–70, 76, 86–87, 90, 92, 101, 117, 121, 123–26
  adornment: amulets, 4, 27, 29–30, 42–44, 46, 48, 50, 52–54, 56–61, 65–66, 69–70, 95; finger rings, 44–45, 61; gems, 4, 44–46, 48, 57, 59–68, 70; *lamellae*, 55–57; pendant, 61
  agency, 11–12, 30, 67, 70, 72–73, 75–76, 84–86, 90–93, 95
  apotropaic, 20, 42–44, 56, 58, 64, 66
  authority to perform, 30, 37, 40–41, 70, 72–76, 78–79, 81, 88, 91, 103
  curative, 4, 6, 14, 36, 38–39, 42, 44, 47, 50, 52–54, 56, 58, 61, 66–69, 77, 86, 88, 111, 126–27
  death or mortuary, 12, 75, 95–98, 100, 103–4, 109–18, 121 (*see also* mortuary practices; tombs)
  experts, 30, 49, 54, 58–59, 61, 66–67, 70, 87, 96, 103, 117–21, 126
  gestures (*see* gestures)
  immersion, 24
  protective, 2, 6, 11, 16, 23, 26, 29, 35–37, 39, 41–42, 44–48, 50, 52–53, 55–59, 61, 65–69, 72, 76, 87–88, 93, 110–11, 122, 126–27
  signaling identity, 87–88, 92, 94, 122
  speech, 44, 47
  theory, 11, 73, 93
  washing, 31–32, 35, 38, 125

  as women's work, 11, 16–17, 25, 41, 47, 53, 70–72, 75–76, 79, 84–85, 88, 91
ritualization, 73–74, 77, 79, 88, 93
  empowerment through, 74, 76, 79, 83, 85, 88, 92–93
Rome, Roman empire
  catacombs, 33, 98, 109–10, 113; Callistus, 99
  deities, 21, 35, 112
  emperor, 77, 83, 115, 118; Augustus, 76–77; Diocletian, 106, 108, 114; Maxentius, 115–16; Tiberius, 20; Trajan (and Plotina), 21; Valerian, 100
  patronage/sponsorship of religious entities, 115, 121
  Roman identity, 17

sacrifice, 8, 17, 24, 40, 48–49, 51–53, 77, 99, 101–2
Salzman, Michele, 117–8
sanctification, 37–39, 81, 86, 88
Sanzo, Joseph, 43, 54, 59, 66–67, 70
Sarah, wife of Abraham, 83
Schüssler Fiorenza, Elisabeth, 74
scribes, 28, 49, 69–70
Sepphoris, 17, 24–26
  mosaics, 25–26
  trash heaps, 25
Sessa, Kristina, 33, 76
Severus of Antioch, 54
sex, 32–33
Sheckler, Allyson, 66
shrines, 1, 11, 15–18, 21–25, 31–32, 79, 90–92, 95, 103, 119
  of martyrs, 95
Silvanus, 14, 89
sleep, 31–32
  death as, 97–99
Smith, J. Z., 49, 123
Solomon's ring, 57
sorcerers, 39
spells, 4, 29–30, 39, 48–50, 52, 55–59, 67, 69–70
  administration of, 49
  handbook of, 30
  purchase of, 49
  recipes for, 39, 49
Spera, Lucrezia, 112–3
Spier, Jeffrey, 45–46, 64
spirits, 6–7, 20–21, 29, 31, 36–37, 41–42, 55–57, 75–76, 90, 98–100, 110, 118–9
  Agathos Daimon, 20
  alien, 41
  of ancestors, 21, 90
  evil, 42, 55–57

guardian, 21, 76
Holy Spirit, 29, 31, 36–37, 57
of place, 21
possession, 119
S. Sebastiano, 98, 109–11, 116
statues/statuettes, 15, 18–21, 52
imperial, 21
status, 40, 44, 71–74, 76–77, 79–82, 84, 96, 107, 117–18, 120, 125
"status culture," 117
stepped pools, 24
Stern, Karen, 26
Stowers, Stanley K., 5–9, 13, 50, 68, 95, 117, 121, 123
structural positions, 74–75
subject positions, 74–75, 83
subordinate people
agency of, 12, 41, 72, 74–76, 78–79, 86, 90–91, 93
believers, 81–83, 89
empowerment of, 41, 74, 76, 79, 83, 85, 89, 92–93
influence of, 82–85
resistance, 73, 79, 84, 92, 93, 117
suffering, 36, 49, 55–56, 61, 83, 101
superstition, 52, 71, 76
supervision of religious practices, 1–3, 15, 17, 32, 40–41, 47, 70–71, 77–79, 86, 91, 96, 102, 109, 119–20, 124
supplication, 1, 14–15, 28–29, 31, 49, 54, 65–66
syncretism, 11, 25–26, 29, 49, 58, 66, 69–70, 72, 82, 85, 88, 92, 124

Tacitus, 91
temple, 9, 11, 19–20, 24–27, 44, 46, 80, 99
believer's body as, 80
service, 24–25
Tertullian, 30, 32–42, 46–47, 50–53, 67, 72–73, 79, 84–89, 91–93, 99–100, 102–3, 122, 126
tolerance, 76, 80, 82, 88, 91, 112, 124, 126
thanksgiving, 2, 6, 14, 29, 98
Thecla, 1, 28–29, 33, 87
Thymiateria, 20
tombs, 1–2, 9–10, 16, 24, 33, 95–121, 125
burial, 16, 70, 95–96, 116, 121; in chamber tombs, 87, 97, 106; in amphorae, 106; in ash chests, 96; in pit graves, 96; in mausolea, 109, 112, 115; in sarcophagi, 33, 96, 98, 106, 119; privileged, 107
as extension of the household, 16, 97
features: *loculae* (grave coverings), 99; *mensae*, 98, 103–9, 119; slabs, 98, 104, 106, 108–9

and rituals, 2, 16, 95, 97–103 (*see also* meals; mortuary practices; offerings)
spaces: burial grounds, 101, 106, 116; catacombs, 33, 98, 109–10, 113; cemeteries, 100–101, 103, 105–7, 109–10, 113–14, 116, 118–22, 124; courtyards, 111–12; for gathering, 99, 102, 109–11, 113
shared meals at, 16, 97, 99, 102, 104–5, 109–10, 113; *triclia*, 109–14, 116
See also burial; mortuary practices
travel, 2, 26, 42, 48, 92
Trnka-Amrhein, Yvona, 57
Trouillot, Michel-Rolph, 123

Ullucci, Daniel, 117, 119

Vatican *tropaion*, 120
Via Appia, 109, 112, 114–16
Via Praenestina, 115
voces magicae, 59

wealth. *See* economic interests
White, L. Michael, 104
wine, 23, 31, 39–42, 88, 97–99, 102
women, 3–4, 11–12, 14, 16–18, 23, 25–26, 28, 32–34, 37, 39–43, 47, 51, 53, 55, 69, 70–74, 76–88, 91–93, 98–101, 124–27
influence within household, 81, 83–86
wives, 3–4, 16, 23, 32, 39–41, 47, 70–77, 79, 81–88, 92–93, 126
See also subordinate people
worship in the ancient Mediterranean
civic, 21
communal, 3, 16, 43, 58, 99–100
of lightning, 34
rituals, 2–3, 31, 34–35, 39

Xenophon, 77

Yasin, Ann Marie, 108